SEVEN SEAS ENTERTAINMENT PRESENTS

ARPEGGIO
OF BLUE STEEL
story and art by **ARK PERFORMANCE**   VOLUME 8

TRANSLATION
Greg Moore

ADAPTATION
Ysabet Reinhardt MacFarlane

LETTERING AND LAYOUT
Paweł Szczęszek

LOGO DESIGN
Courtney Williams

COVER DESIGN
Nicky Lim

PROOFREADER
Lee Otter

PRODUCTION MANAGER
Lissa Pattillo

EDITOR-IN-CHIEF
Adam Arnold

PUBLISHER
Jason DeAngelis

AOKI HAGANENO ARPEGGIO VOLUME 8
© Ark Performance 2013
Originally published in Japan in 2013 by SHONENGAHOSHA Co., Ltd., Tokyo.
English translation rights arranged through TOHAN CORPORATION, Tokyo.

Seven Seas books may be purchased in bulk for educational, business, or
promotional use. For information on bulk purchases, please contact Macmillan
Corporate & Premium Sales Department at 1-800-221-7945 (ext 5442)
or write specialmarkets@macmillan.com.

Seven Seas and the Seven Seas logo are
Seven Seas Entertainment, LLC. All right

ISBN: 978-1-626923-26-3

Printed in Canada

First Printing: September 2016

10 9 8 7 6 5 4 3 2 1

FOLLOW US ONLINE: *www.go*

READING DIRECTIONS

This book reads from *right to left*, Japanese style.
If this is your first time reading manga, you start
reading from the top right panel on each page and
take it from there. If you get lost, just follow the
numbered diagram here. It may seem backwards at
first, but you'll get the hang of it! Have fun!!

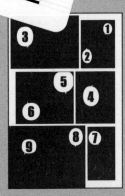

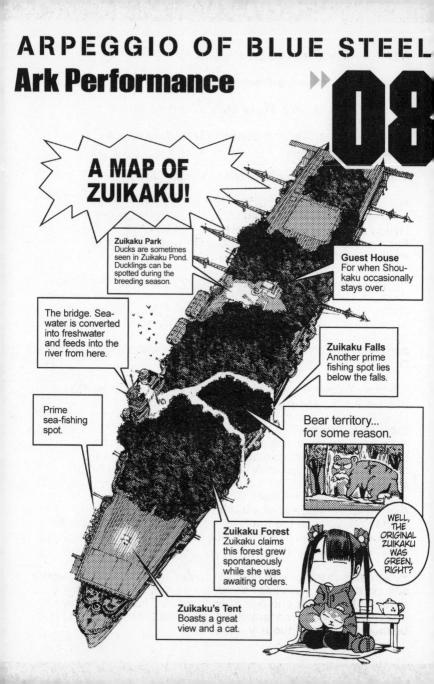

ARPEGGIO OF BLUE STEEL

Ark Performance

08

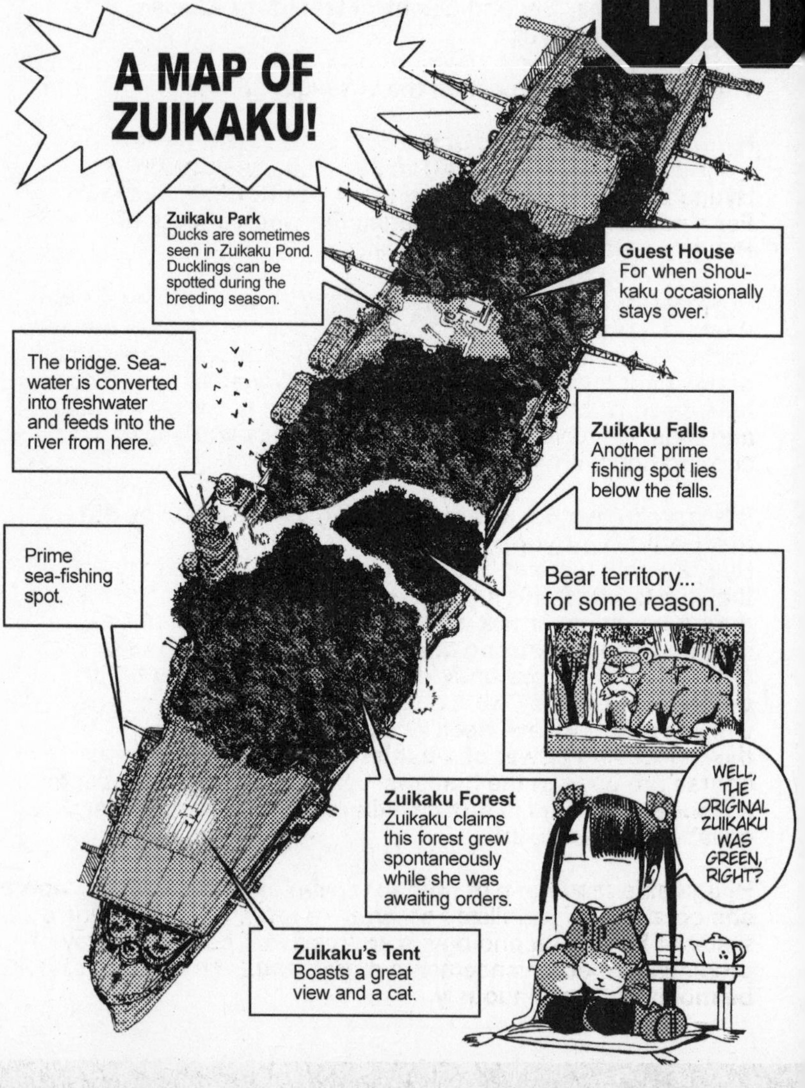
A MAP OF ZUIKAKU!
Guest House For when Shoukaku occasionally stays over.
Zuikaku Park Ducks are sometimes seen in Zuikaku Pond. Ducklings can be spotted during the breeding season.
The bridge. Seawater is converted into freshwater and feeds into the river from here.
Zuikaku Falls Another prime fishing spot lies below the falls.
Bear territory... for some reason.
Prime sea-fishing spot.
WELL, THE ORIGINAL ZUIKAKU WAS GREEN, RIGHT?
Zuikaku Forest Zuikaku claims this forest grew spontaneously while she was awaiting orders.
Zuikaku's Tent Boasts a great view and a cat.

[Fleet Assessment Report No. 00013]

From: First Submarine Fleet I-400, I-402

To: Supreme Flagship Super Battleship Yamato

Subject: Former Second Oriental Fleet Large-Class
Flag Battleship Hyuga

This is an interim report on the vessel in question.

Hyuga was the flagship of the Second Oriental Fleet until
a series of battles with I-401 in July 2055, culminating in
Hyuga being sunk after being lured into Bou-no-misakioki.
For a prolonged period thereafter, the whereabouts of
Hyuga's core remained unknown.

However, during Heavy Cruiser Takao's later battle with I-401,
it was determined that 401 was now equipped with a miniatur-
ized version of Hyuga's super-graviton cannon. The structure
of this canon made it clear that the modification would not
have been possible without assistance from Hyuga herself,
and thus, we have concluded that Hyuga is working in
cooperation with 401.

It is now known, thanks to data willingly uploaded by 401,
that Battleship Hyuga has acknowledged 401 as flagship.
Hyuga's ship has not been restored, but all signs indicate
that she is under 401's command. 401's use of option vessels
during her snipe attack on U-2501 also suggest that this
collaboration is a strong one. The precise makeup of the
option vessels is currently unknown, but there is a high
probability that they were super-graviton cannon vessels,
which could not have been designed or developed without
the processing power of a battleship-class core, and of
course are beyond the humans' current level of technological
advancement. This is further evidence of Battleship Hyuga's
collaboration with 401.

Hyuga also made use of human technology on Iwo Jima, where
she created and mobilized an army of robot troops. Hyuga's
study of human technology is aggressive. There is no way of
predicting what advancements might result. This vessel should
be monitored continuously.

FOG FLEET POWER DIAGRAM

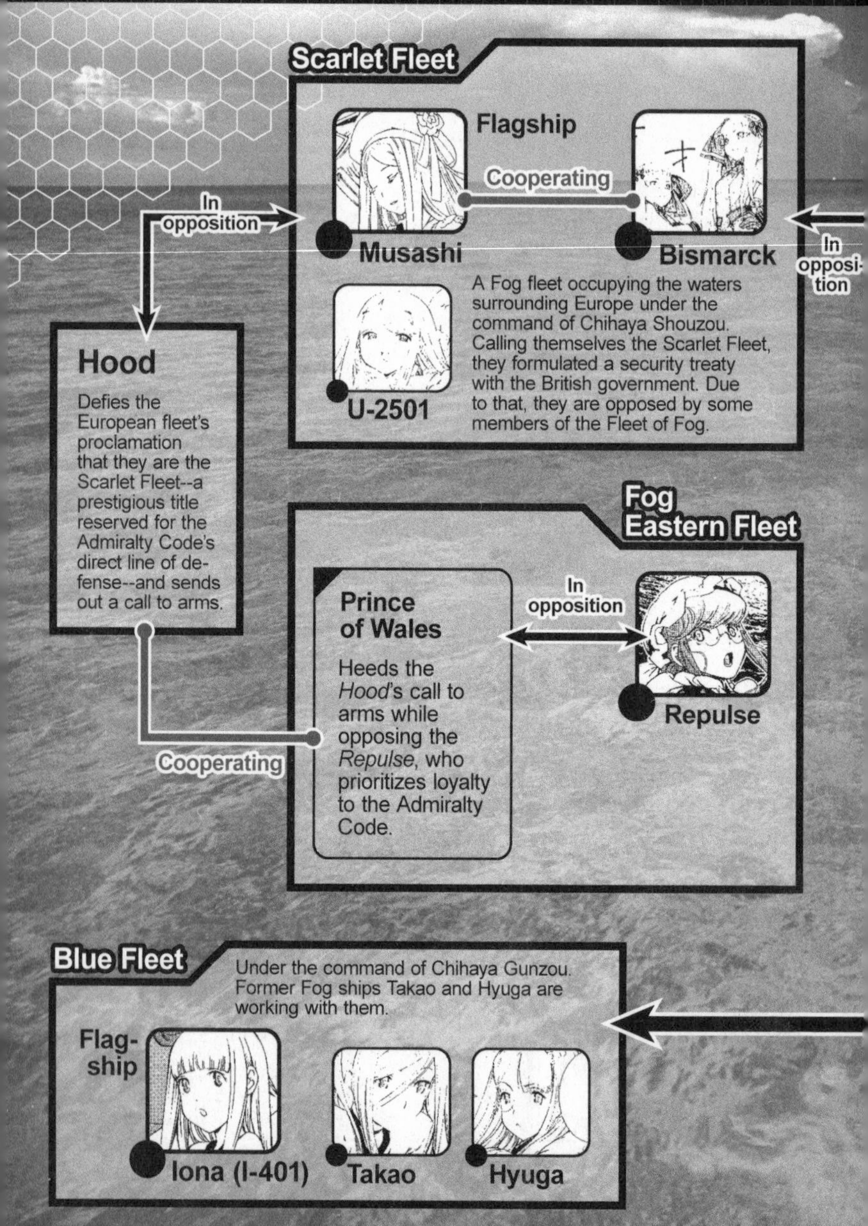
Scarlet Fleet
Flagship
Cooperating
Musashi
Bismarck
In opposition
In opposi-tion
A Fog fleet occupying the waters surrounding Europe under the command of Chihaya Shouzou. Calling themselves the Scarlet Fleet, they formulated a security treaty with the British government. Due to that, they are opposed by some members of the Fleet of Fog.
U-2501
Hood
Defies the European fleet's proclamation that they are the Scarlet Fleet--a prestigious title reserved for the Admiralty Code's direct line of de-fense--and sends out a call to arms.
Fog Eastern Fleet
Prince of Wales
Heeds the *Hood*'s call to arms while opposing the *Repulse*, who prioritizes loyalty to the Admiralty Code.
In opposition
Repulse
Cooperating
Blue Fleet
Under the command of Chihaya Gunzou. Former Fog ships Takao and Hyuga are working with them.
Flag-ship
Iona (I-401)
Takao
Hyuga

Eastern Fleet of Fog

Supreme Flagship

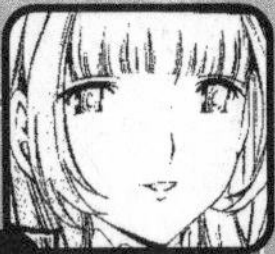

Yamato

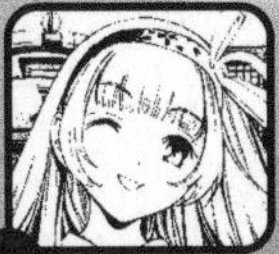

Kotono

The fleet commanded by Supreme Flagship *Yamato*. This fleet once kept the far eastern seas surrounding Japan sealed off, but it underwent significant changes after engaging in battle with the *I-401*. Kotono is the supreme flagship's additional mental model.

Direct report line to supreme flagship

Supreme Flagship Fleet

A fleet which serves as Supreme Flagship Yamato's direct line of defense and faithfully enacts her will. They are often tasked with top secret missions.

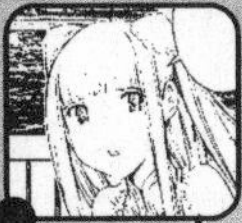

I-400

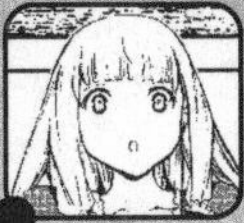

I-402

Monitoring

First Oriental Fleet

A Fog fleet that patrols the waters off Japan's shores. Currently under the command of the *Ise*, as Flagship *Kongo* and the *Hiei* head off to face the *I-401*.

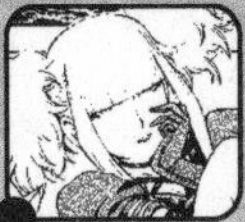

Kongo

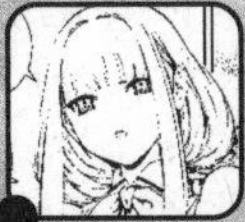

Hiei

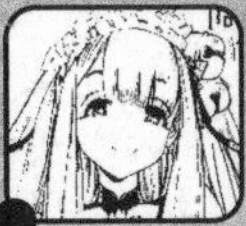

Ise

Splinter Fleet

Having lost their ships, Haruna and Kirishima take shelter on Maya and reconvene with Osakabe Makie. They're about to embark on a search for the Admiralty Code.

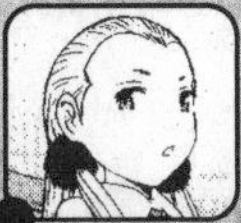

Haruna

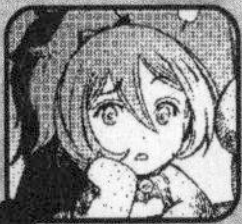

Kirishima

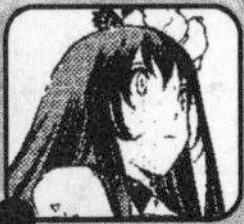

Maya

Second Oriental Fleet

A patrol fleet under the command of the *Nagato*. Details unknown.

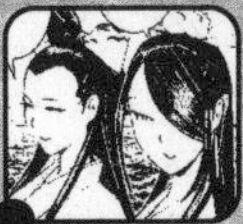

Nagato

Ocean Assault and Suppression Fleet

This fleet includes the *Zuikaku*, the *Shoukaku*, and others, and is stationed in the Sea of Okhotsk.

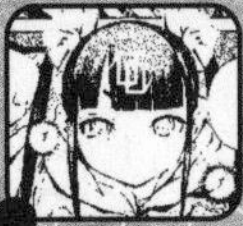

Zuikaku

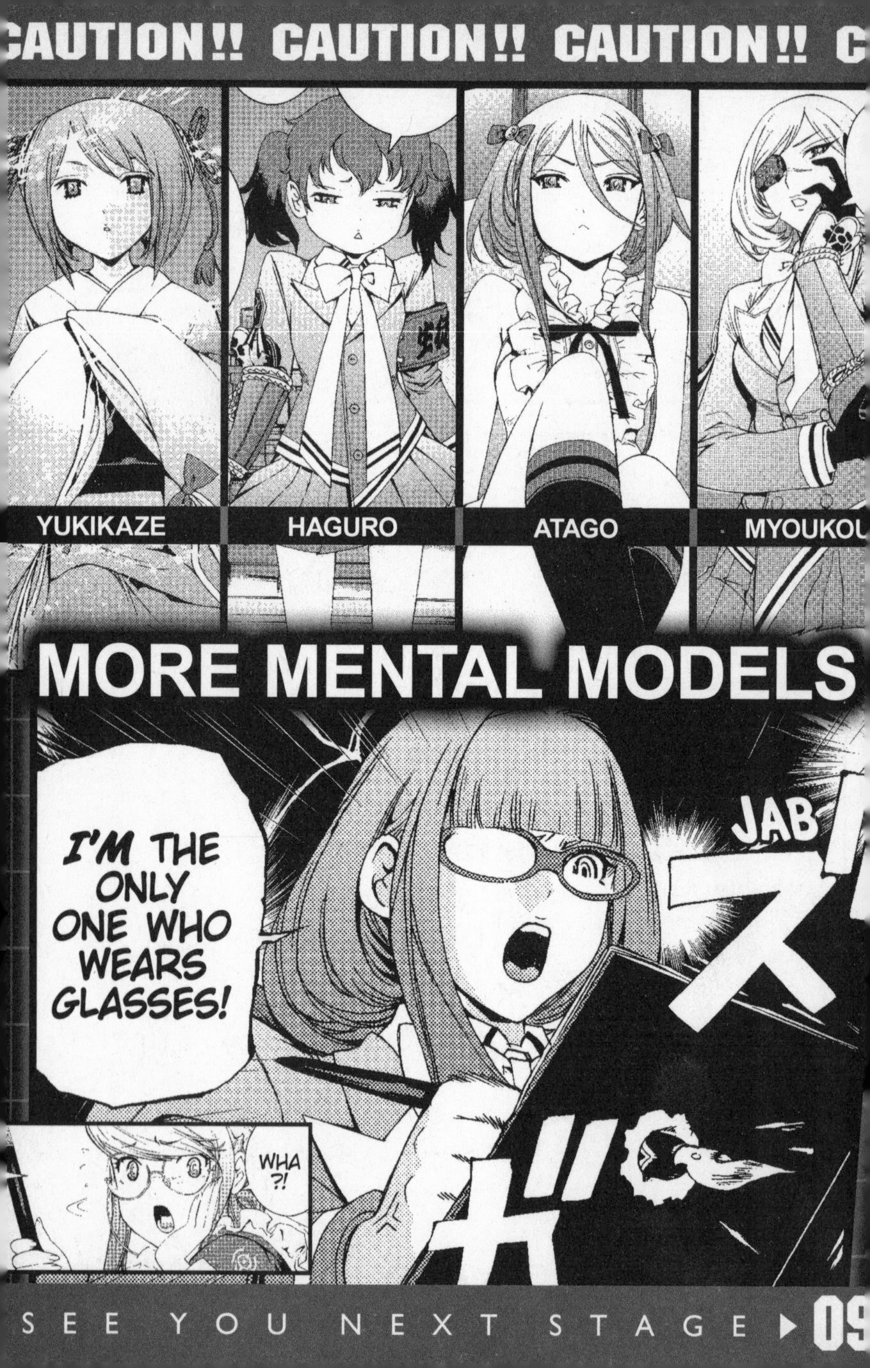
CAUTION!! CAUTION!! CAUTION!!
MYOUKOU
ATAGO
HAGURO
YUKIKAZE
MORE MENTAL MODELS
JAB
I'M THE ONLY ONE WHO WEARS GLASSES!
WHA?!
SEE YOU NEXT STAGE ▶ 09

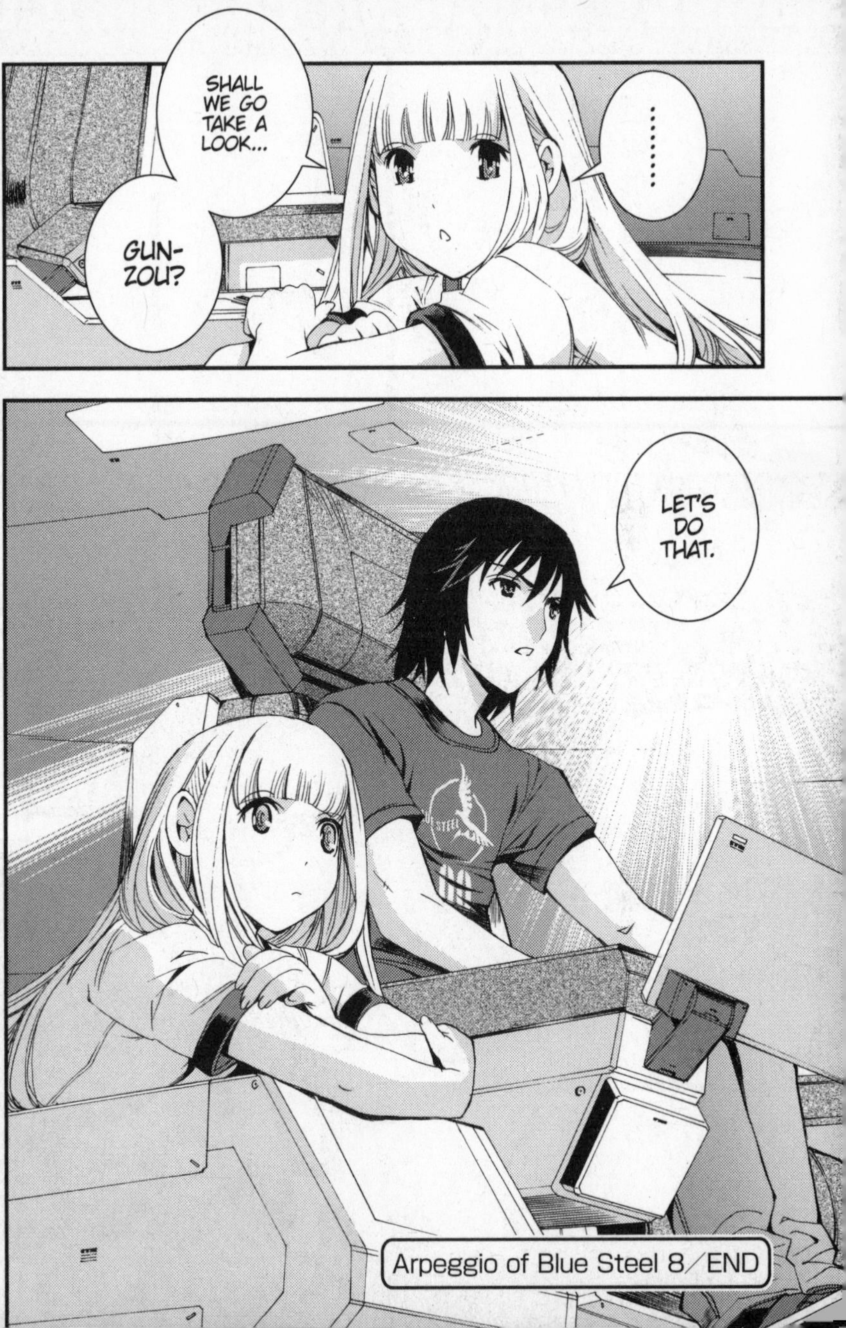
......
SHALL WE GO TAKE A LOOK...
GUN-ZOU?
LET'S DO THAT.
Arpeggio of Blue Steel 8/END

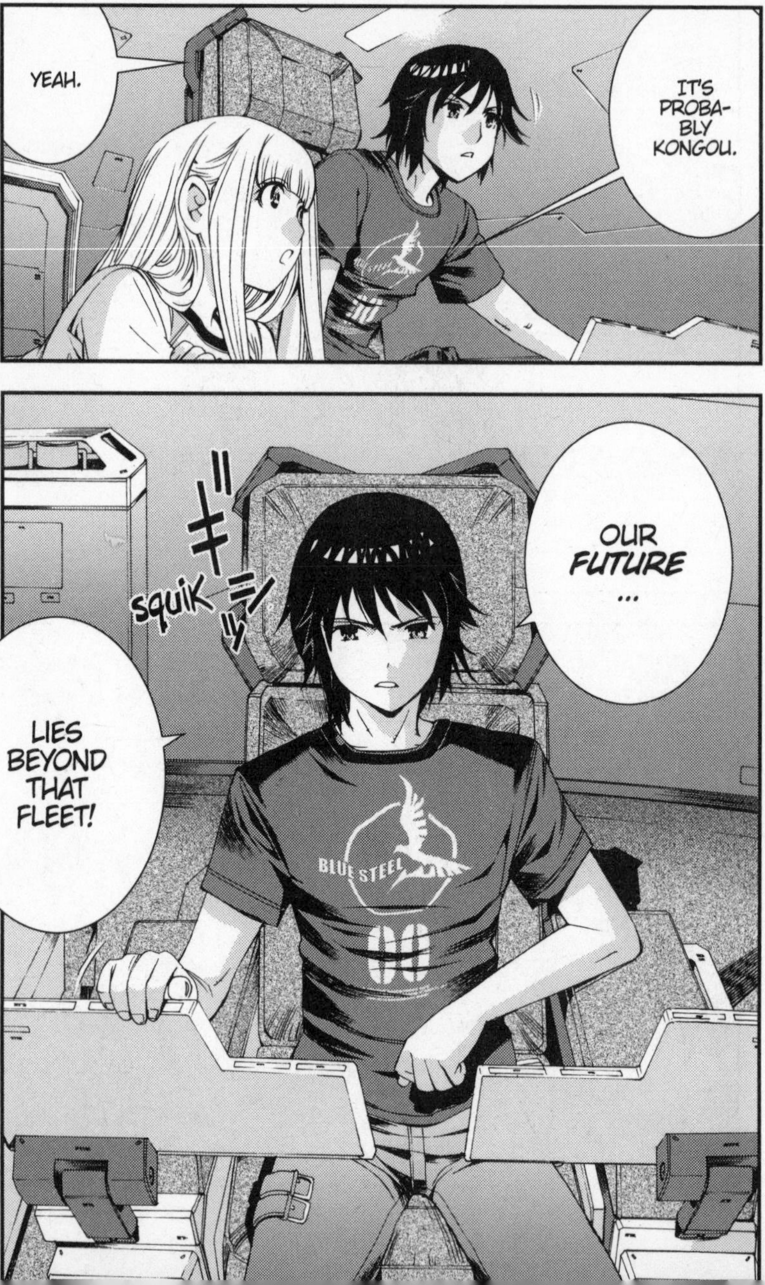
IT'S PROBA-BLY KONGOU.
YEAH.
OUR FUTURE ...
squik
LIES BEYOND THAT FLEET!
BLUE STEEL

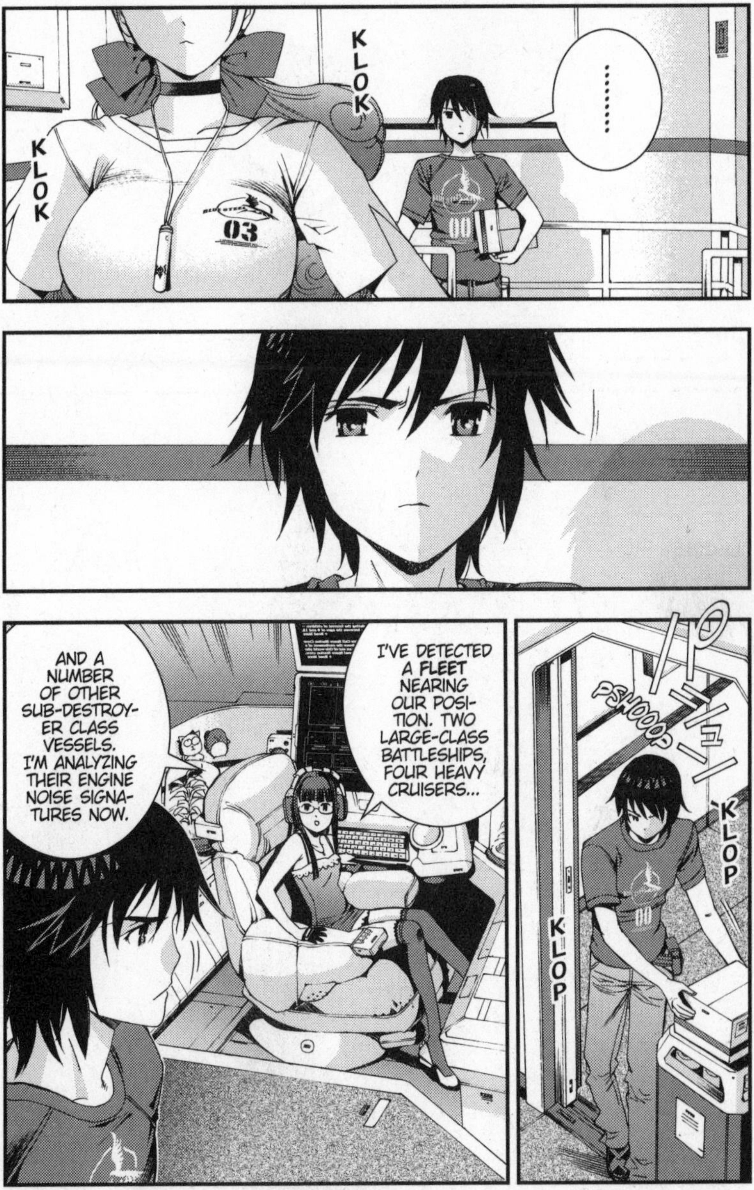

......
KLOK KLOK
KLOK KLOK
PSHOOP
KLOP
KLOP
I'VE DETECTED A FLEET NEARING OUR POSITION. TWO LARGE-CLASS BATTLESHIPS, FOUR HEAVY CRUISERS...
AND A NUMBER OF OTHER SUB-DESTROYER CLASS VESSELS. I'M ANALYZING THEIR ENGINE NOISE SIGNATURES NOW.

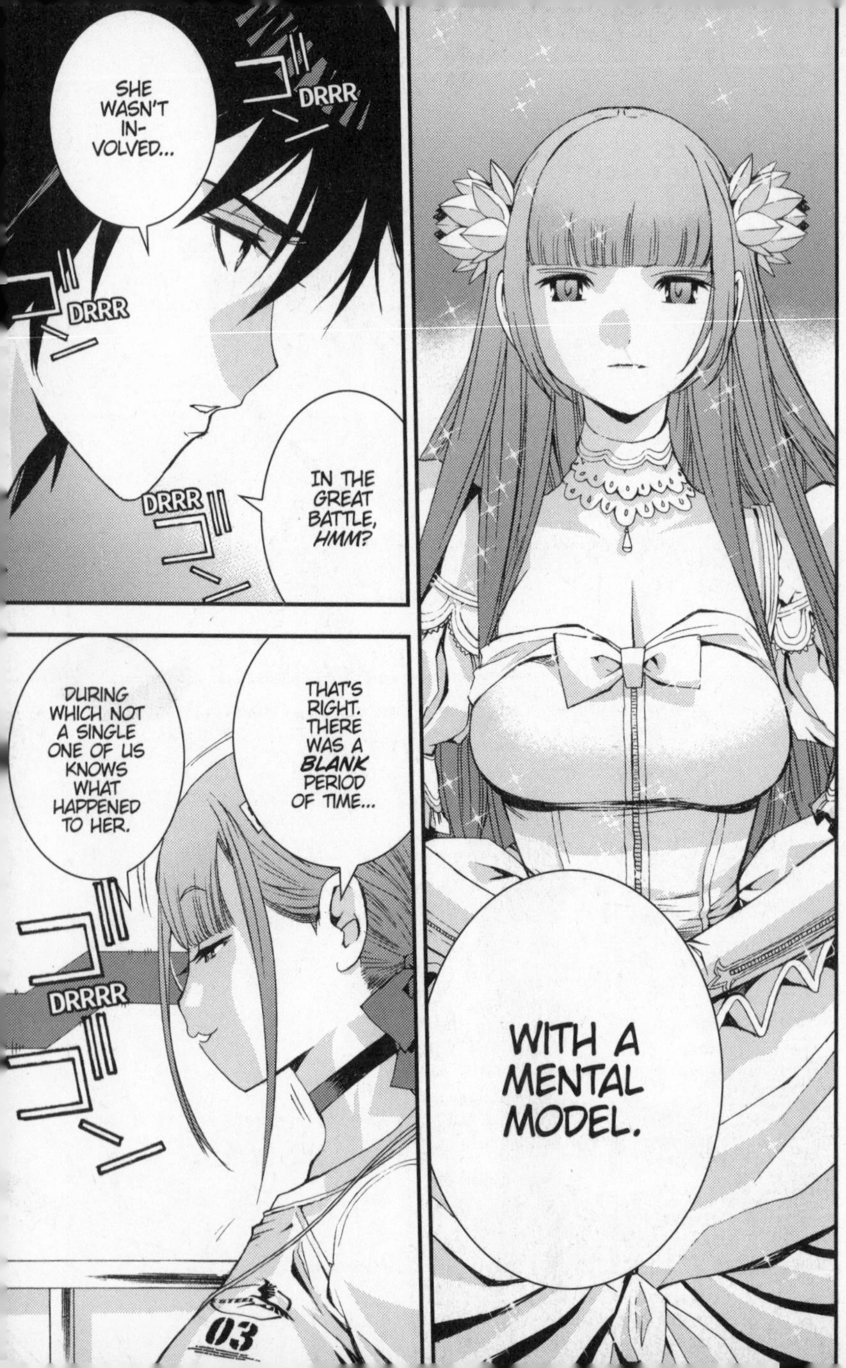
WITH A MENTAL MODEL.
SHE WASN'T IN-VOLVED...
DRRR
DRRR
IN THE GREAT BATTLE, *HMM?*
DRRR
THAT'S RIGHT. THERE WAS A *BLANK* PERIOD OF TIME...
DURING WHICH NOT A SINGLE ONE OF US KNOWS WHAT HAPPENED TO HER.
DRRRR
03

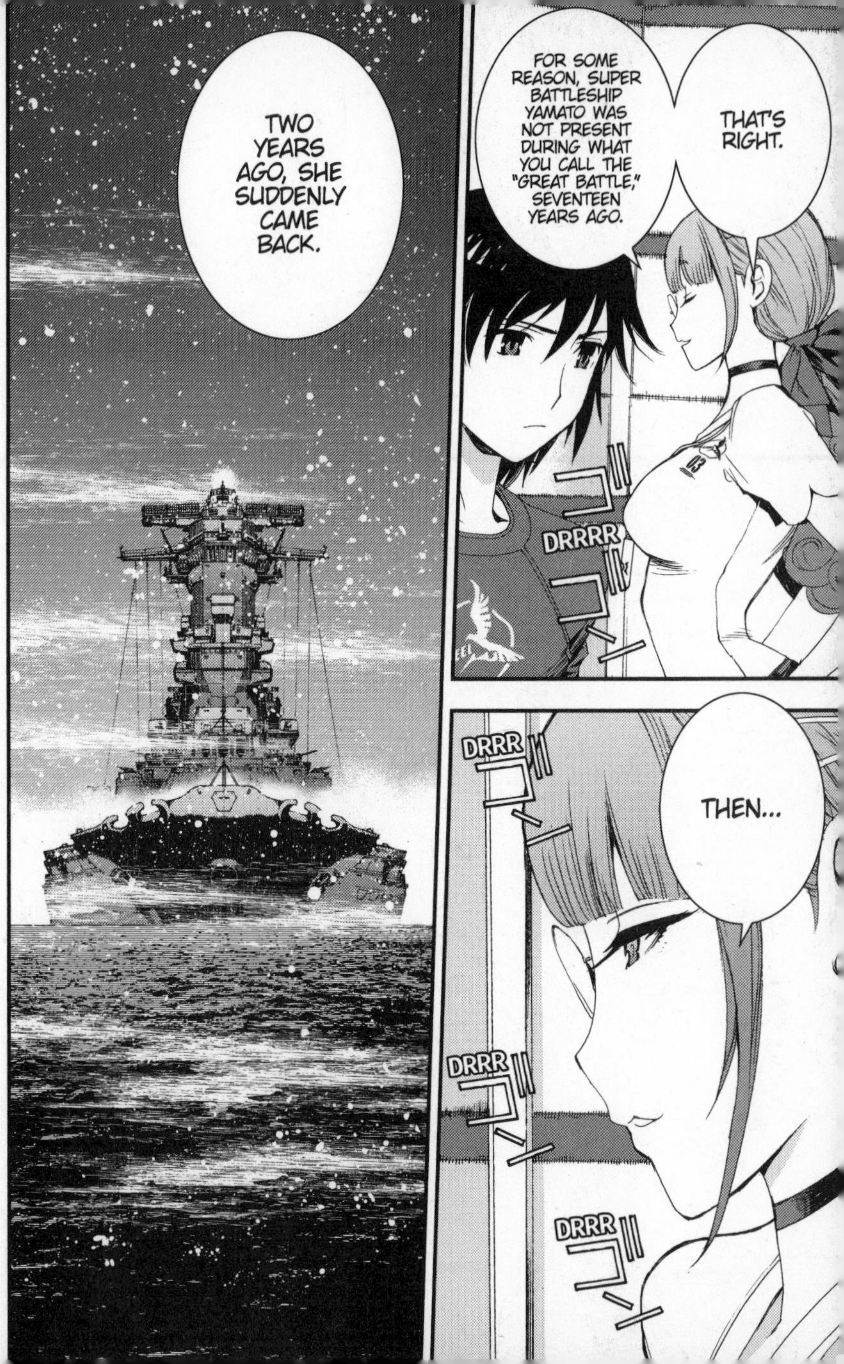
FOR SOME REASON, SUPER BATTLESHIP YAMATO WAS NOT PRESENT DURING WHAT YOU CALL THE "GREAT BATTLE," SEVENTEEN YEARS AGO.
THAT'S RIGHT.
DRRRR
DRRR
THEN...
DRRR
DRRR
TWO YEARS AGO, SHE SUDDENLY CAME BACK.

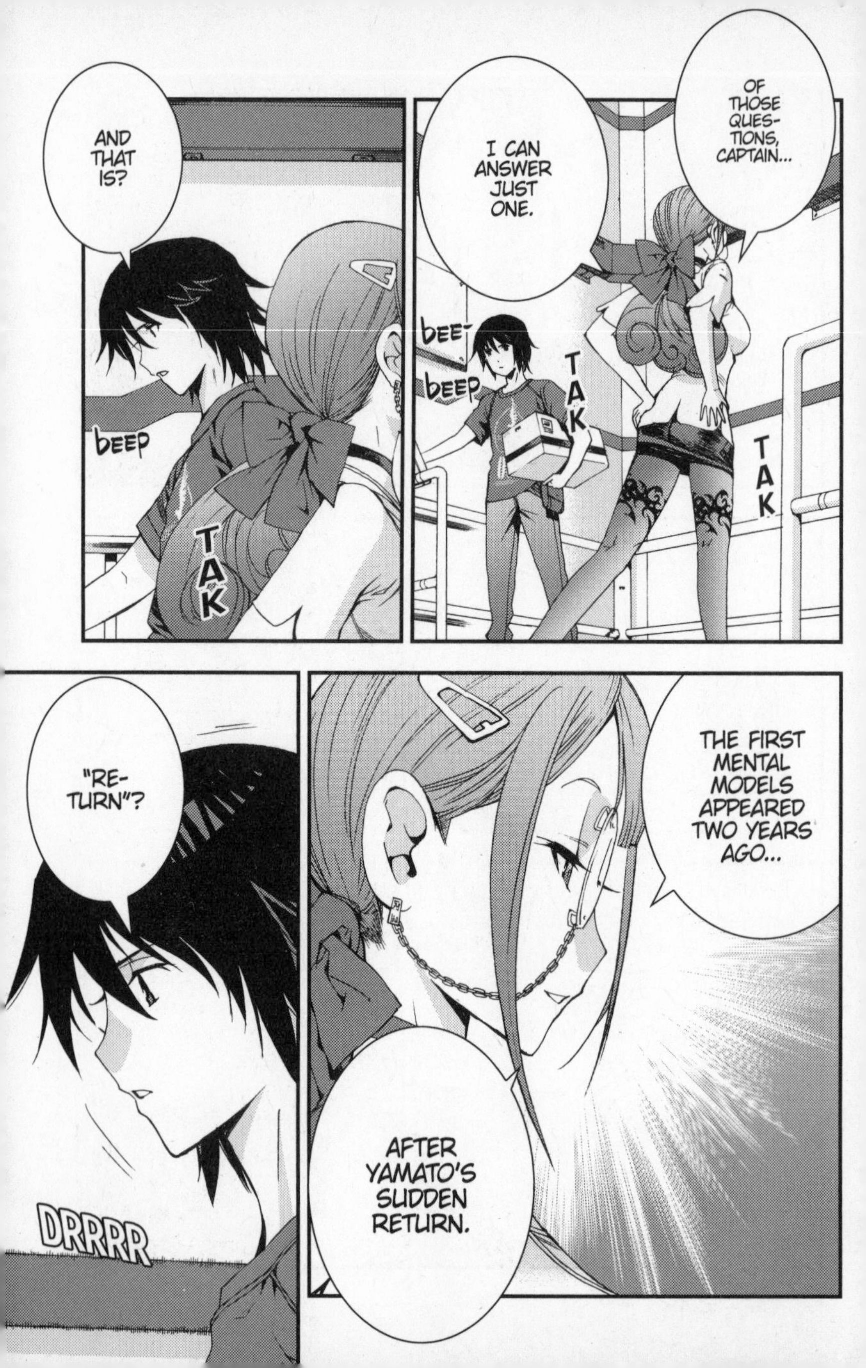
OF THOSE QUES-TIONS, CAPTAIN...
I CAN ANSWER JUST ONE.
bee-beep
TAK
TAK
AND THAT IS?
beep
TAK
THE FIRST MENTAL MODELS APPEARED TWO YEARS AGO...
AFTER YAMATO'S SUDDEN RETURN.
"RE-TURN"?
DRRRR

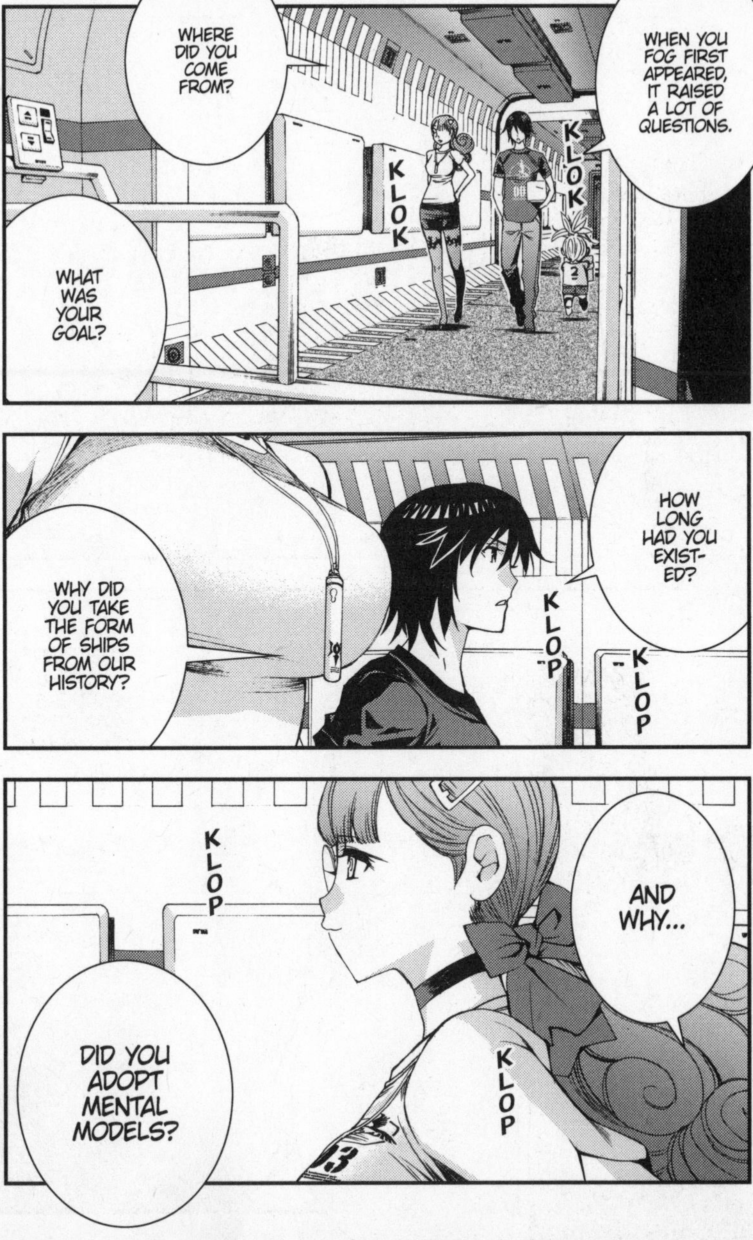
WHEN YOU FOG FIRST APPEARED, IT RAISED A LOT OF QUESTIONS.
KLOK
WHERE DID YOU COME FROM?
KLOK
WHAT WAS YOUR GOAL?
HOW LONG HAD YOU EXIST-ED?
KLOP
KLOP
WHY DID YOU TAKE THE FORM OF SHIPS FROM OUR HISTORY?
AND WHY...
KLOP
KLOP
DID YOU ADOPT MENTAL MODELS?

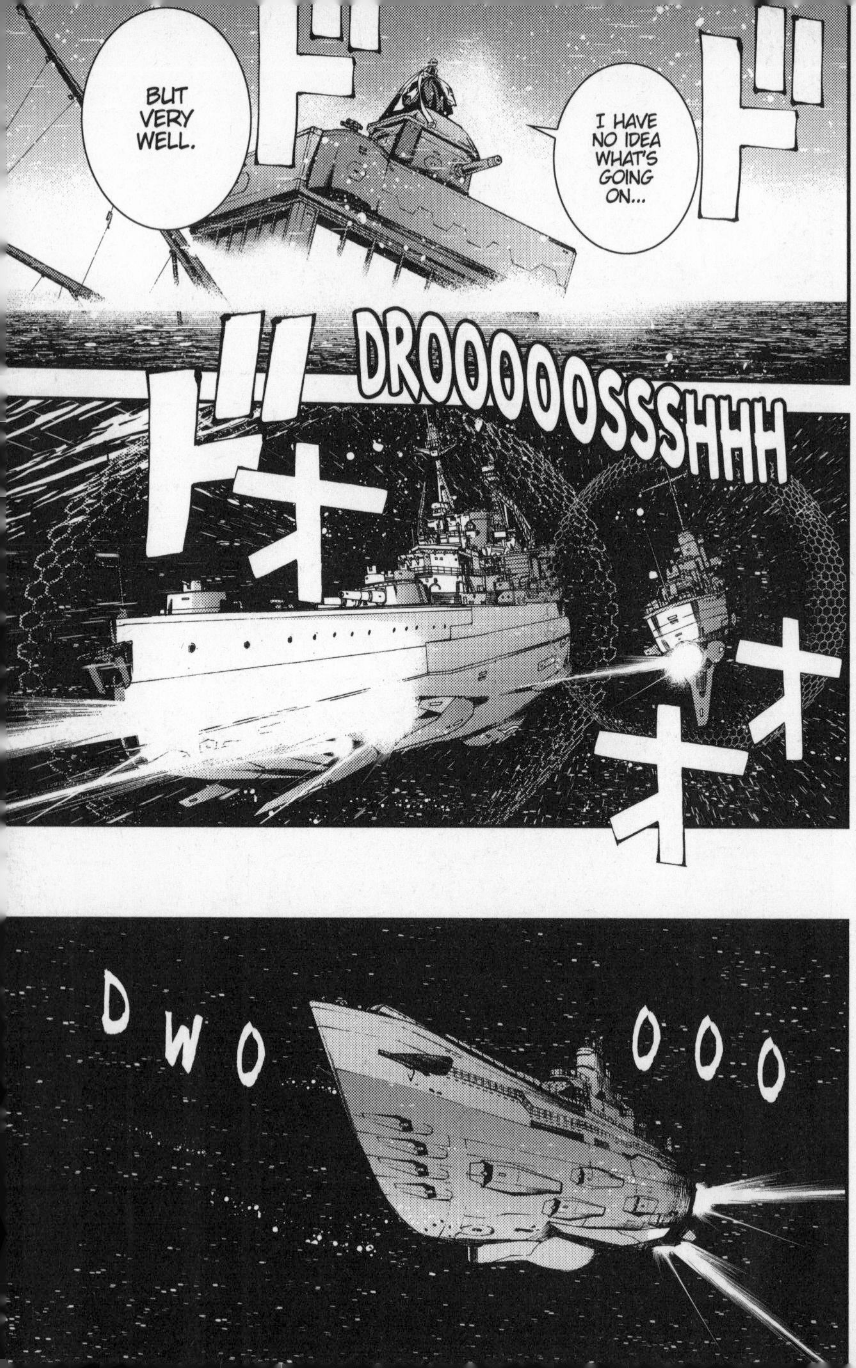
ドド
I HAVE NO IDEA WHAT'S GOING ON...
BUT VERY WELL.
DROOOOOOSSSHHH
ドオオオ
DWO OOO

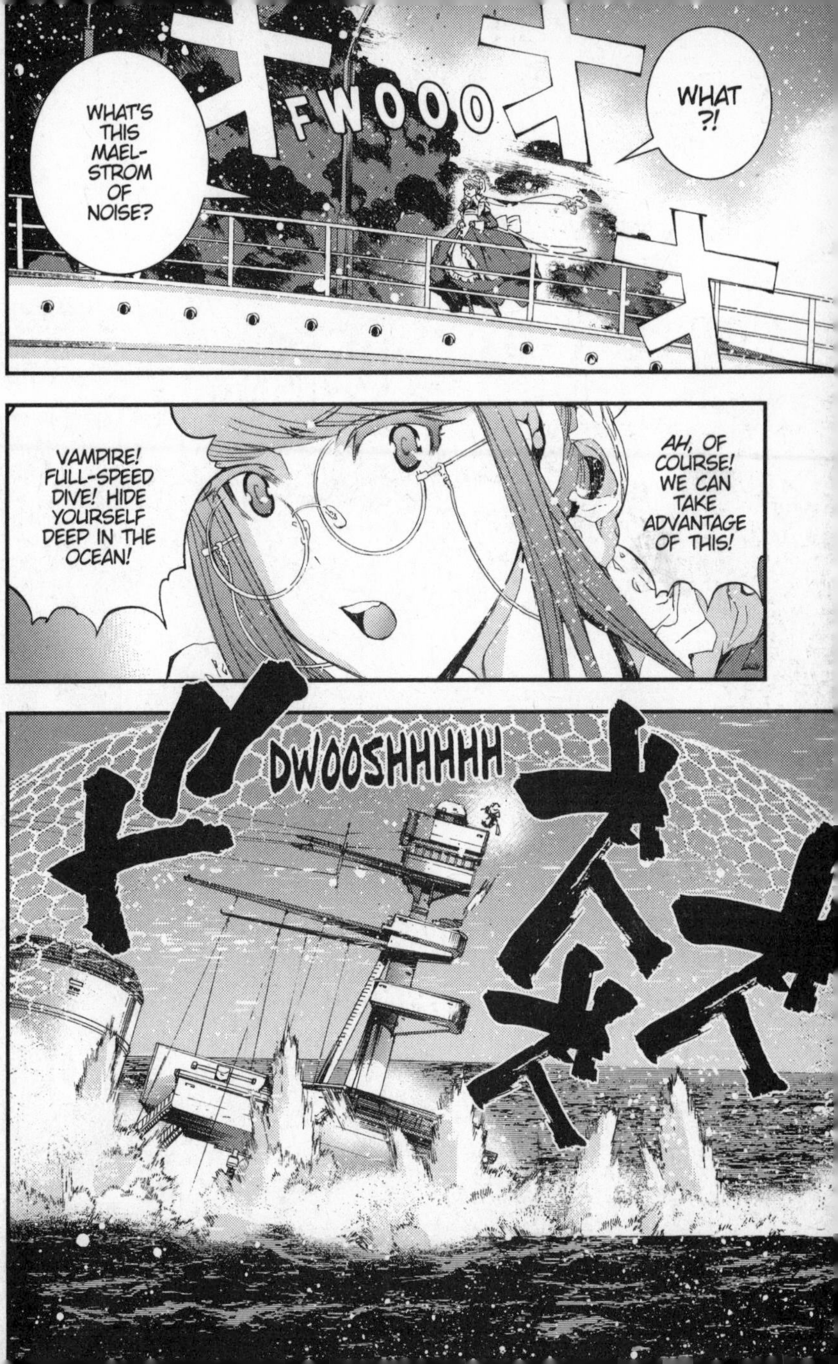
WHAT ?!
FWOOO
WHAT'S THIS MAEL-STROM OF NOISE?
AH, OF COURSE! WE CAN TAKE ADVANTAGE OF THIS!
VAMPIRE! FULL-SPEED DIVE! HIDE YOURSELF DEEP IN THE OCEAN!
DWOOSHHHHH

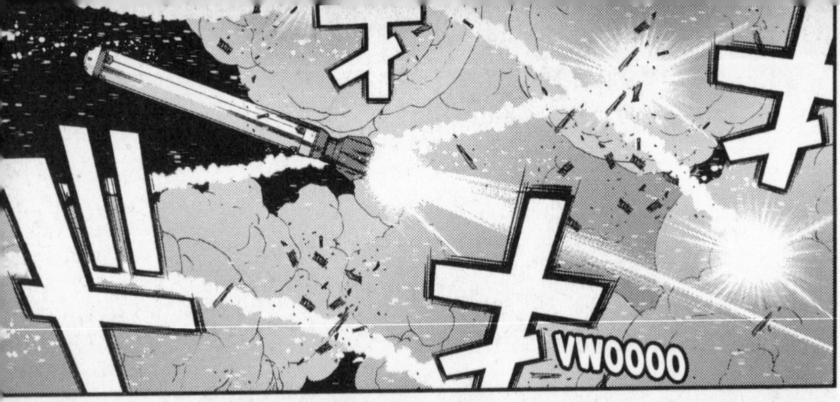
VWOOOO

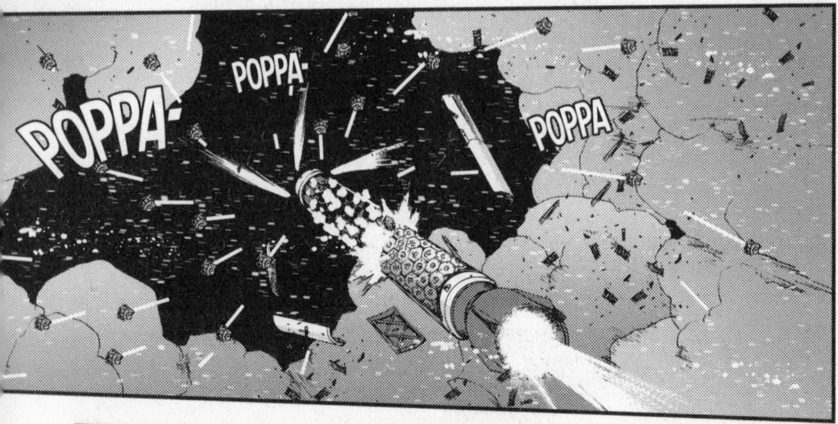
POPPA
POPPA-
POPPA-

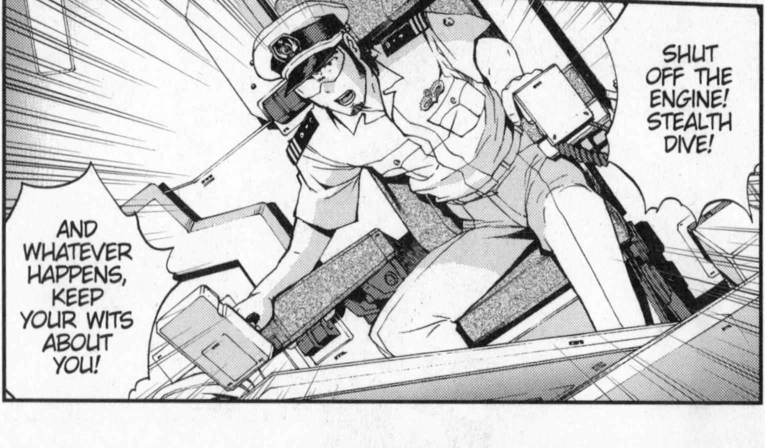
SHUT OFF THE ENGINE! STEALTH DIVE!
AND WHATEVER HAPPENS, KEEP YOUR WITS ABOUT YOU!

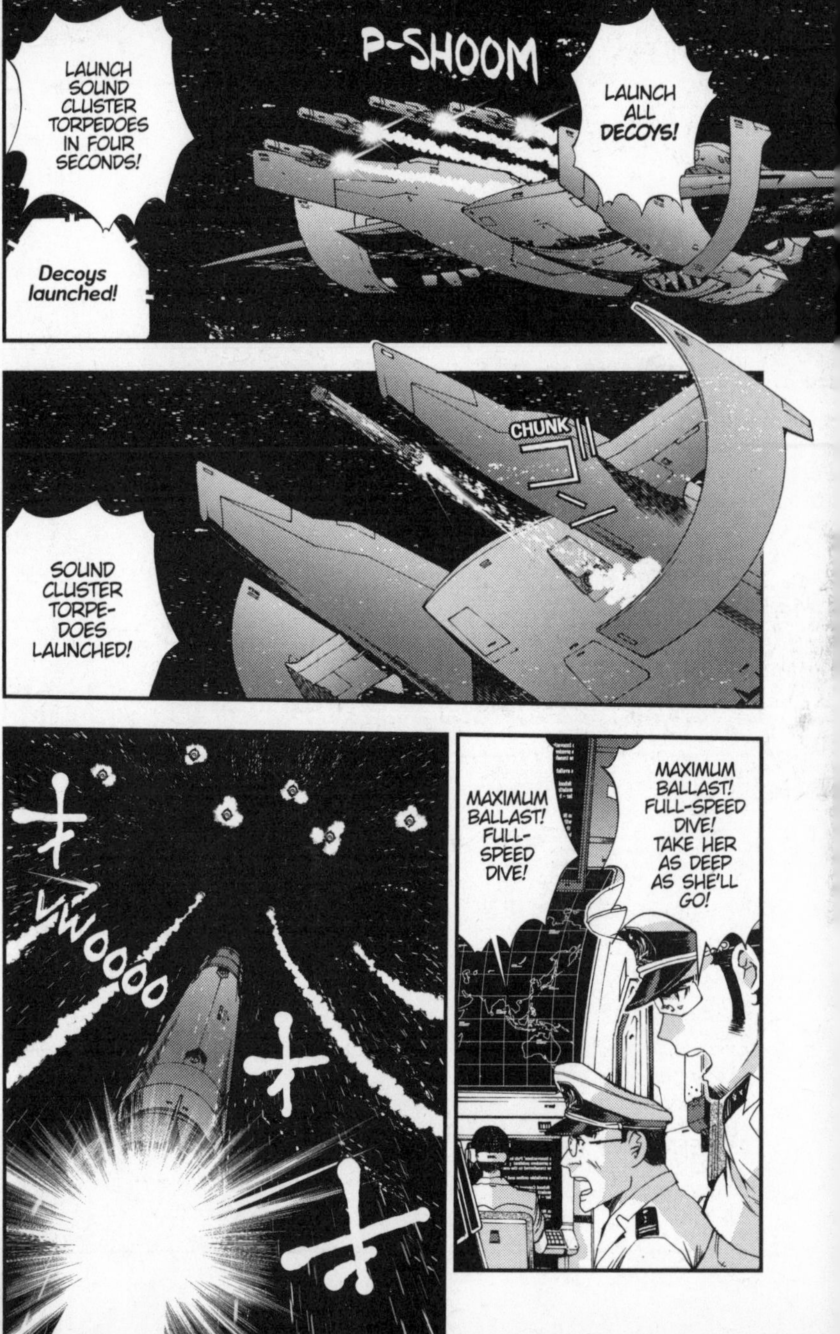

LAUNCH ALL DECOYS!
P-SHOOM
LAUNCH SOUND CLUSTER TORPEDOES IN FOUR SECONDS!
Decoys launched!
CHUNK
SOUND CLUSTER TORPE-DOES LAUNCHED!
MAXIMUM BALLAST! FULL-SPEED DIVE! TAKE HER AS DEEP AS SHE'LL GO!
MAXIMUM BALLAST! FULL-SPEED DIVE!
VWOOOO

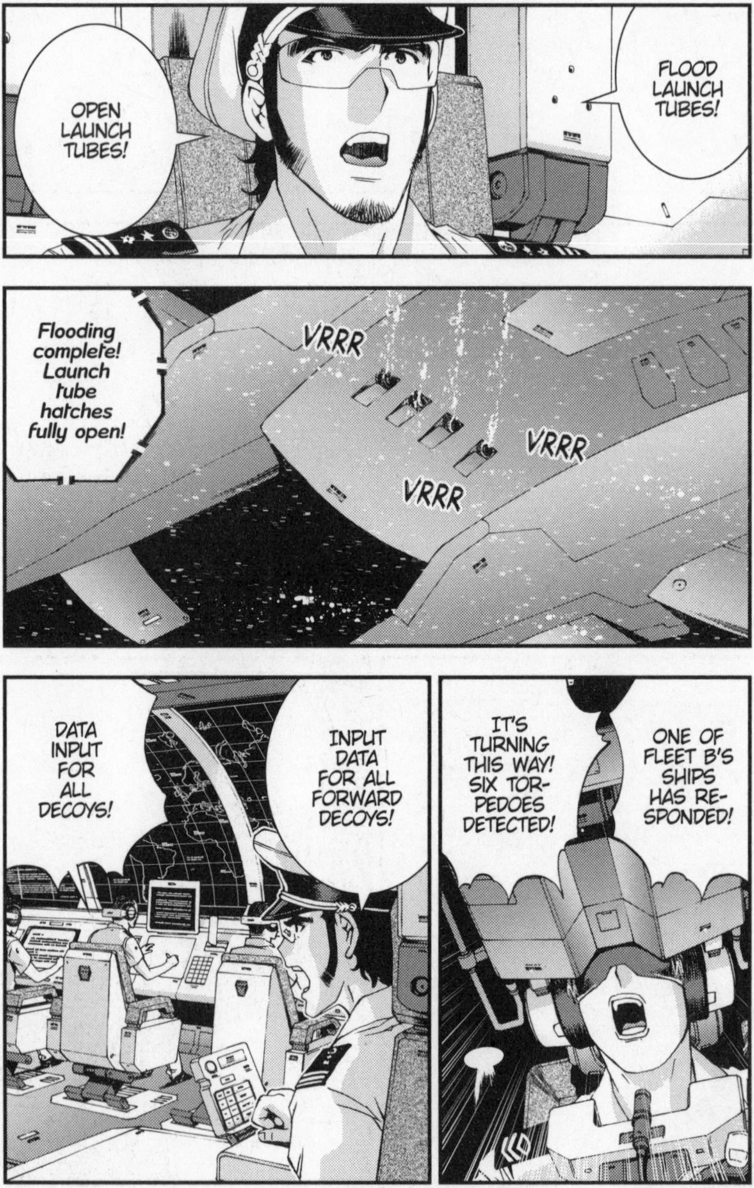
FLOOD LAUNCH TUBES!
OPEN LAUNCH TUBES!
Flooding complete! Launch tube hatches fully open!
VRRR
VRRR
VRRR
ONE OF FLEET B'S SHIPS HAS RE-SPONDED!
IT'S TURNING THIS WAY! SIX TOR-PEDOES DETECTED!
INPUT DATA FOR ALL FORWARD DECOYS!
DATA INPUT FOR ALL DECOYS!

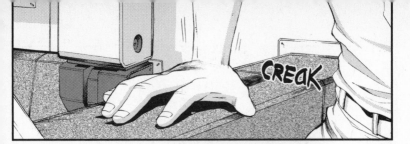

CREAK
SOUND CLUSTER TORPEDOES ARE READY FOR LAUNCH! WHAT'S OUR TARGET?
RIGHT BETWEEN FLEETS A AND B. HAVE THE MINI-WARHEADS FAN OUT IN THE WIDEST POSSIBLE PATTERN.
AYE, AYE. SOUND CLUSTER TORPEDOES, MOVEMENT PATTERN C! SCATTER PATTERN B-6!
blip
FLEET B
FLEET A
blip
TARGETING MIDPOINT BETWEEN FLEETS A AND B!
ALL COORDINATES ARE LOCKED!
COORDINATES LOCKED AND CONFIRMED! CAPTAIN, WE'RE READY WHEN YOU ARE!

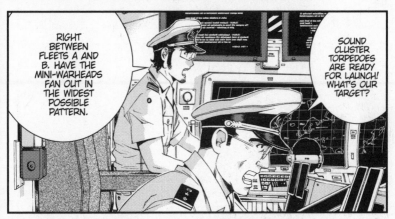

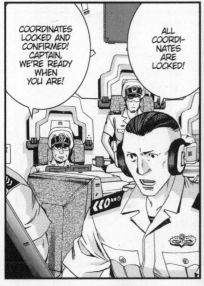

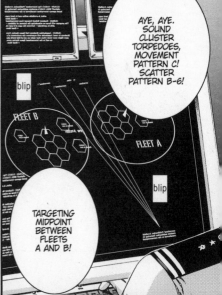

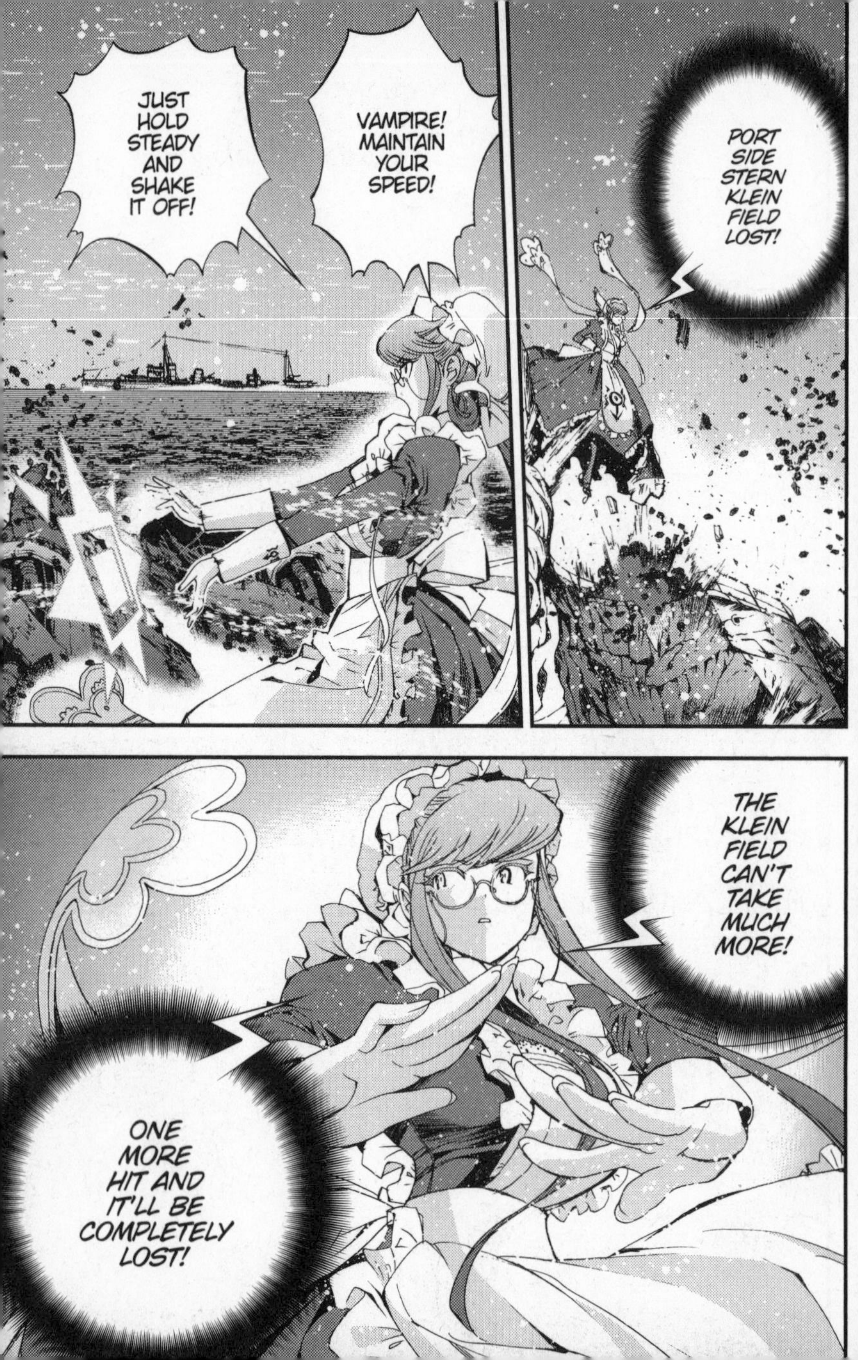
PORT SIDE STERN KLEIN FIELD LOST!
VAMPIRE! MAINTAIN YOUR SPEED!
JUST HOLD STEADY AND SHAKE IT OFF!
THE KLEIN FIELD CAN'T TAKE MUCH MORE!
ONE MORE HIT AND IT'LL BE COMPLETELY LOST!

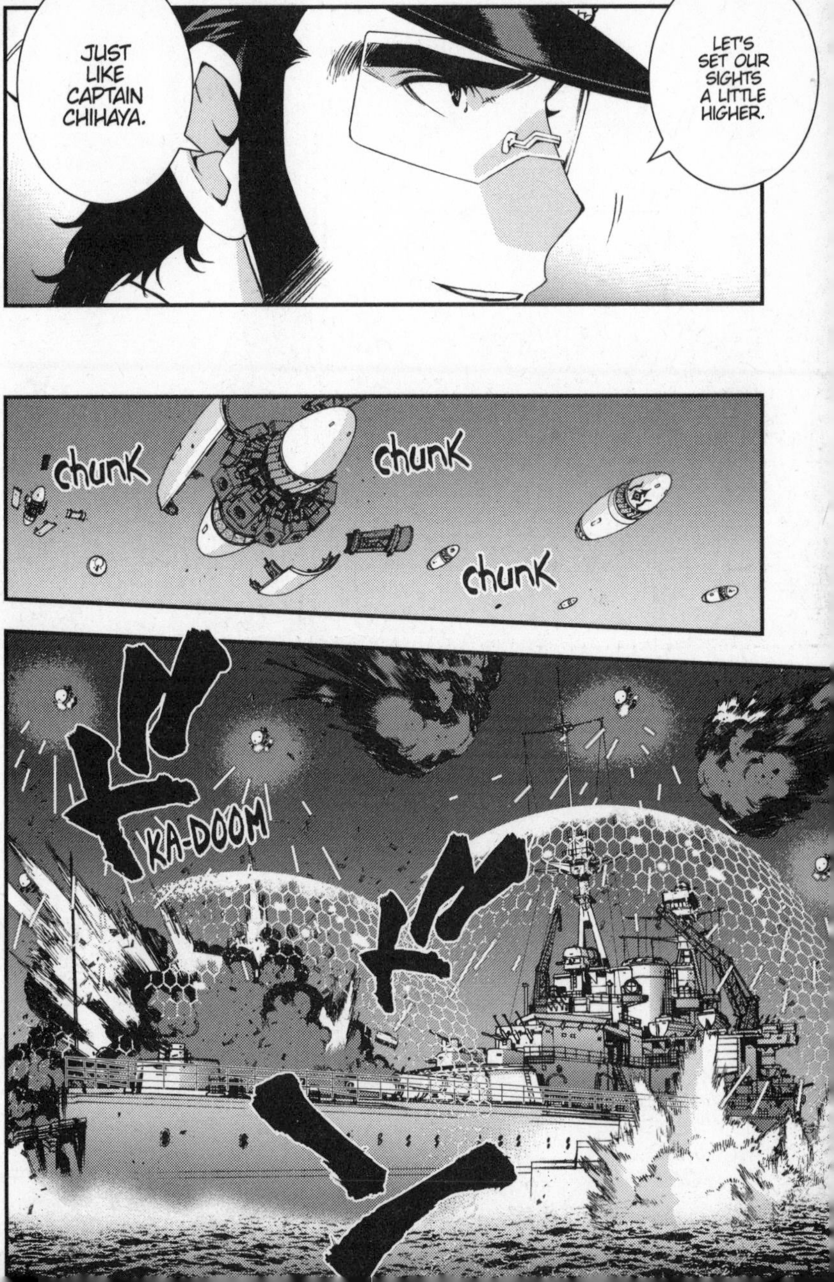
LET'S SET OUR SIGHTS A LITTLE HIGHER.
JUST LIKE CAPTAIN CHIHAYA.
chunk
chunk
chunk
KA-DOOM

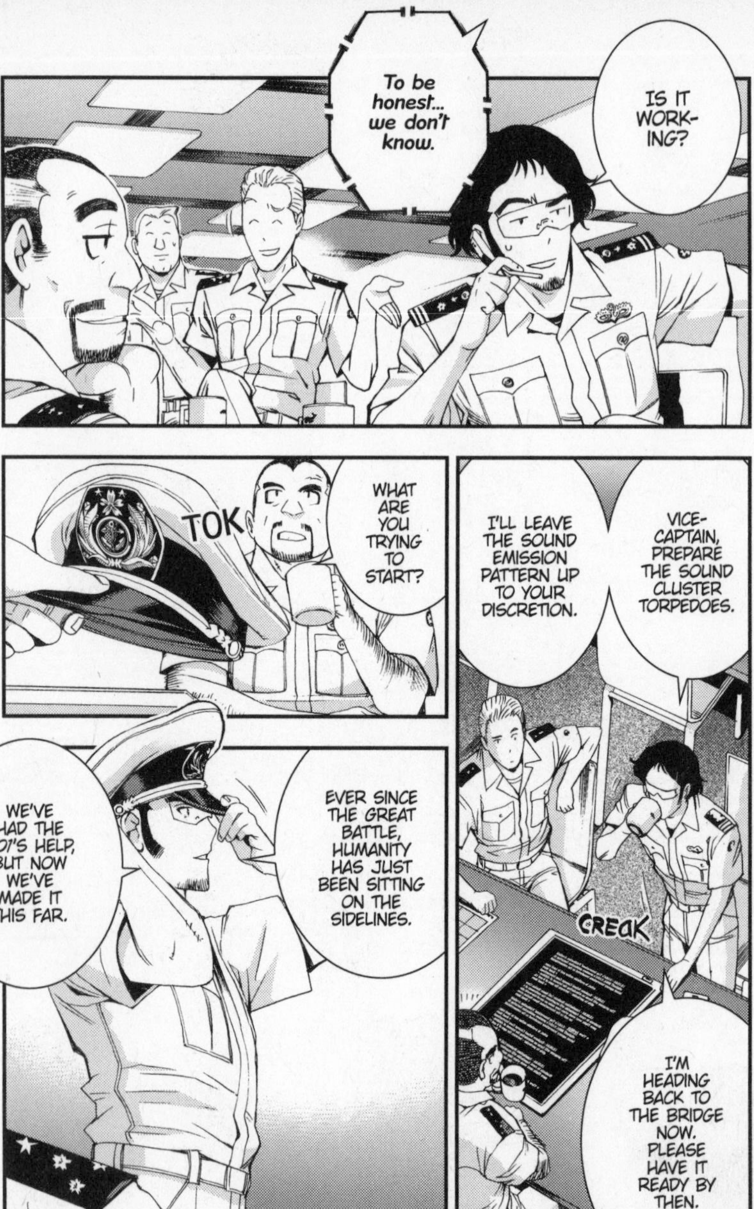
IS IT WORKING?
To be honest... we don't know.
VICE-CAPTAIN, PREPARE THE SOUND CLUSTER TORPEDOES.
I'LL LEAVE THE SOUND EMISSION PATTERN UP TO YOUR DISCRETION.
CREAK
I'M HEADING BACK TO THE BRIDGE NOW. PLEASE HAVE IT READY BY THEN.
WHAT ARE YOU TRYING TO START?
TOK
EVER SINCE THE GREAT BATTLE, HUMANITY HAS JUST BEEN SITTING ON THE SIDELINES.
WE'VE HAD THE 401'S HELP, BUT NOW WE'VE MADE IT THIS FAR.

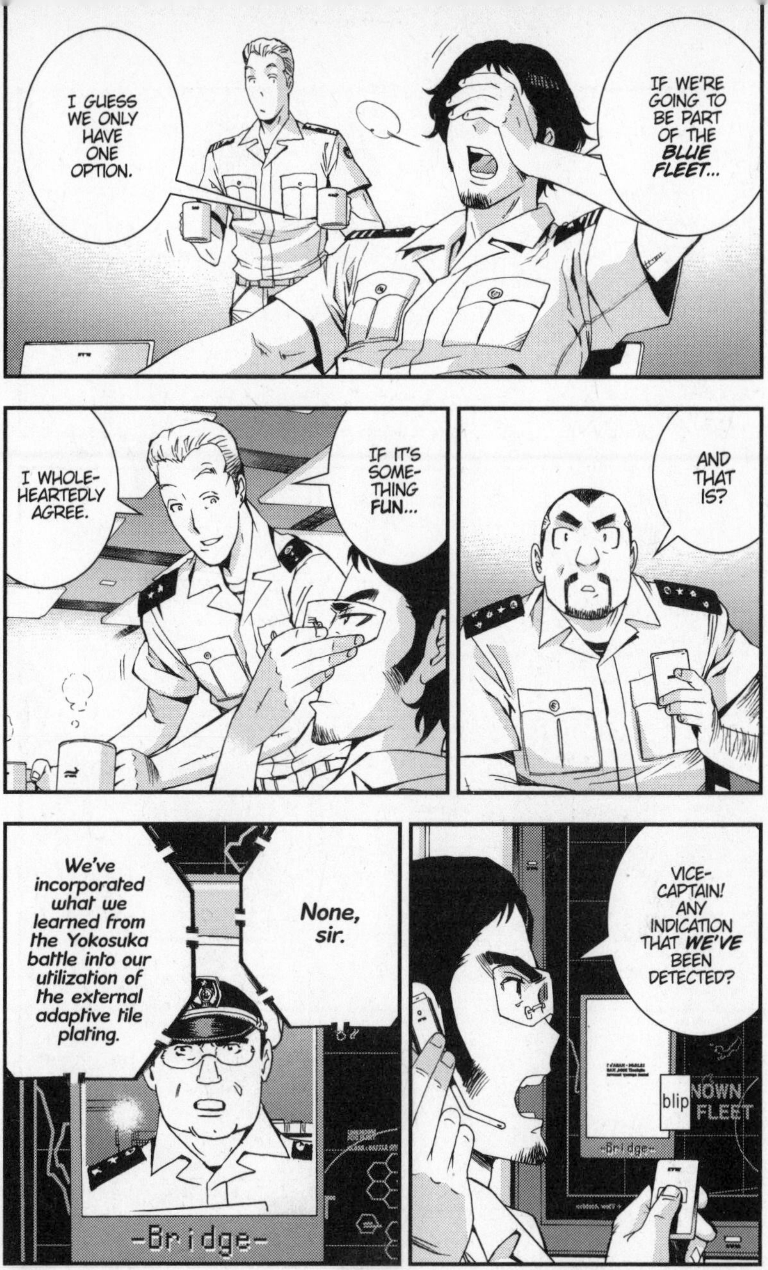
IF WE'RE GOING TO BE PART OF THE ***BLUE FLEET***...
I GUESS WE ONLY HAVE ONE OPTION.
AND THAT IS?
IF IT'S SOMETHING FUN...
I WHOLEHEARTEDLY AGREE.
VICE-CAPTAIN! ANY INDICATION THAT ***WE'VE*** BEEN DETECTED?
blip
-Bridge-
None, sir.
We've incorporated what we learned from the Yokosuka battle into our utilization of the external adaptive tile plating.
-Bridge-

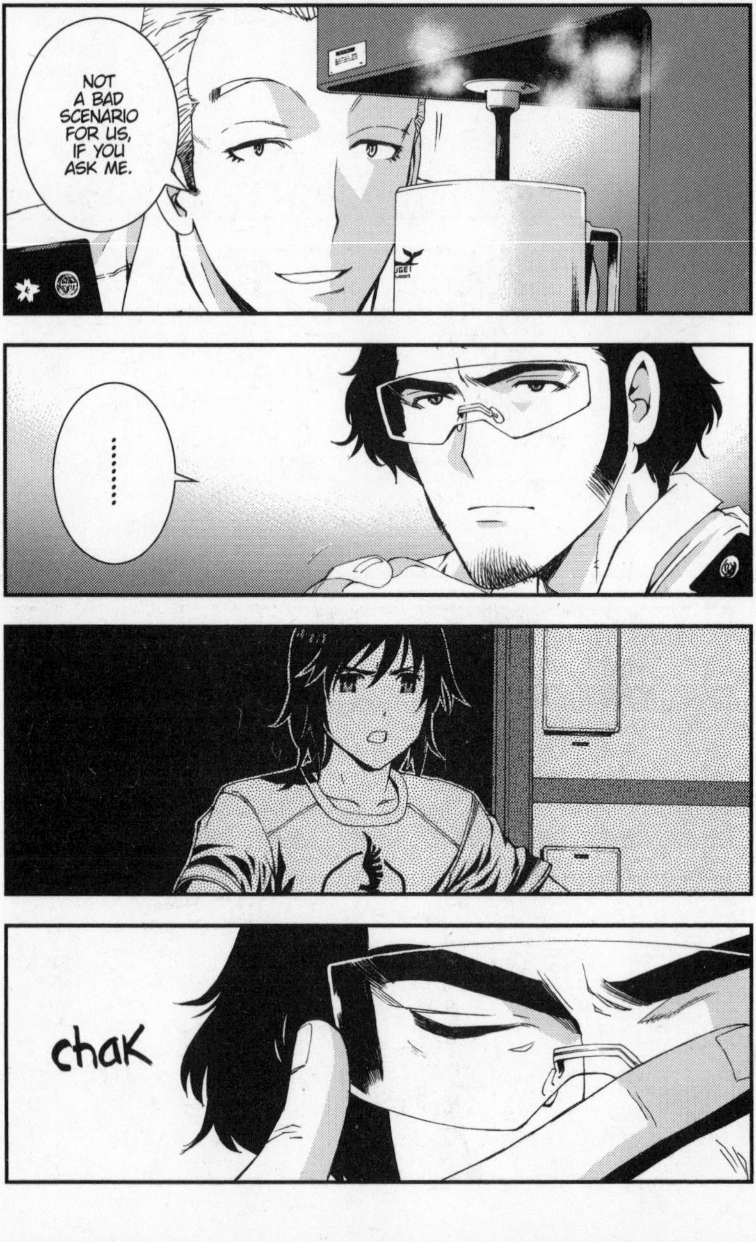
NOT A BAD SCENARIO FOR US, IF YOU ASK ME.
......
chak

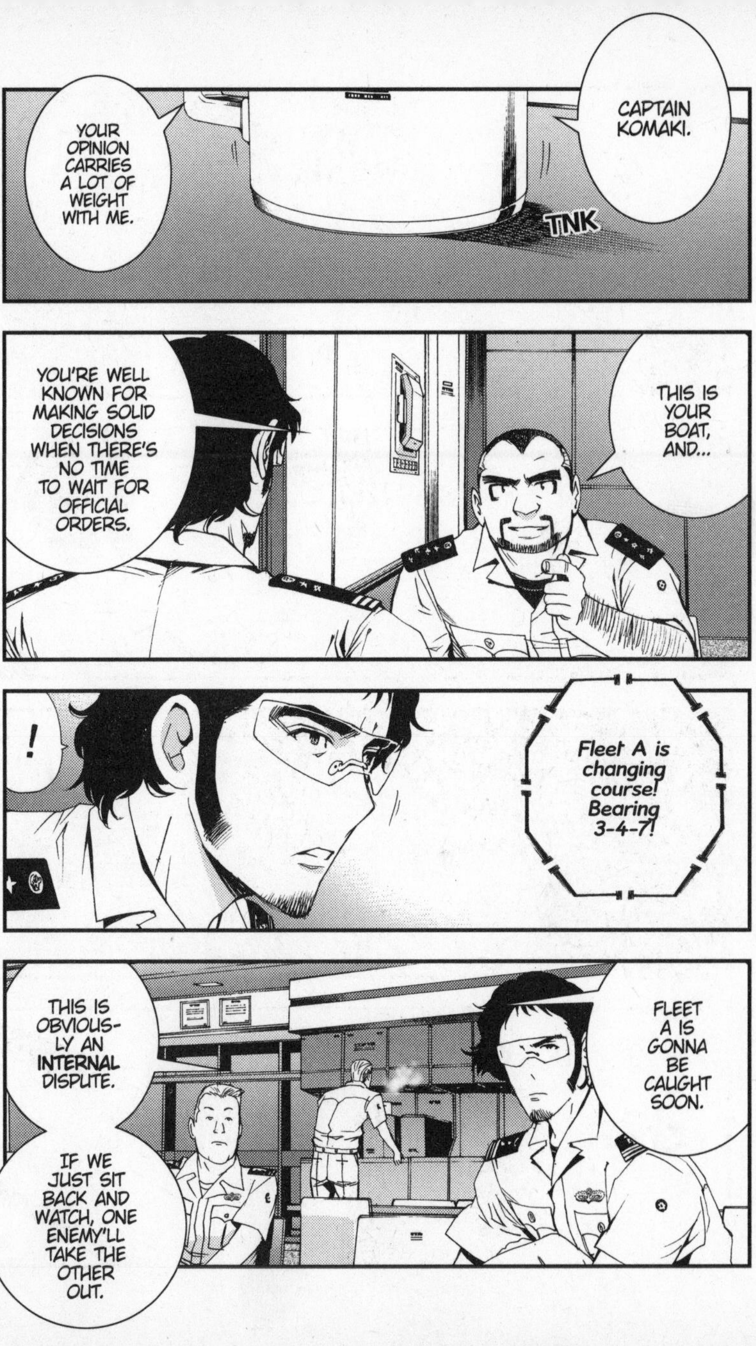
CAPTAIN KOMAKI.
TNK
YOUR OPINION CARRIES A LOT OF WEIGHT WITH ME.
THIS IS YOUR BOAT, AND...
YOU'RE WELL KNOWN FOR MAKING SOLID DECISIONS WHEN THERE'S NO TIME TO WAIT FOR OFFICIAL ORDERS.
Fleet A is changing course! Bearing 3-4-7!
!
FLEET A IS GONNA BE CAUGHT SOON.
THIS IS OBVIOUS-LY AN INTERNAL DISPUTE.
IF WE JUST SIT BACK AND WATCH, ONE ENEMY'LL TAKE THE OTHER OUT.

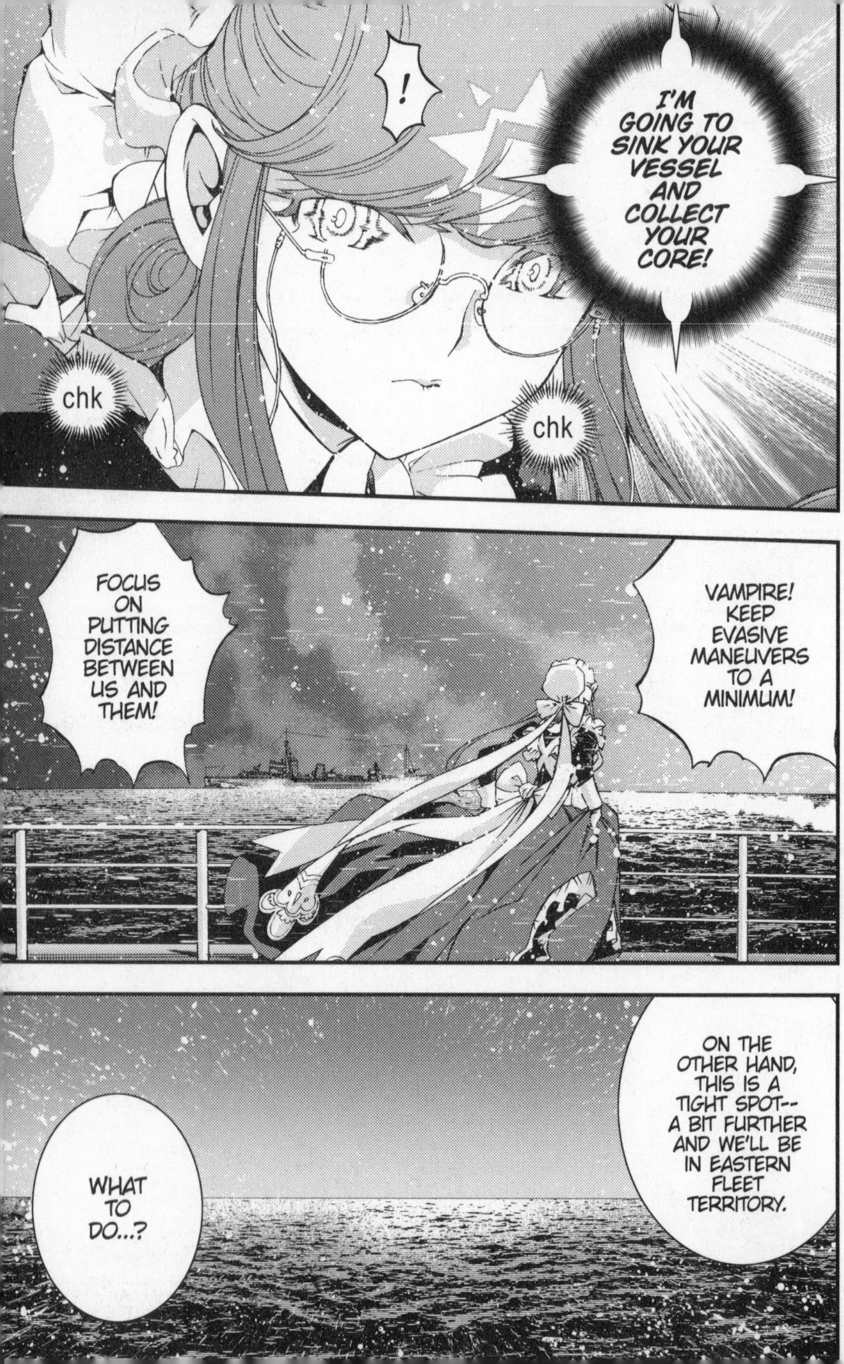
I'M GOING TO SINK YOUR VESSEL AND COLLECT YOUR CORE!
!
chk
chk
VAMPIRE! KEEP EVASIVE MANEUVERS TO A MINIMUM!
FOCUS ON PUTTING DISTANCE BETWEEN US AND THEM!
ON THE OTHER HAND, THIS IS A TIGHT SPOT-- A BIT FURTHER AND WE'LL BE IN EASTERN FLEET TERRITORY.
WHAT TO DO...?

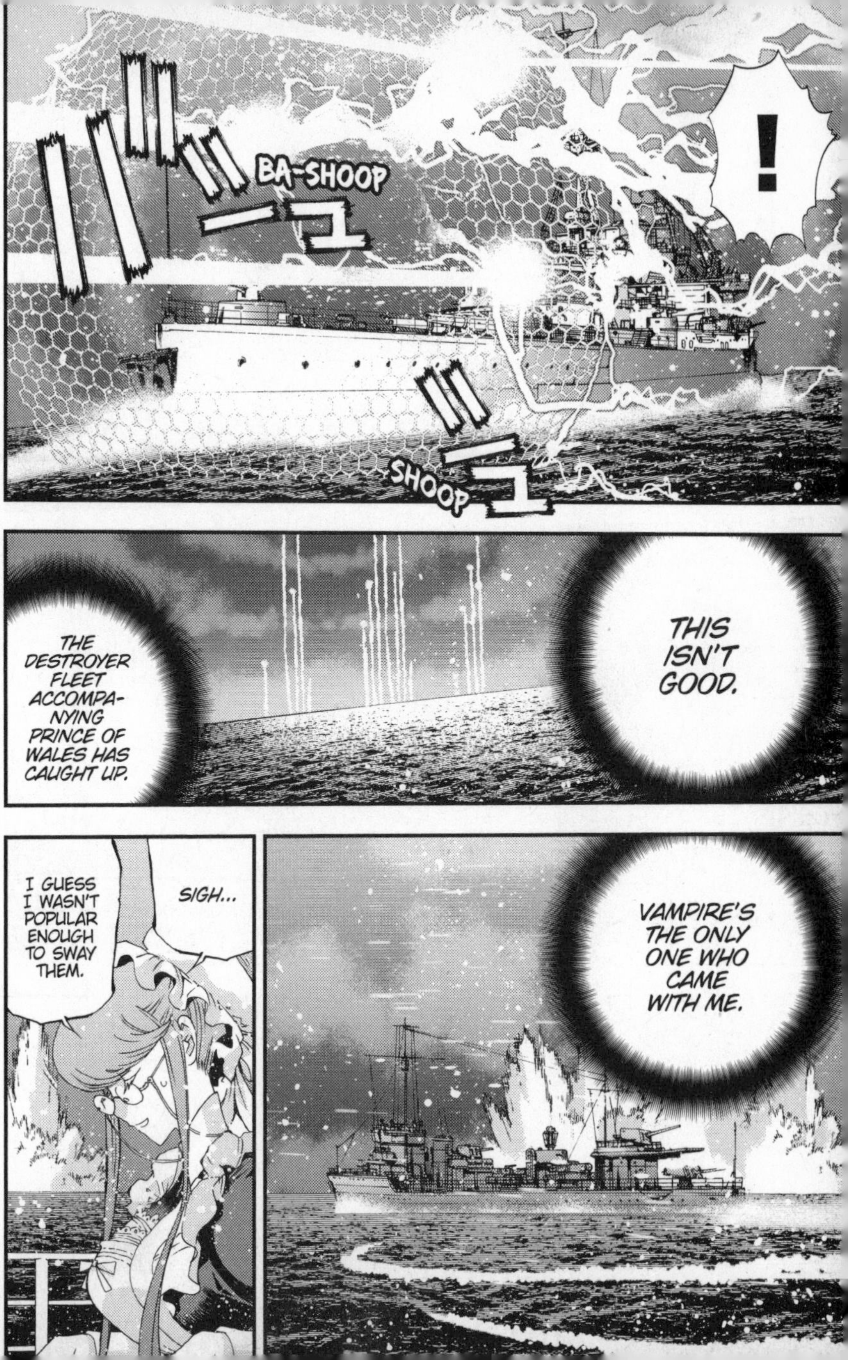
!
BA-SHOOP
SHOOP
THIS ISN'T GOOD.
THE DESTROYER FLEET ACCOMPANYING PRINCE OF WALES HAS CAUGHT UP.
VAMPIRE'S THE ONLY ONE WHO CAME WITH ME.
SIGH...
I GUESS I WASN'T POPULAR ENOUGH TO SWAY THEM.

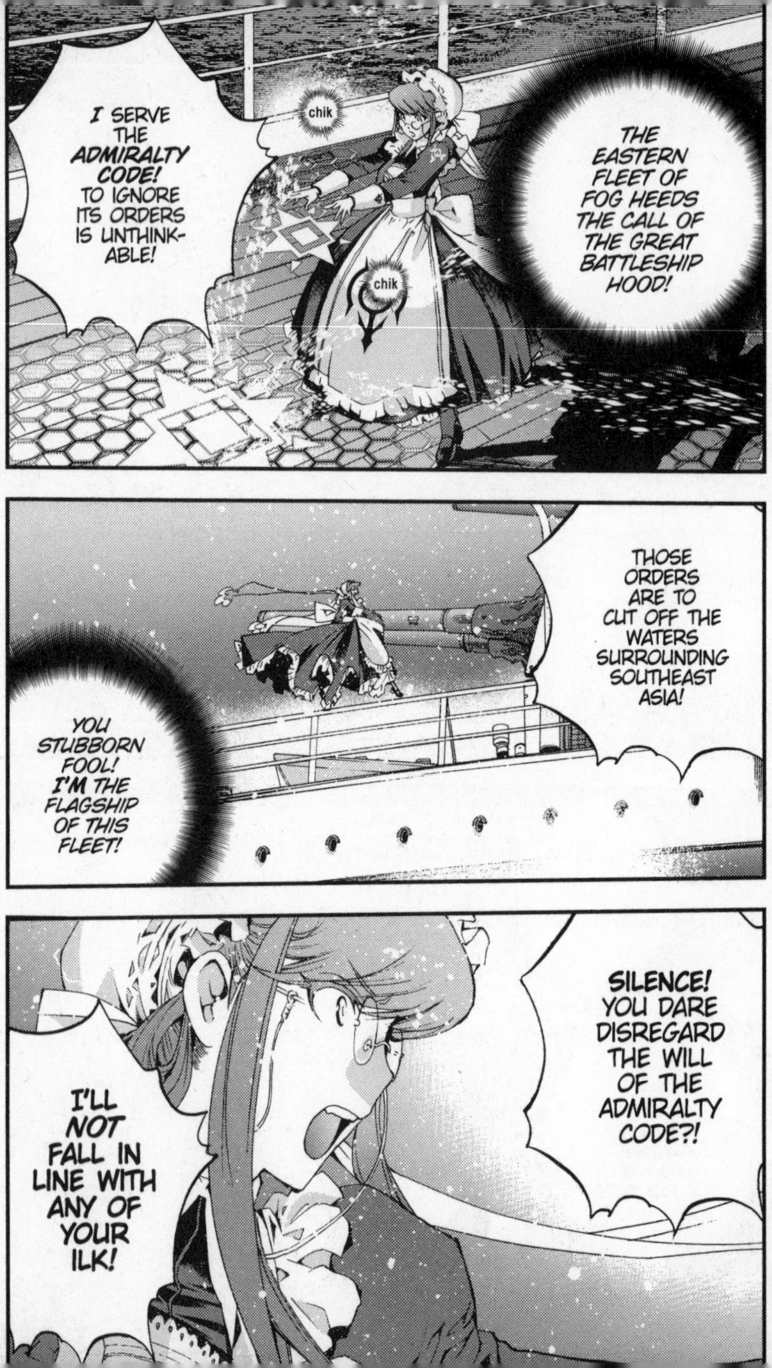
THE EASTERN FLEET OF FOG HEEDS THE CALL OF THE GREAT BATTLESHIP HOOD!
chik
I SERVE THE ADMIRALTY CODE! TO IGNORE ITS ORDERS IS UNTHINK-ABLE!
chik
THOSE ORDERS ARE TO CUT OFF THE WATERS SURROUNDING SOUTHEAST ASIA!
YOU STUBBORN FOOL! I'M THE FLAGSHIP OF THIS FLEET!
SILENCE! YOU DARE DISREGARD THE WILL OF THE ADMIRALTY CODE?!
I'LL NOT FALL IN LINE WITH ANY OF YOUR ILK!

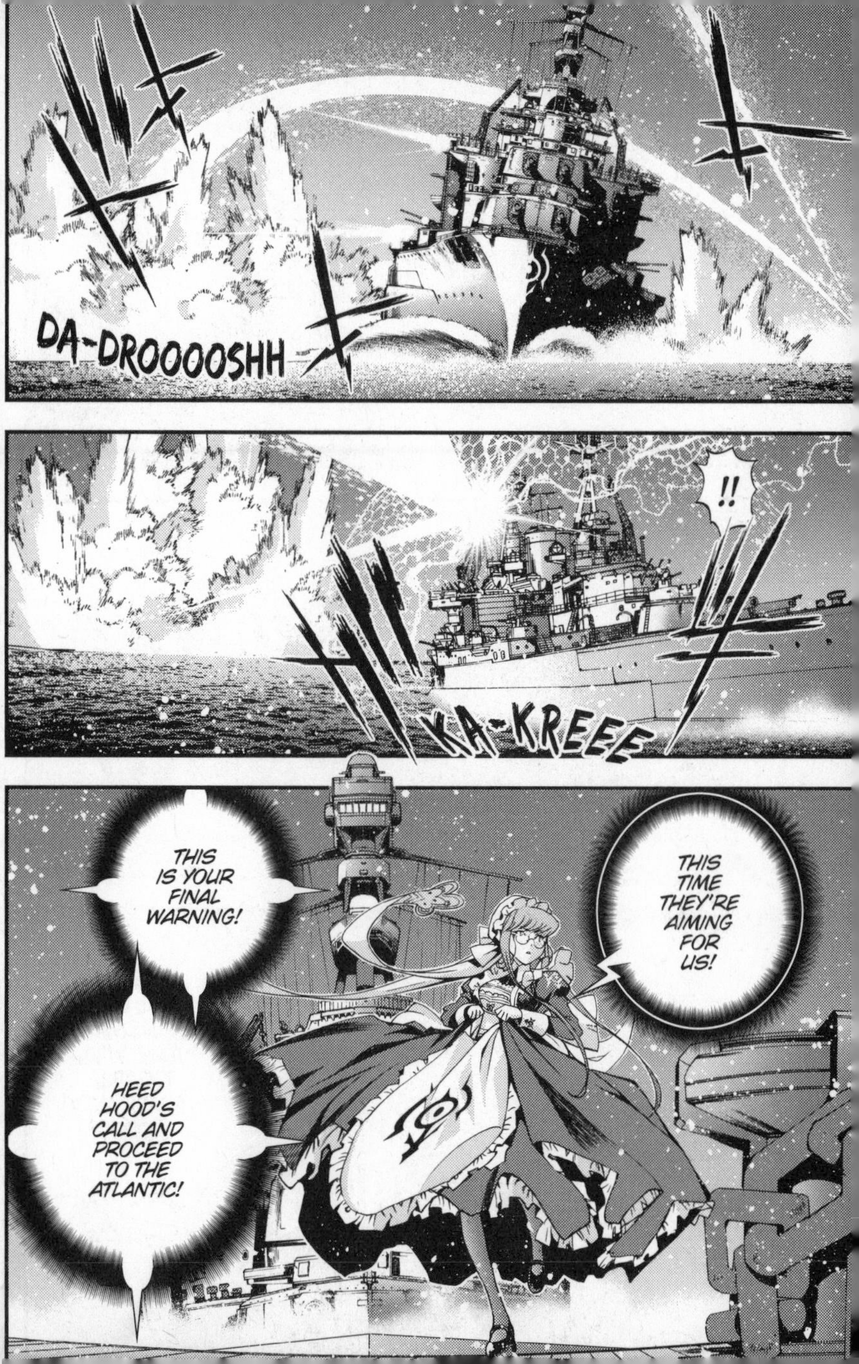
DA-DROOOOOSHH
!!
KA-KREEE
THIS TIME THEY'RE AIMING FOR US!
THIS IS YOUR FINAL WARNING!
HEED HOOD'S CALL AND PROCEED TO THE ATLANTIC!

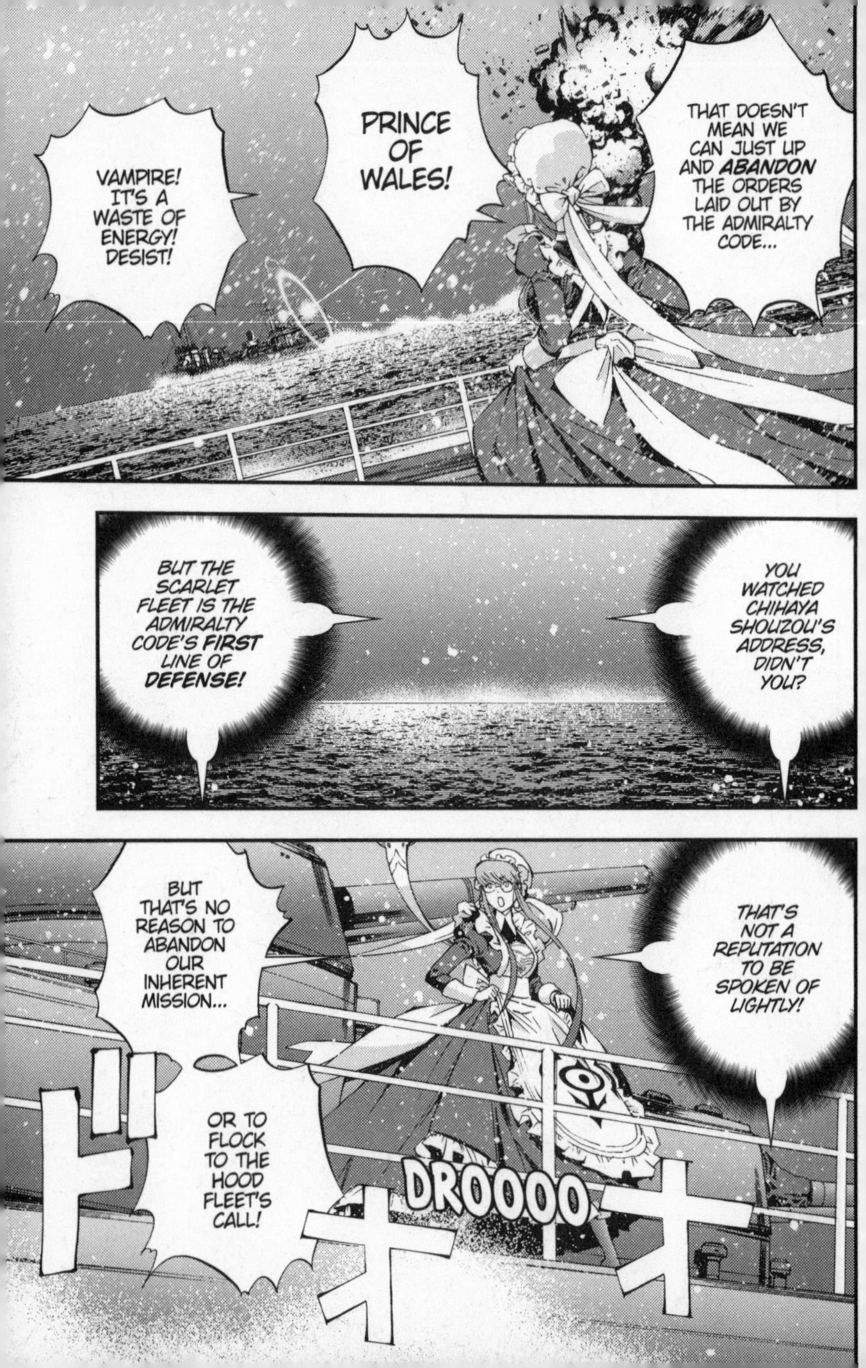
THAT DOESN'T MEAN WE CAN JUST UP AND ABANDON THE ORDERS LAID OUT BY THE ADMIRALTY CODE...
PRINCE OF WALES!
VAMPIRE! IT'S A WASTE OF ENERGY! DESIST!
YOU WATCHED CHIHAYA SHOUZOU'S ADDRESS, DIDN'T YOU?
BUT THE SCARLET FLEET IS THE ADMIRALTY CODE'S FIRST LINE OF DEFENSE!
THAT'S NOT A REPUTATION TO BE SPOKEN OF LIGHTLY!
BUT THAT'S NO REASON TO ABANDON OUR INHERENT MISSION...
OR TO FLOCK TO THE HOOD FLEET'S CALL!
ドオオ
DROOOO

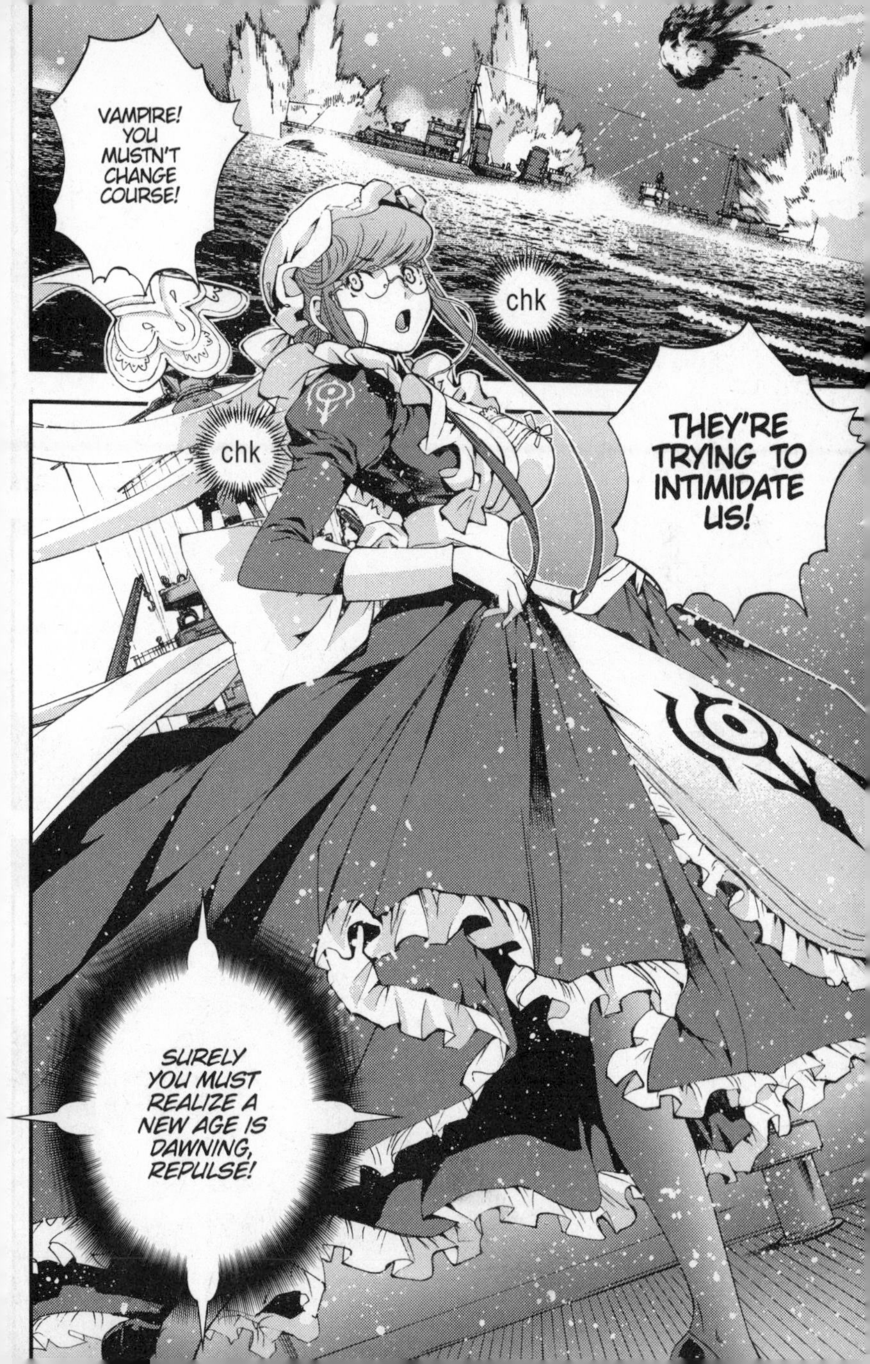

VAMPIRE! YOU MUSTN'T CHANGE COURSE!
chk
THEY'RE TRYING TO INTIMIDATE US!
chk
SURELY YOU MUST REALIZE A NEW AGE IS DAWNING, REPULSE!

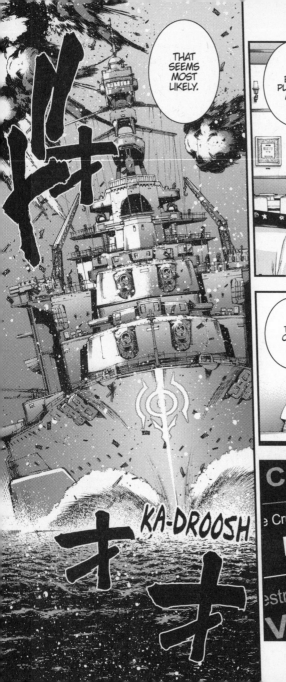

THAT SEEMS MOST LIKELY.

KA-DROOSH

THE SHIP BEING PURSUED MUST BE...

UNDER-STOOD. IN WHICH CASE, BASED ON THIS FORMATION CHART PROVIDED BY THE HYUGA...

THIS ONE?

Class

e Cruiser

Repulse

estroyer

Vamp

A BATTLE CRUISER-- THE REPULSE.

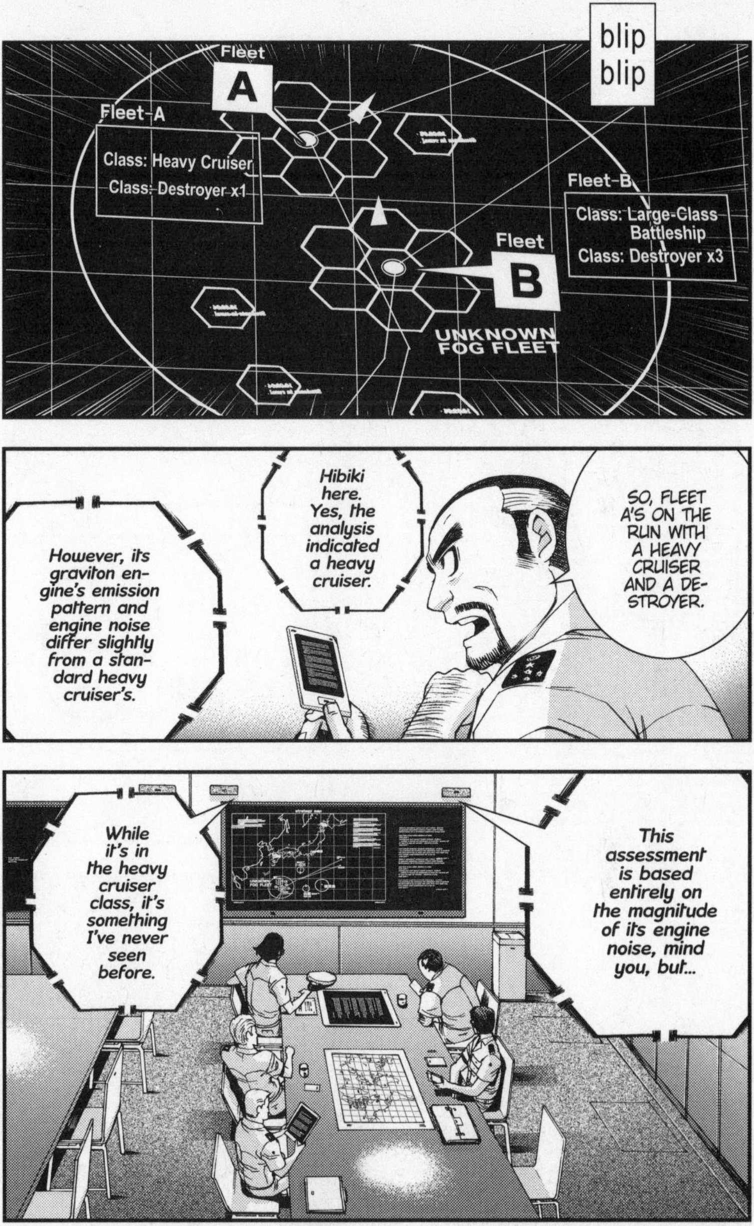
blip blip
Fleet A
Fleet-A
Class: Heavy Cruiser
Class: Destroyer x1
Fleet-B
Class: Large-Class Battleship
Class: Destroyer x3
Fleet B
UNKNOWN FOG FLEET
SO, FLEET A'S ON THE RUN WITH A HEAVY CRUISER AND A DESTROYER.
Hibiki here. Yes, the analysis indicated a heavy cruiser.
However, its graviton engine's emission pattern and engine noise differ slightly from a standard heavy cruiser's.
This assessment is based entirely on the magnitude of its engine noise, mind you, but...
While it's in the heavy cruiser class, it's something I've never seen before.

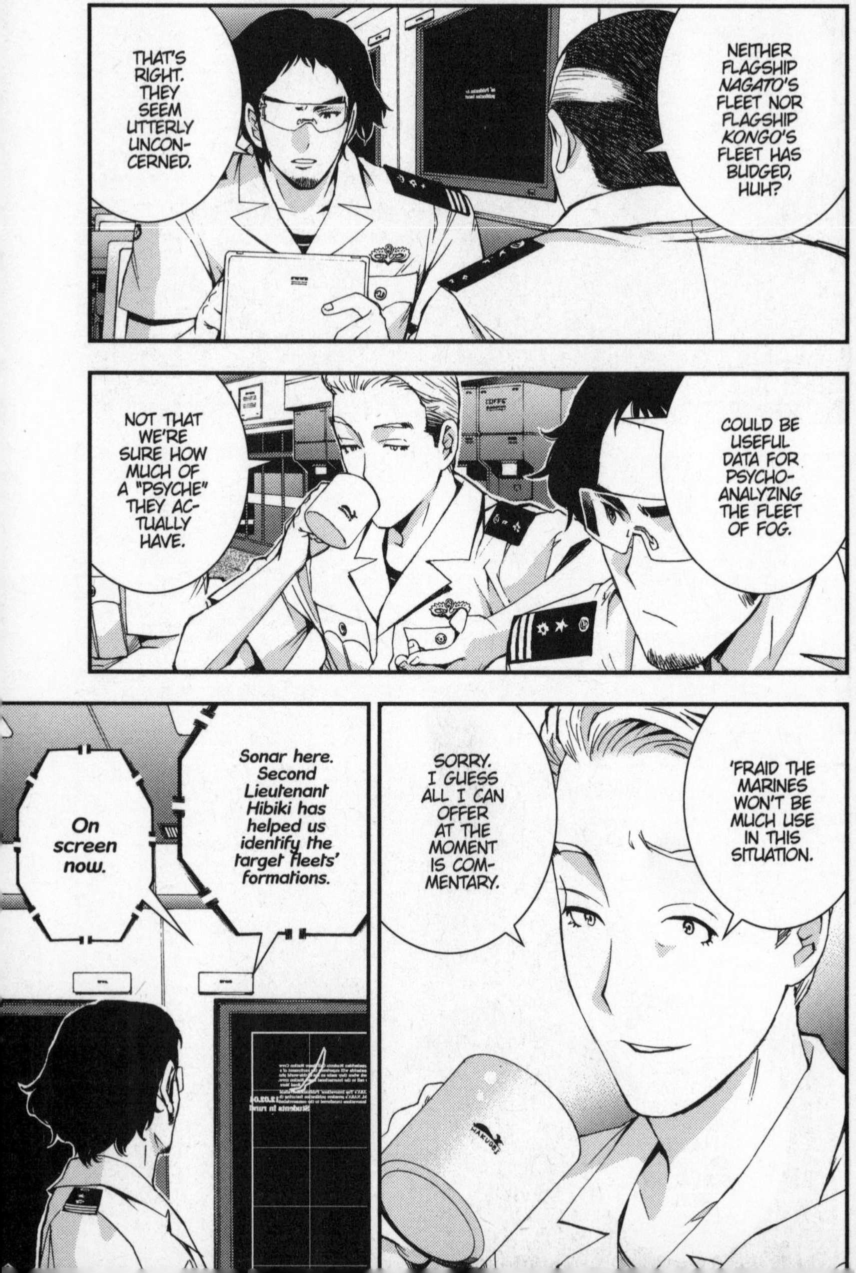
NEITHER FLAGSHIP *NAGATO*'S FLEET NOR FLAGSHIP *KONGO*'S FLEET HAS BUDGED, HUH?
THAT'S RIGHT. THEY SEEM UTTERLY UNCON-CERNED.
COULD BE USEFUL DATA FOR PSYCHO-ANALYZING THE FLEET OF FOG.
NOT THAT WE'RE SURE HOW MUCH OF A "PSYCHE" THEY AC-TUALLY HAVE.
'FRAID THE MARINES WON'T BE MUCH USE IN THIS SITUATION.
SORRY. I GUESS ALL I CAN OFFER AT THE MOMENT IS COM-MENTARY.
Sonar here. Second Lieutenant Hibiki has helped us identify the target fleets' formations.
On screen now.

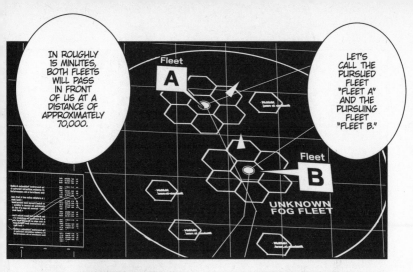

LET'S CALL THE PURSUED FLEET "FLEET A" AND THE PURSUING FLEET "FLEET B."
IN ROUGHLY 15 MINUTES, BOTH FLEETS WILL PASS IN FRONT OF US AT A DISTANCE OF APPROXIMATELY 70,000.
Fleet A
Fleet B
UNKNOWN FOG FLEET
AND THEIR FORMATION?
STILL UN-KNOWN.
THERE'S TOO MUCH NOISE. THEY APPEAR TO BE IN COMBAT.
THIS IS AN ENLARGED MAP WITH OUR SHIP AT THE CENTER.
I-401
blip
THE 401 IS EN ROUTE TO THE RENDEZVOUS POINT, AS PLANNED.
Fleet A
BATTLE CRUISER
Fleet B
UNKNOWN FOG FLEET
CLASS : BATTLESHIP
White Whale HAS-03
IT'S LIKELY THAT THEY'VE PICKED UP THE TARGET FLEETS ON THEIR SONAR AS WELL.
blip

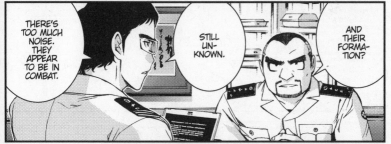

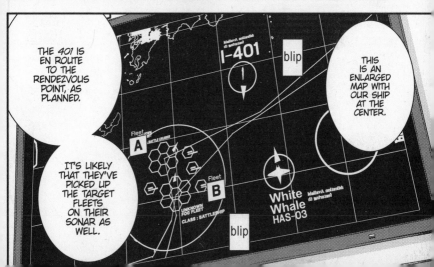

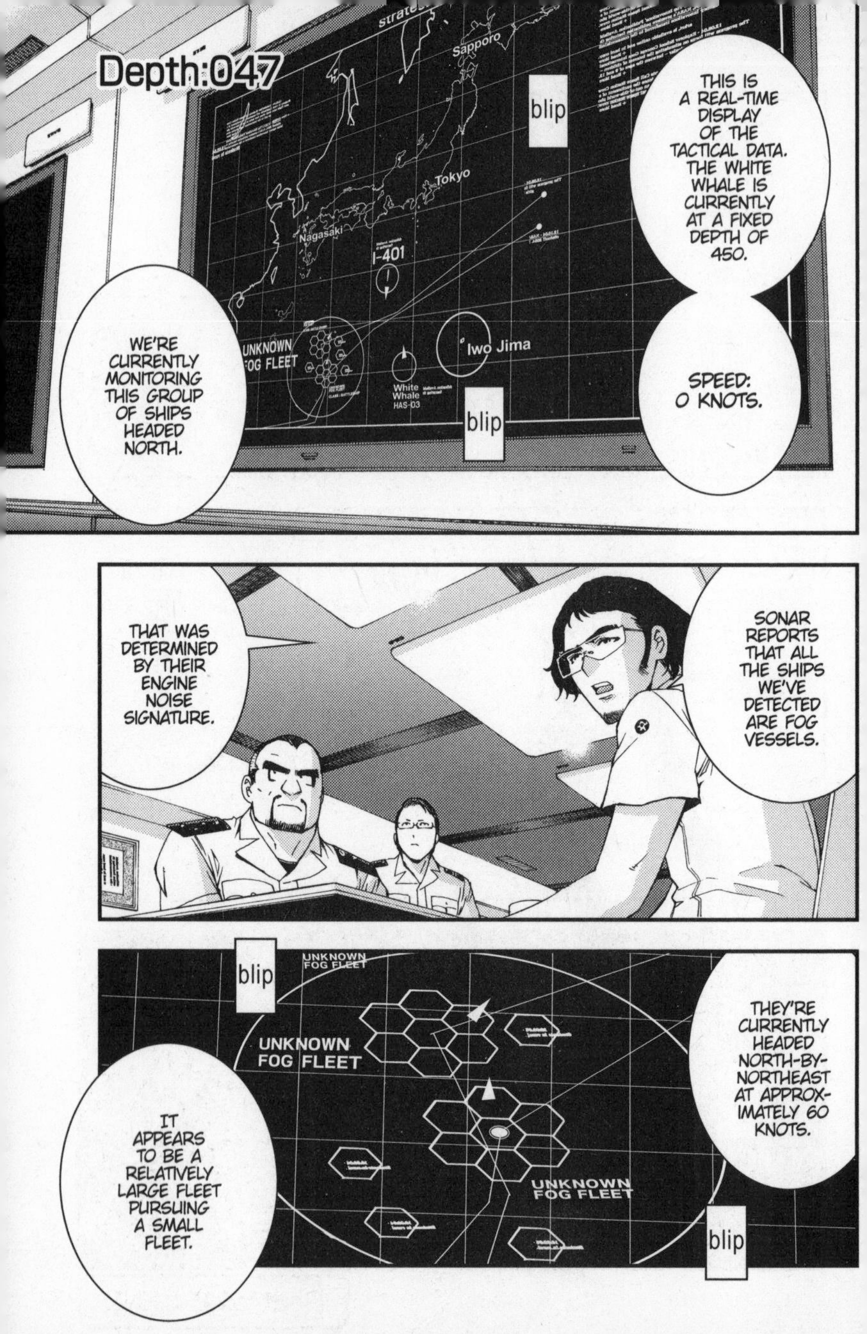
Depth:047
Sapporo
Tokyo
Nagasaki
I-401
UNKNOWN FOG FLEET
Iwo Jima
White Whale HAS-03
blip
blip
THIS IS A REAL-TIME DISPLAY OF THE TACTICAL DATA. THE WHITE WHALE IS CURRENTLY AT A FIXED DEPTH OF 450.
SPEED: 0 KNOTS.
WE'RE CURRENTLY MONITORING THIS GROUP OF SHIPS HEADED NORTH.
SONAR REPORTS THAT ALL THE SHIPS WE'VE DETECTED ARE FOG VESSELS.
THAT WAS DETERMINED BY THEIR ENGINE NOISE SIGNATURE.
blip
UNKNOWN FOG FLEET
UNKNOWN FOG FLEET
UNKNOWN FOG FLEET
blip
THEY'RE CURRENTLY HEADED NORTH-BY-NORTHEAST AT APPROXIMATELY 60 KNOTS.
IT APPEARS TO BE A RELATIVELY LARGE FLEET PURSUING A SMALL FLEET.

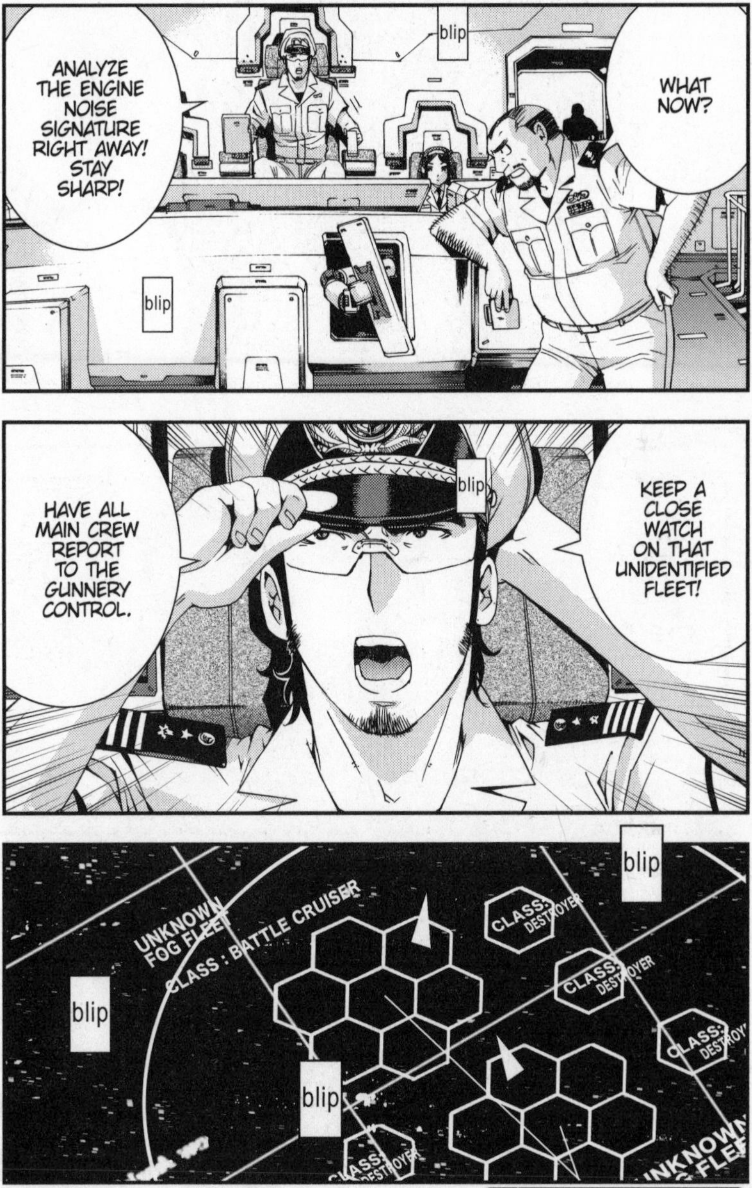
WHAT NOW?
blip
ANALYZE THE ENGINE NOISE SIGNATURE RIGHT AWAY! STAY SHARP!
blip
KEEP A CLOSE WATCH ON THAT UNIDENTIFIED FLEET!
blip
HAVE ALL MAIN CREW REPORT TO THE GUNNERY CONTROL.
blip
CLASS: DESTROYER
CLASS: DESTROYER
CLASS: DESTROYER
UNKNOWN FOG FLEET
CLASS : BATTLE CRUISER
UNKNOWN
blip
blip
CLASS: DESTROYER

Depth:046／END

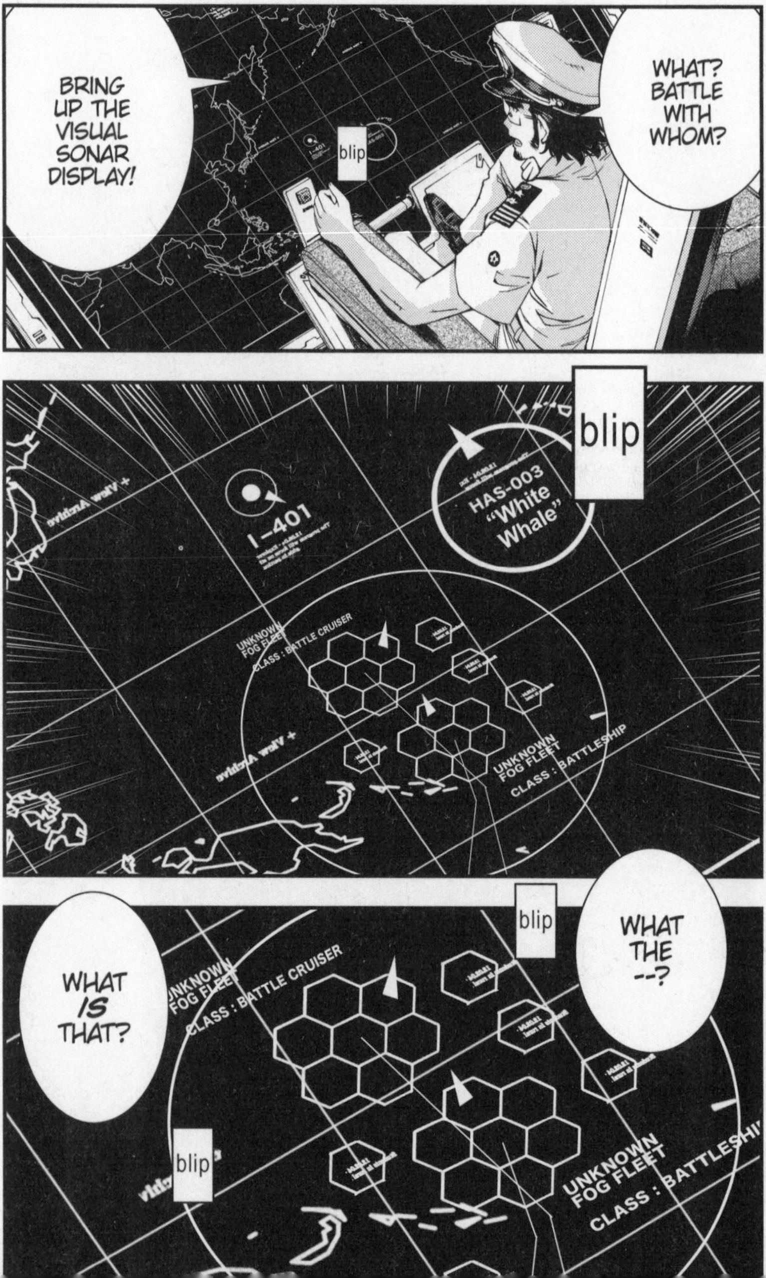
WHAT? BATTLE WITH WHOM?
BRING UP THE VISUAL SONAR DISPLAY!
blip
blip
HAS-003 "White Whale"
I-401
UNKNOWN FOG FLEET CLASS : BATTLE CRUISER
UNKNOWN FOG FLEET CLASS : BATTLESHIP
blip
WHAT THE --?
WHAT IS THAT?
UNKNOWN FOG FLEET CLASS : BATTLE CRUISER
UNKNOWN FOG FLEET CLASS : BATTLESHI
blip

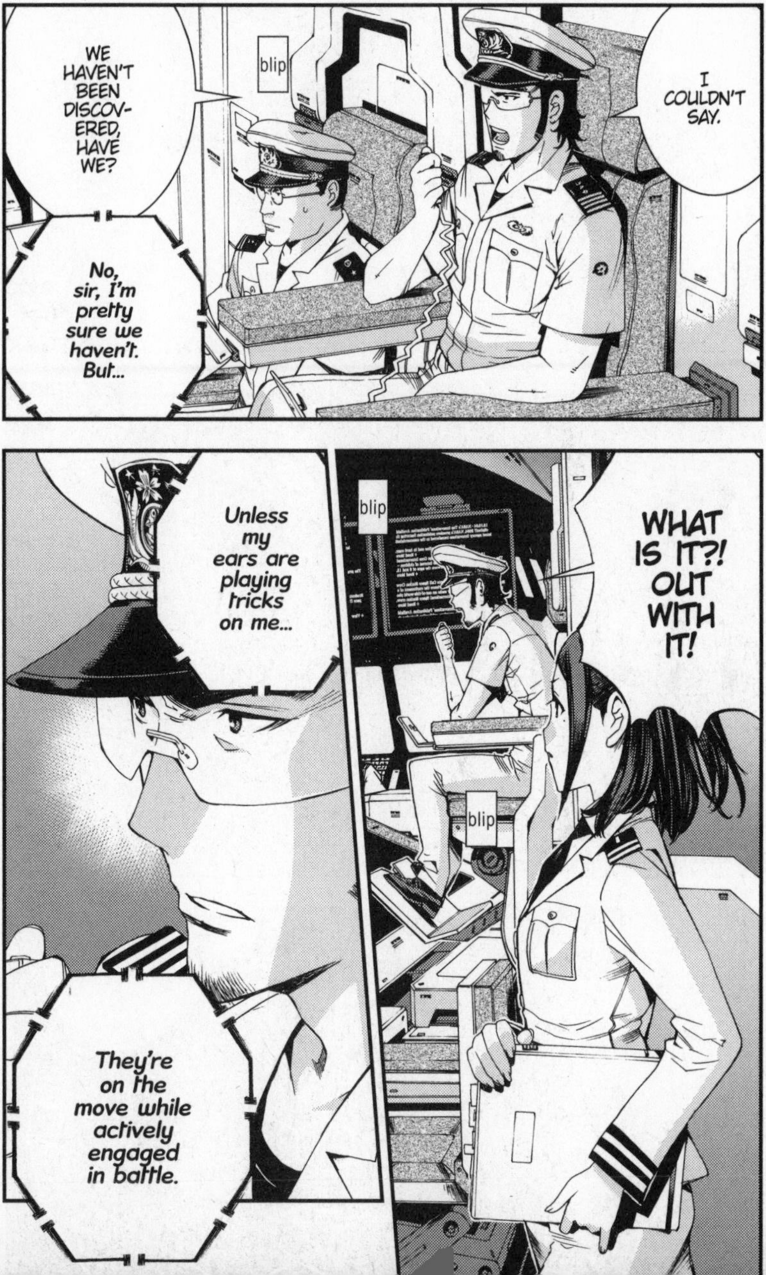

I COULDN'T SAY.
blip
WE HAVEN'T BEEN DISCOVERED, HAVE WE?
No, sir, I'm pretty sure we haven't. But...
WHAT IS IT?! OUT WITH IT!
blip
blip
Unless my ears are playing tricks on me...
They're on the move while actively engaged in battle.

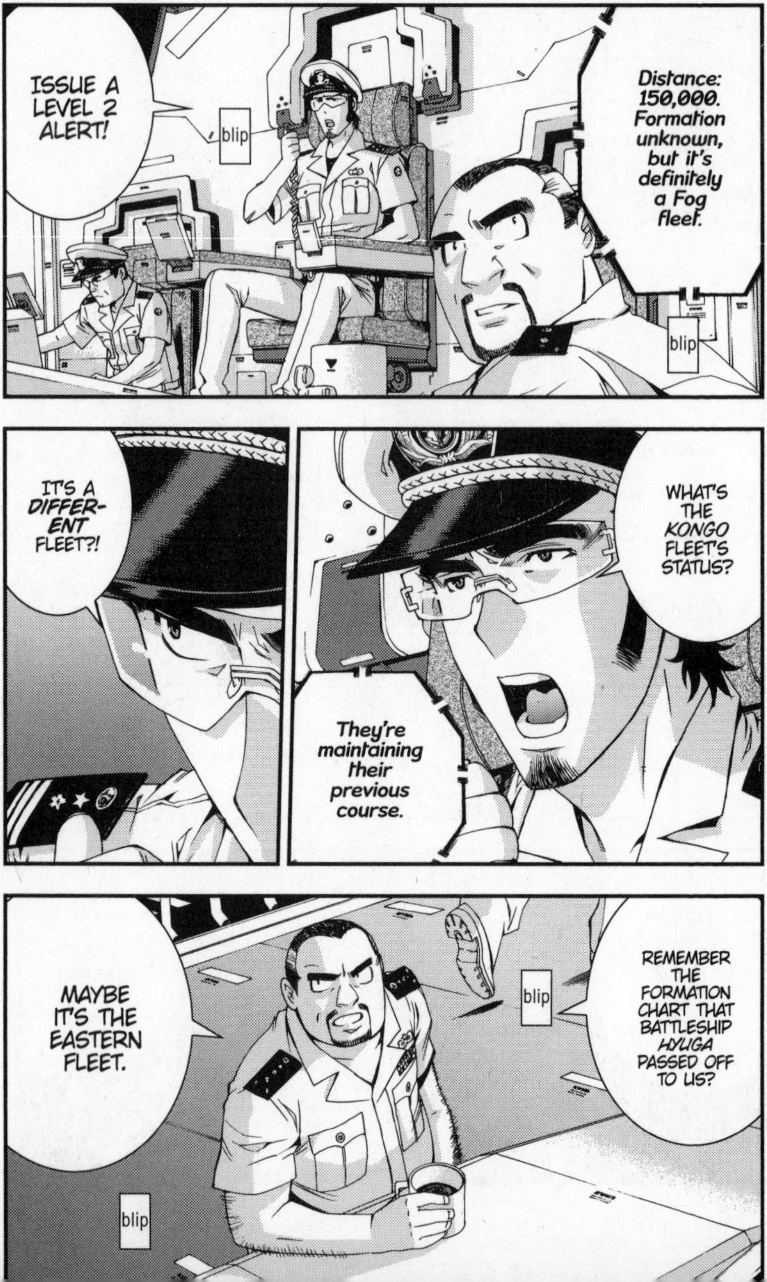
Distance: 150,000. Formation unknown, but it's definitely a Fog fleet.
blip
ISSUE A LEVEL 2 ALERT!
blip
WHAT'S THE *KONGO* FLEET'S STATUS?
They're maintaining their previous course.
IT'S A *DIFFERENT* FLEET?!
REMEMBER THE FORMATION CHART THAT BATTLESHIP *HYUGA* PASSED OFF TO US?
blip
MAYBE IT'S THE EASTERN FLEET.
blip

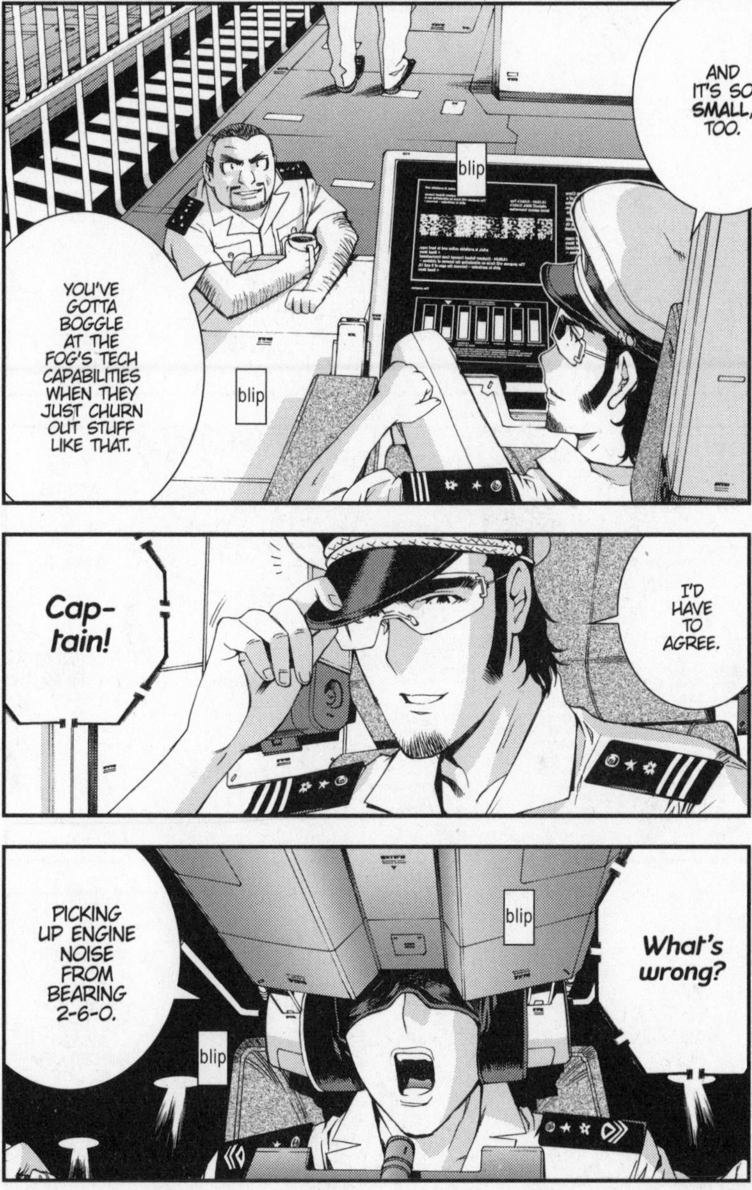
AND IT'S SO SMALL, TOO.
blip
YOU'VE GOTTA BOGGLE AT THE FOG'S TECH CAPABILITIES WHEN THEY JUST CHURN OUT STUFF LIKE THAT.
blip
I'D HAVE TO AGREE.
Cap-tain!
What's wrong?
blip
PICKING UP ENGINE NOISE FROM BEARING 2-6-0.
blip

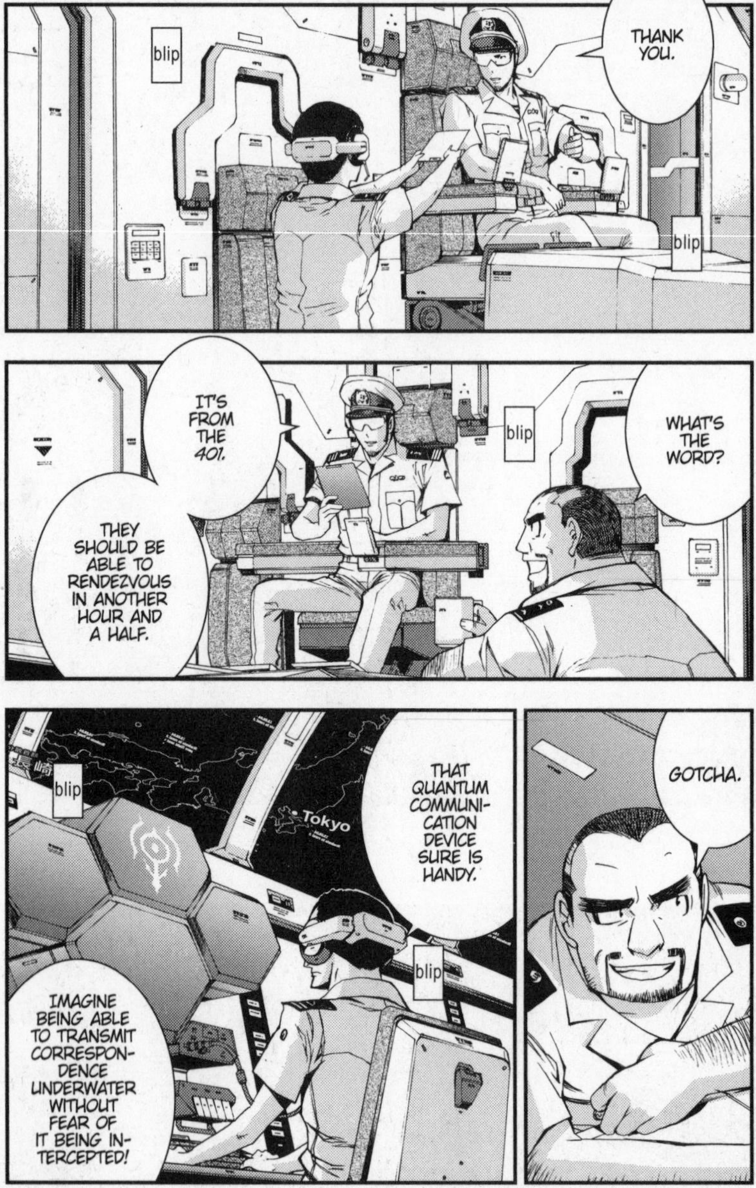
THANK YOU.
blip
blip
WHAT'S THE WORD?
blip
IT'S FROM THE 401.
THEY SHOULD BE ABLE TO RENDEZVOUS IN ANOTHER HOUR AND A HALF.
GOTCHA.
THAT QUANTUM COMMUNI-CATION DEVICE SURE IS HANDY.
blip
Tokyo
blip
IMAGINE BEING ABLE TO TRANSMIT CORRESPON-DENCE UNDERWATER WITHOUT FEAR OF IT BEING IN-TERCEPTED!

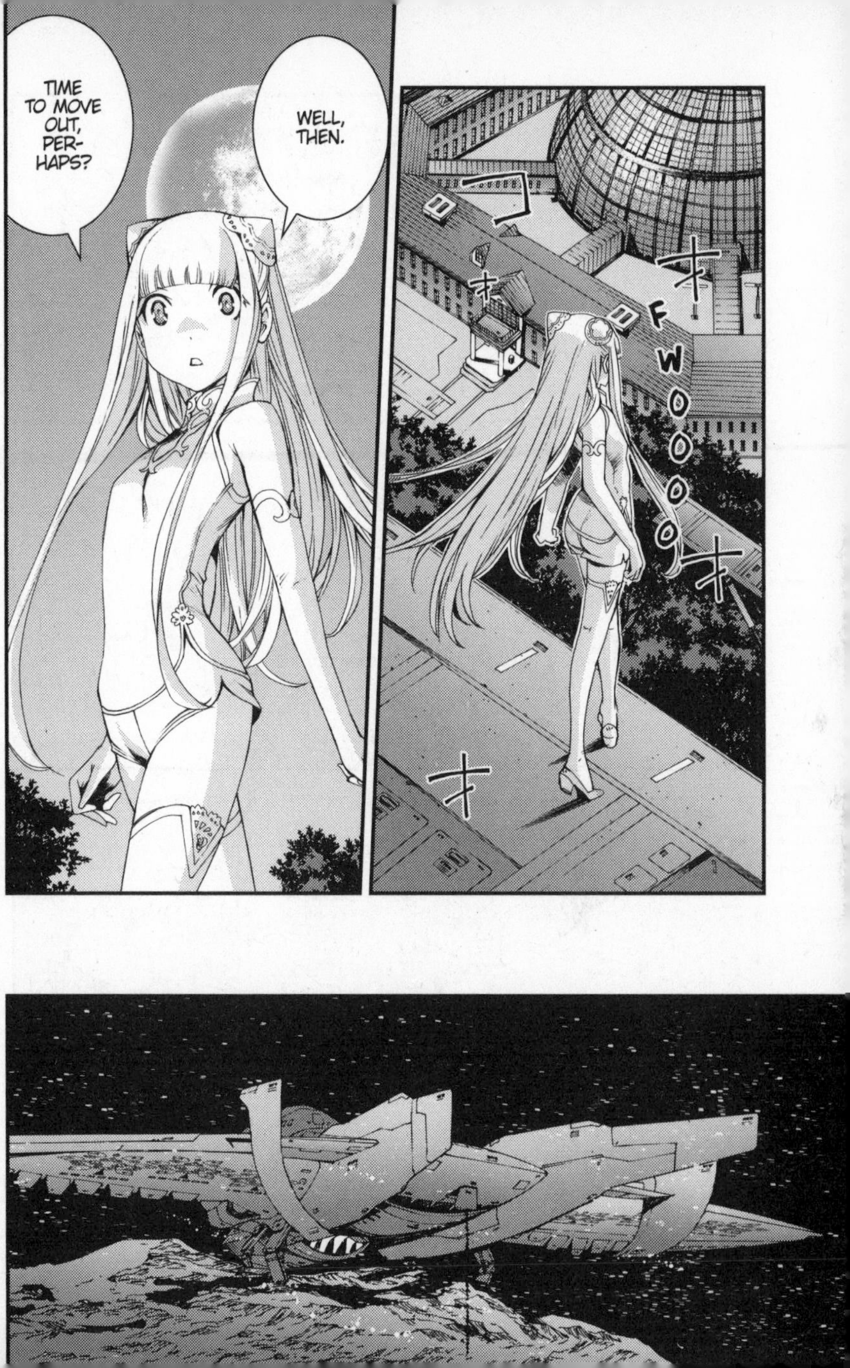
FWOOOOH
WELL, THEN.
TIME TO MOVE OUT, PER-HAPS?

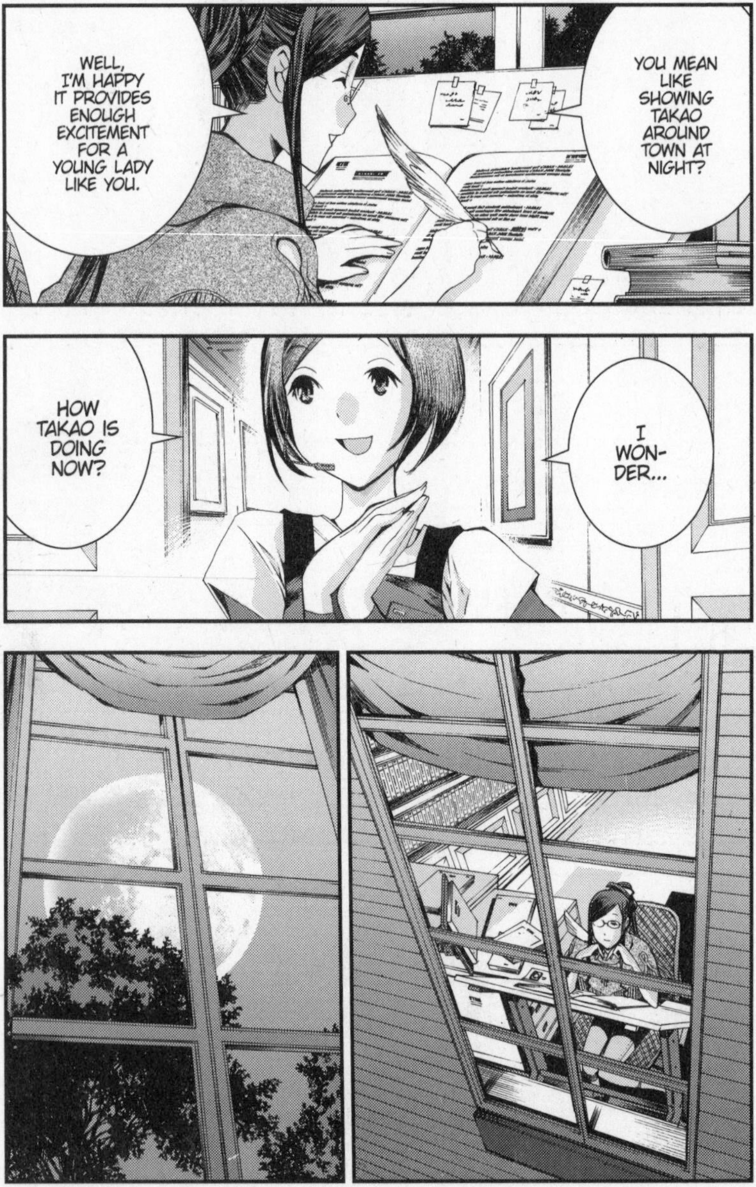
YOU MEAN LIKE SHOWING TAKAO AROUND TOWN AT NIGHT?
WELL, I'M HAPPY IT PROVIDES ENOUGH EXCITEMENT FOR A YOUNG LADY LIKE YOU.
I WON-DER...
HOW TAKAO IS DOING NOW?

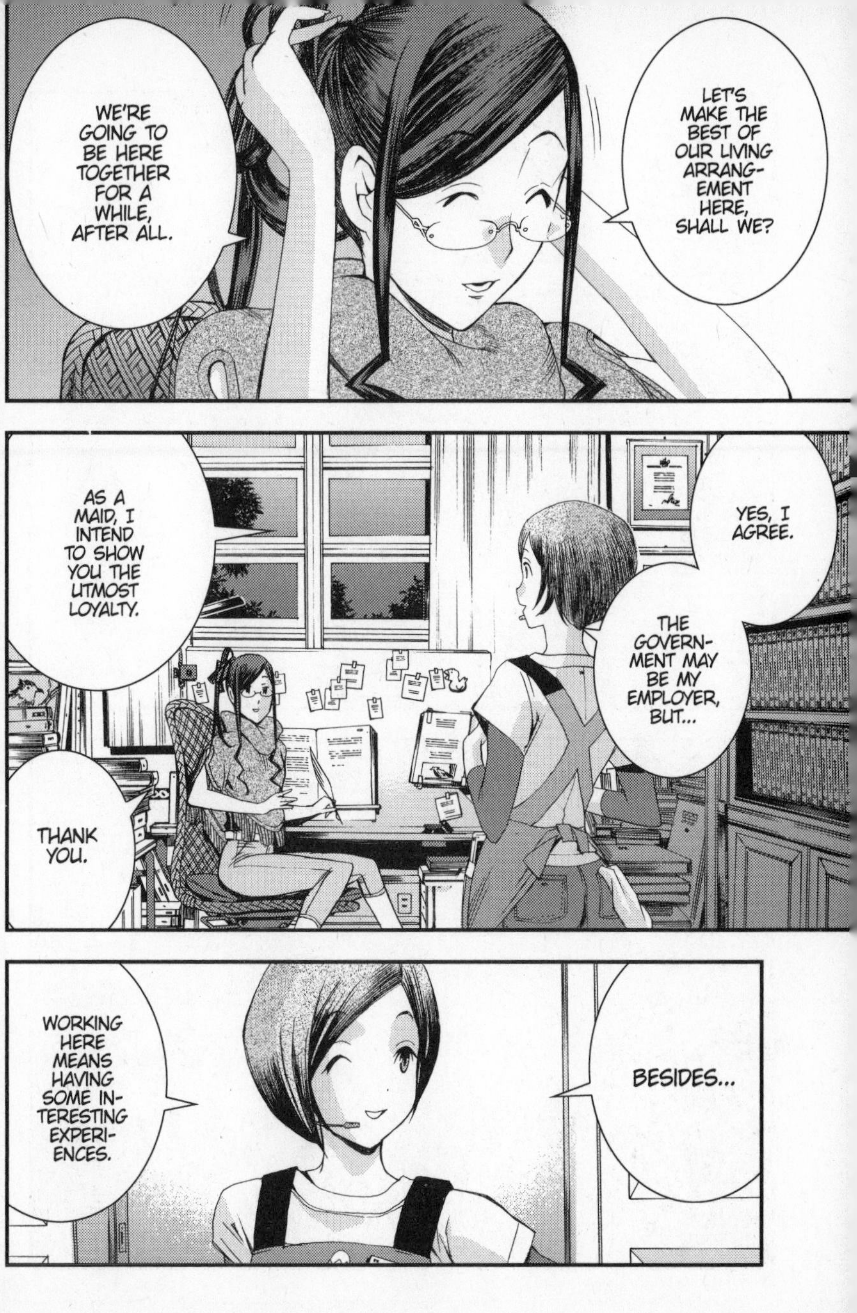
LET'S MAKE THE BEST OF OUR LIVING ARRANGEMENT HERE, SHALL WE?
WE'RE GOING TO BE HERE TOGETHER FOR A WHILE, AFTER ALL.
YES, I AGREE.
THE GOVERNMENT MAY BE MY EMPLOYER, BUT...
AS A MAID, I INTEND TO SHOW YOU THE UTMOST LOYALTY.
THANK YOU.
BESIDES...
WORKING HERE MEANS HAVING SOME INTERESTING EXPERIENCES.

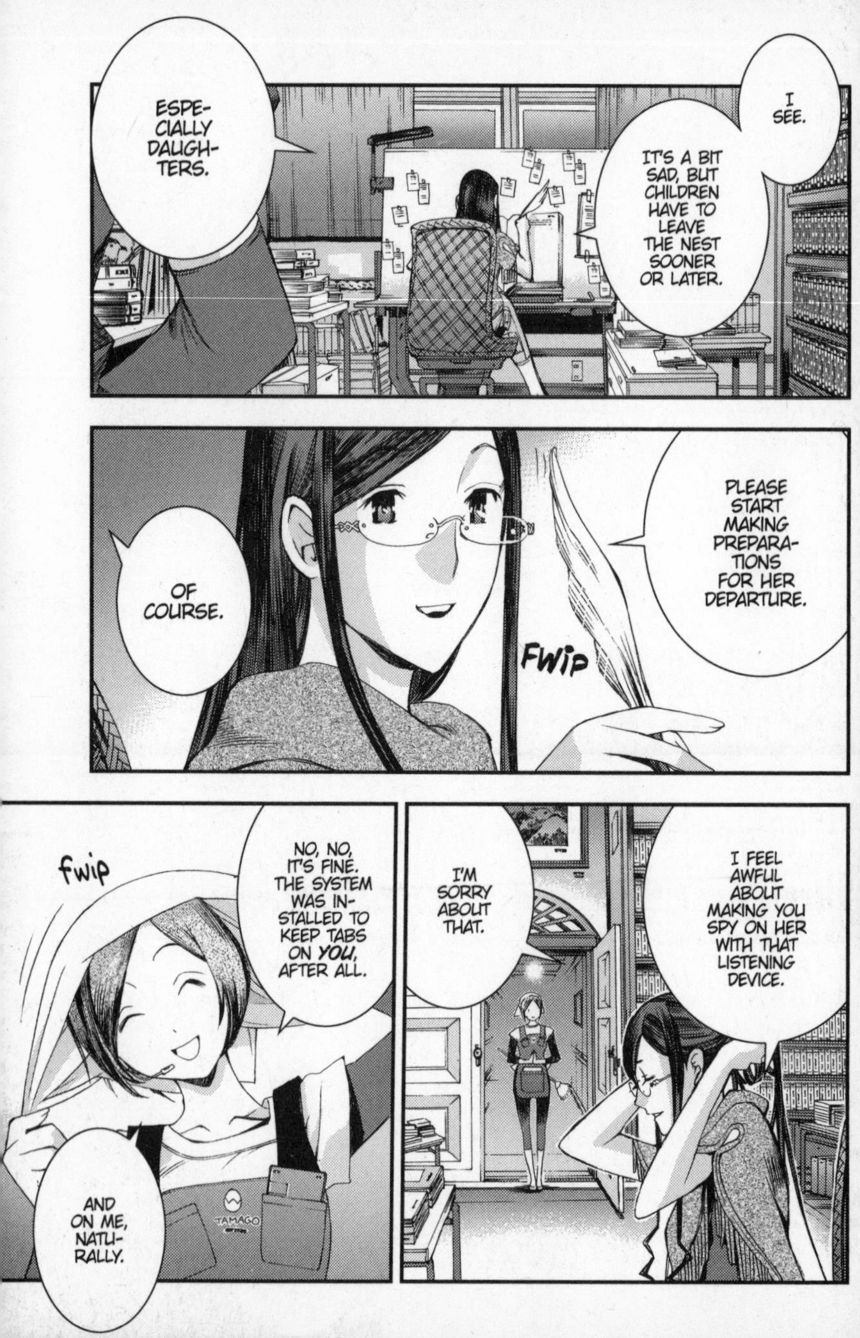
I SEE.
IT'S A BIT SAD, BUT CHILDREN HAVE TO LEAVE THE NEST SOONER OR LATER.
ESPE-CIALLY DAUGH-TERS.
PLEASE START MAKING PREPARA-TIONS FOR HER DEPARTURE.
FWIP
OF COURSE.
I FEEL AWFUL ABOUT MAKING YOU SPY ON HER WITH THAT LISTENING DEVICE.
I'M SORRY ABOUT THAT.
NO, NO, IT'S FINE. THE SYSTEM WAS IN-STALLED TO KEEP TABS ON *YOU*, AFTER ALL.
fwip
TAMAGO
AND ON ME, NATU-RALLY.

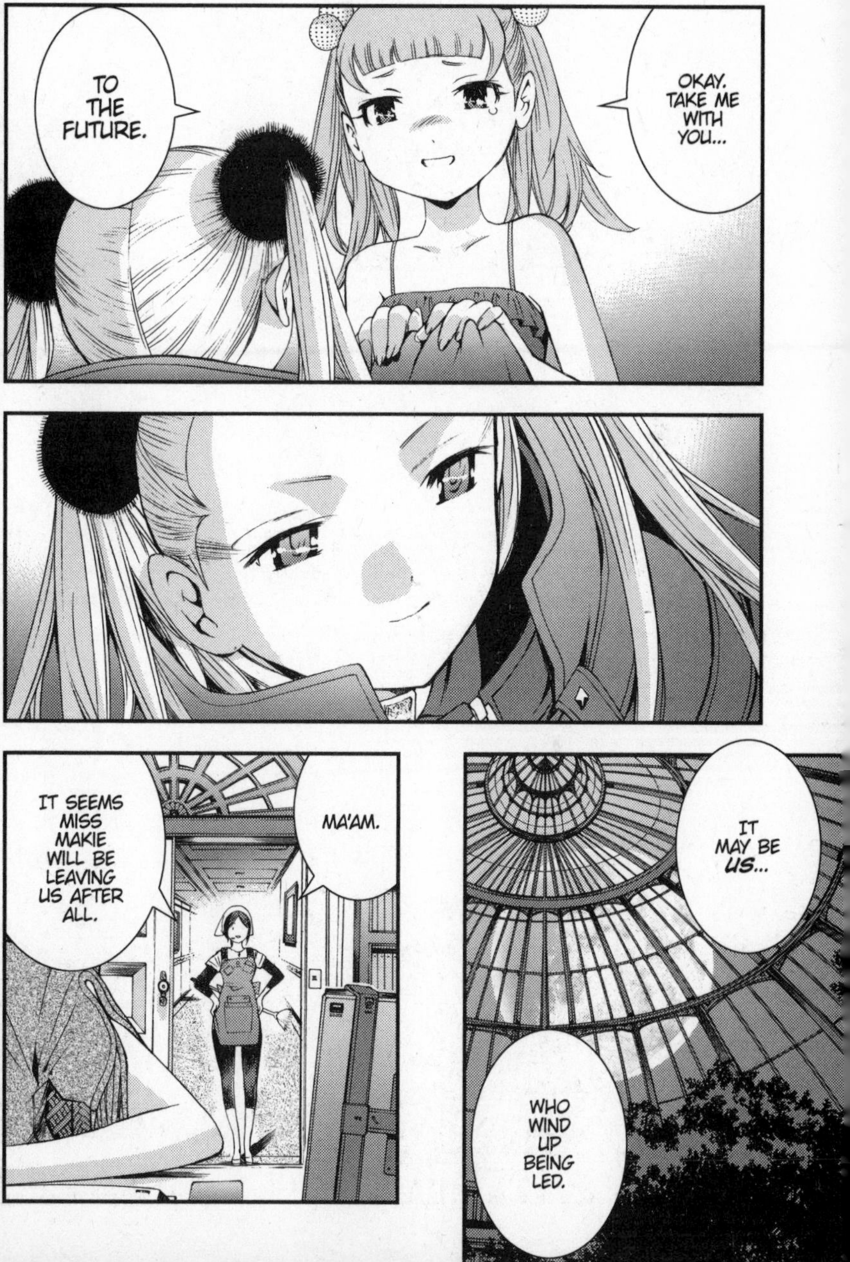
OKAY. TAKE ME WITH YOU...
TO THE FUTURE.
IT MAY BE *US*...
WHO WIND UP BEING LED.
MA'AM.
IT SEEMS MISS MAKIE WILL BE LEAVING US AFTER ALL.

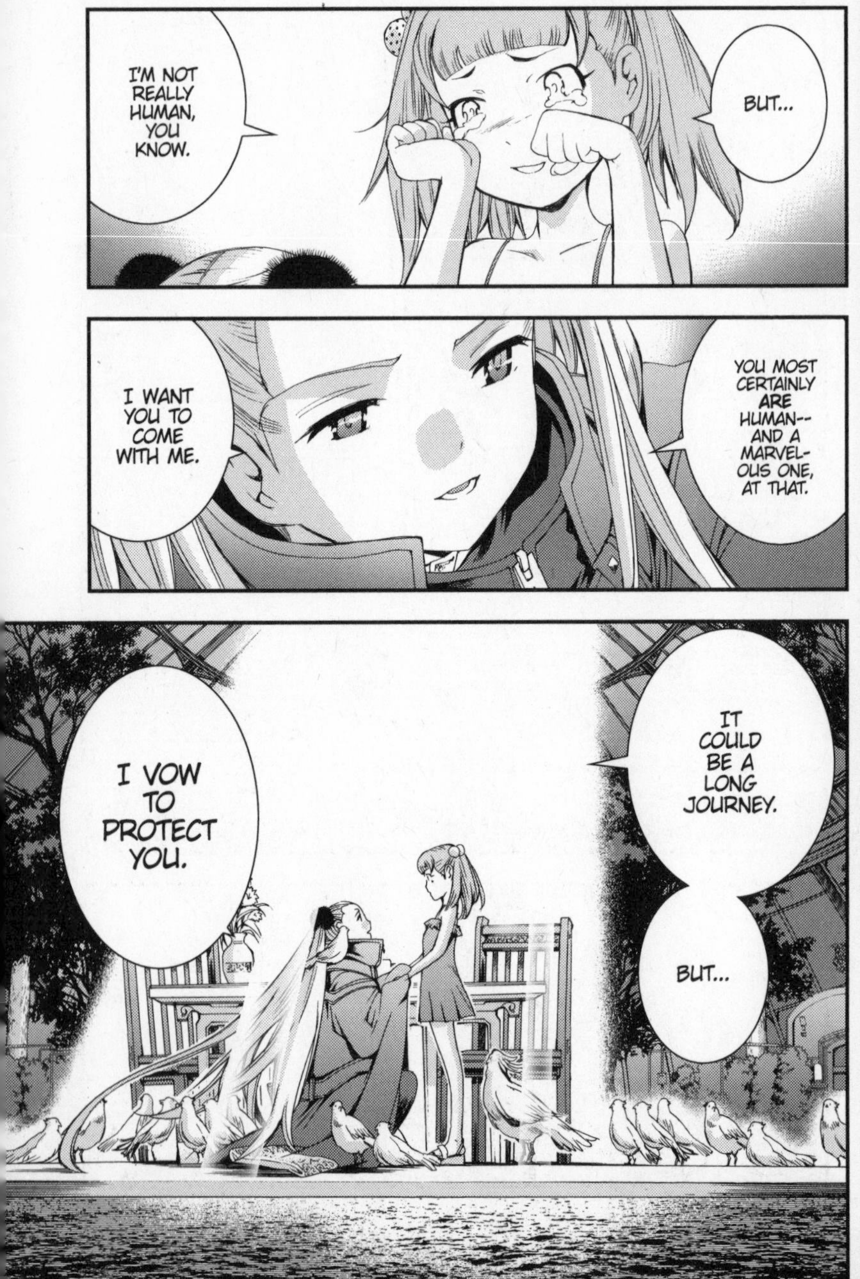
BUT...
I'M NOT REALLY HUMAN, YOU KNOW.
YOU MOST CERTAINLY ARE HUMAN--AND A MARVEL-OUS ONE, AT THAT.
I WANT YOU TO COME WITH ME.
IT COULD BE A LONG JOURNEY.
BUT...
I VOW TO PROTECT YOU.

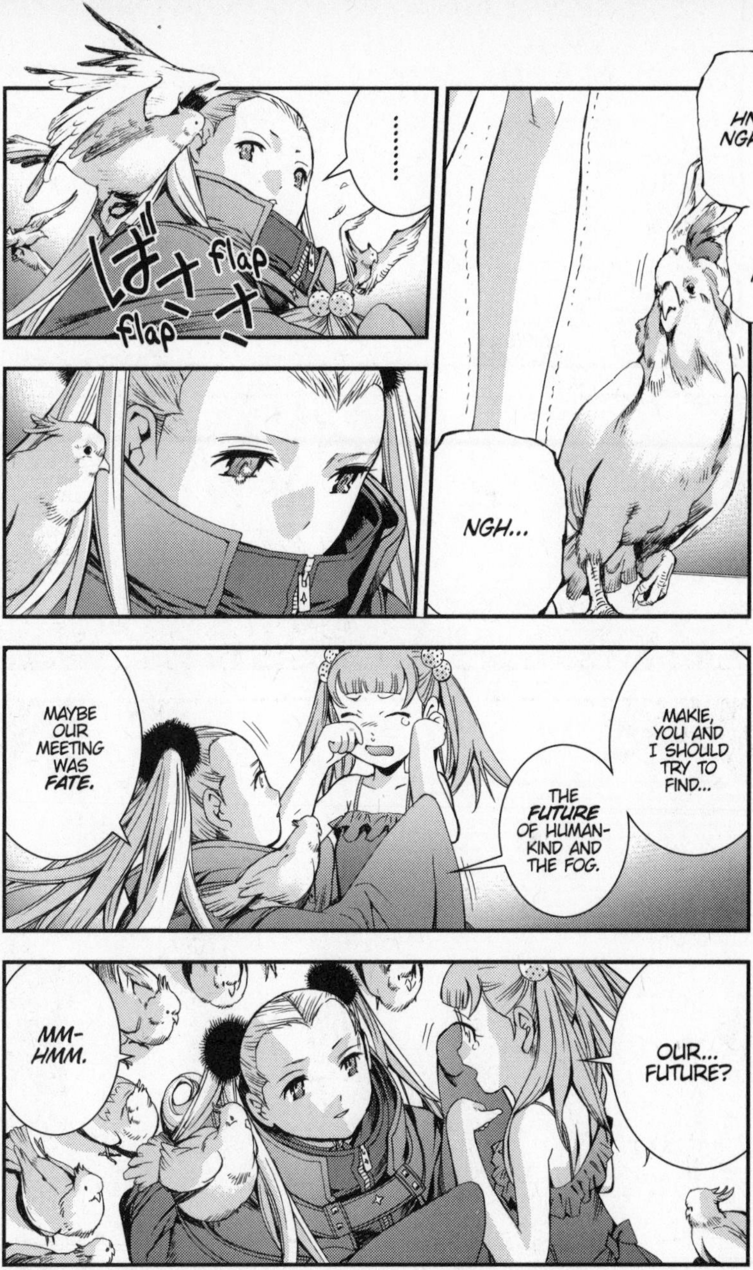
HN-NGH...
NN-NH...
NGH...
......
flap
flap
MAKIE, YOU AND I SHOULD TRY TO FIND...
THE FUTURE OF HUMAN-KIND AND THE FOG.
MAYBE OUR MEETING WAS FATE.
OUR... FUTURE?
MM-HMM.

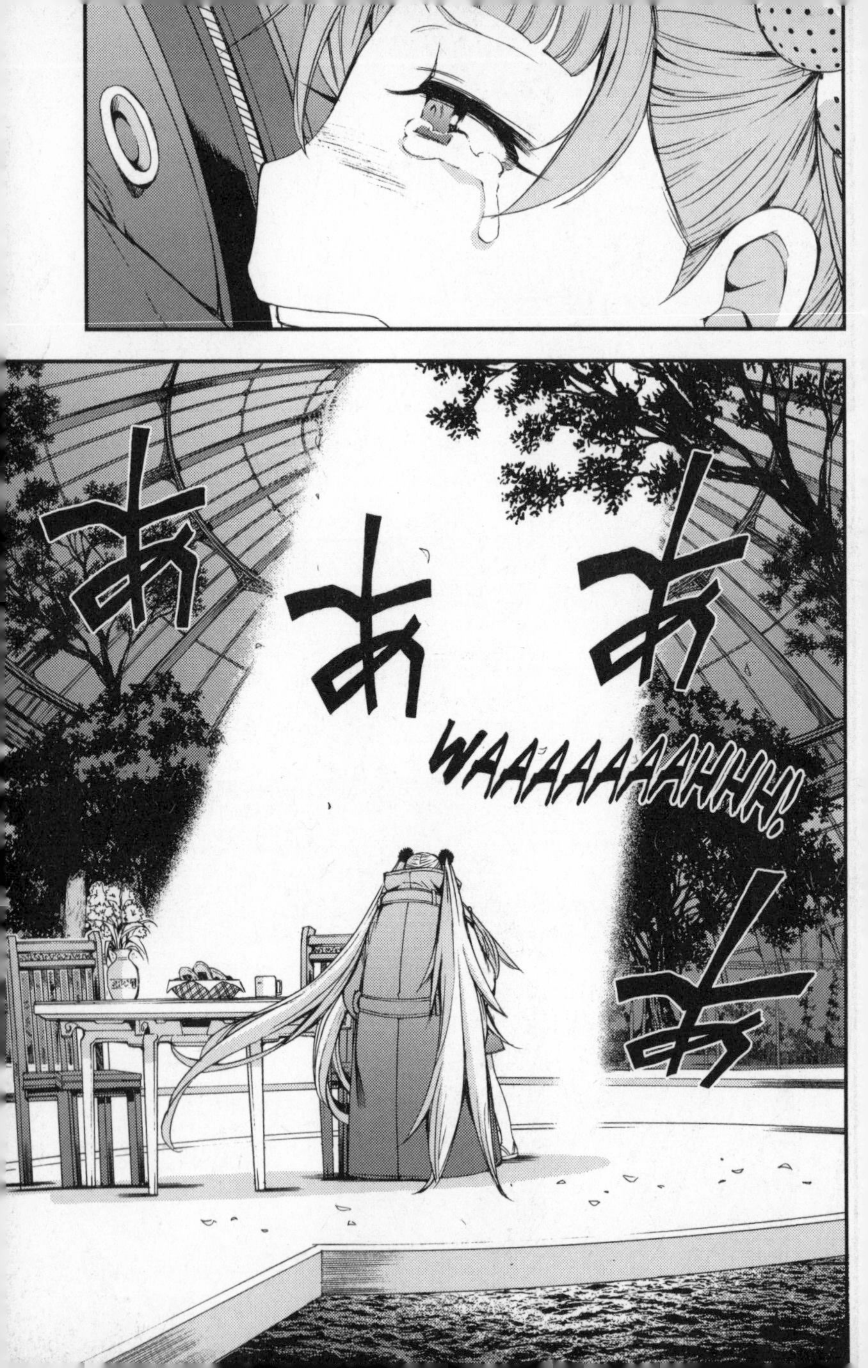
あああーあ
WAAAAAAAHHH!

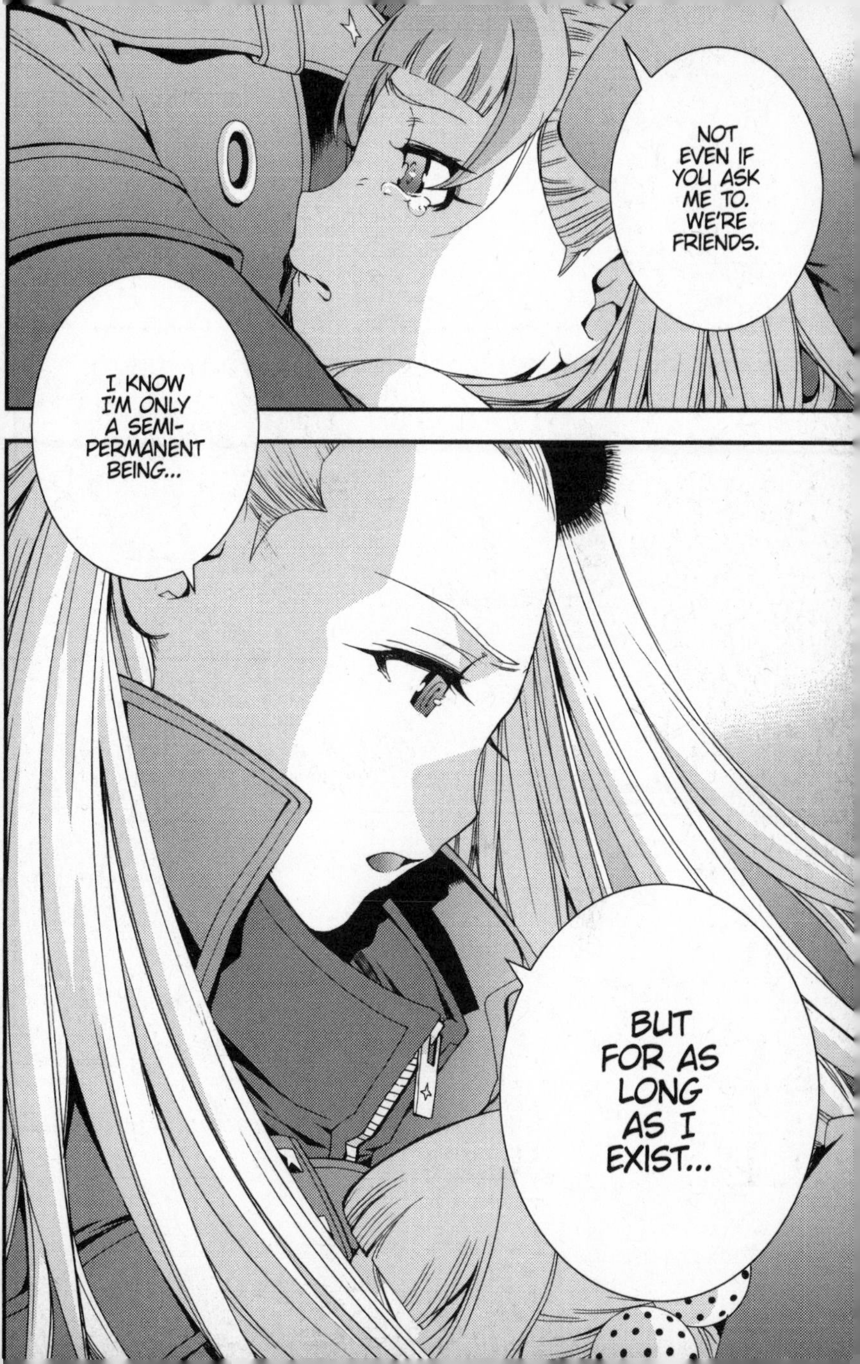
NOT EVEN IF YOU ASK ME TO. WE'RE FRIENDS.
I KNOW I'M ONLY A SEMI-PERMANENT BEING...
BUT FOR AS LONG AS I EXIST...

......

I SEE.

I WON'T KILL YOU, MAKIE.

WHAT-EVER HAPPENS, I WON'T.

I DON'T WANT YOU TO TALK LIKE THAT ANYMORE.

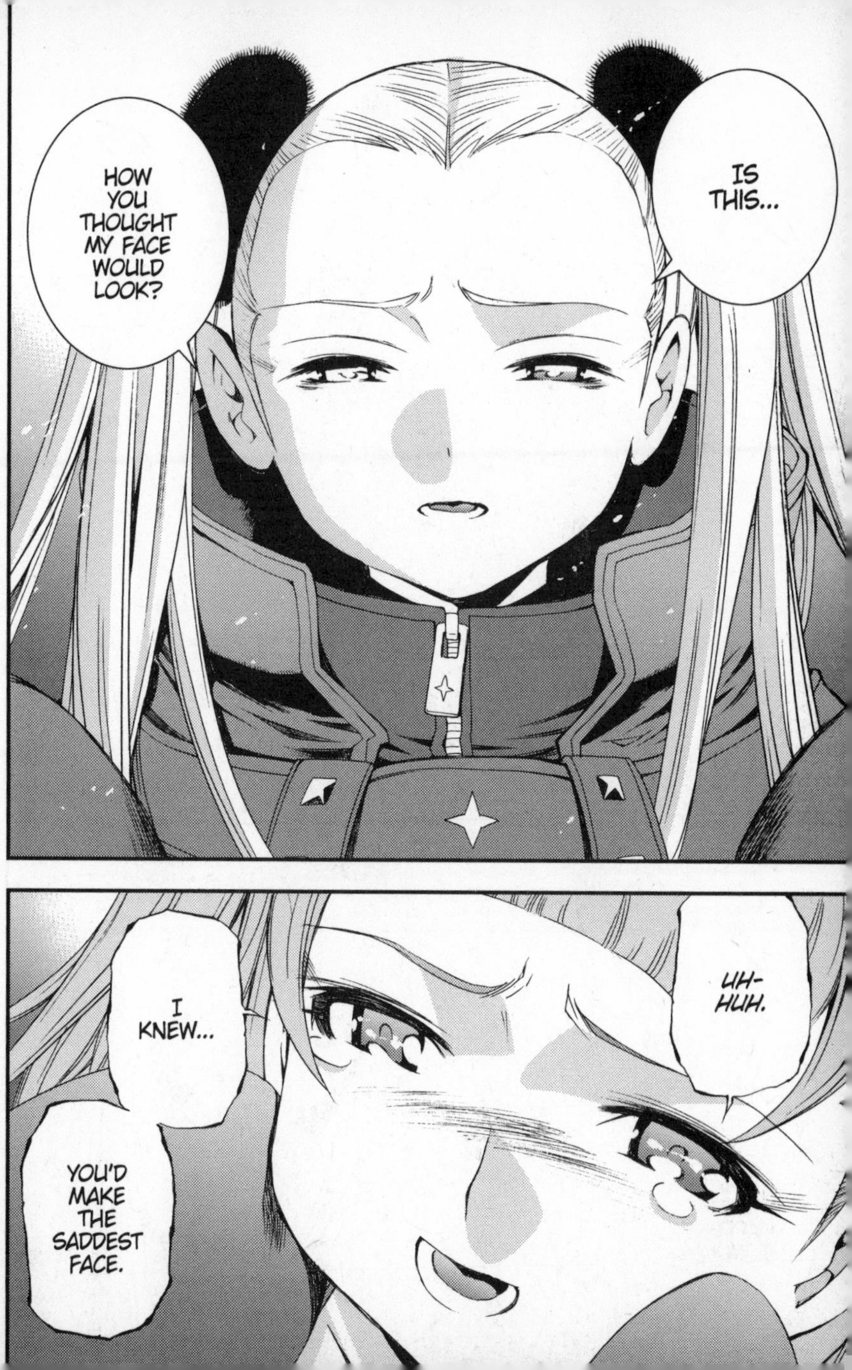
IS THIS...
HOW YOU THOUGHT MY FACE WOULD LOOK?
UH-HUH.
I KNEW...
YOU'D MAKE THE SADDEST FACE.

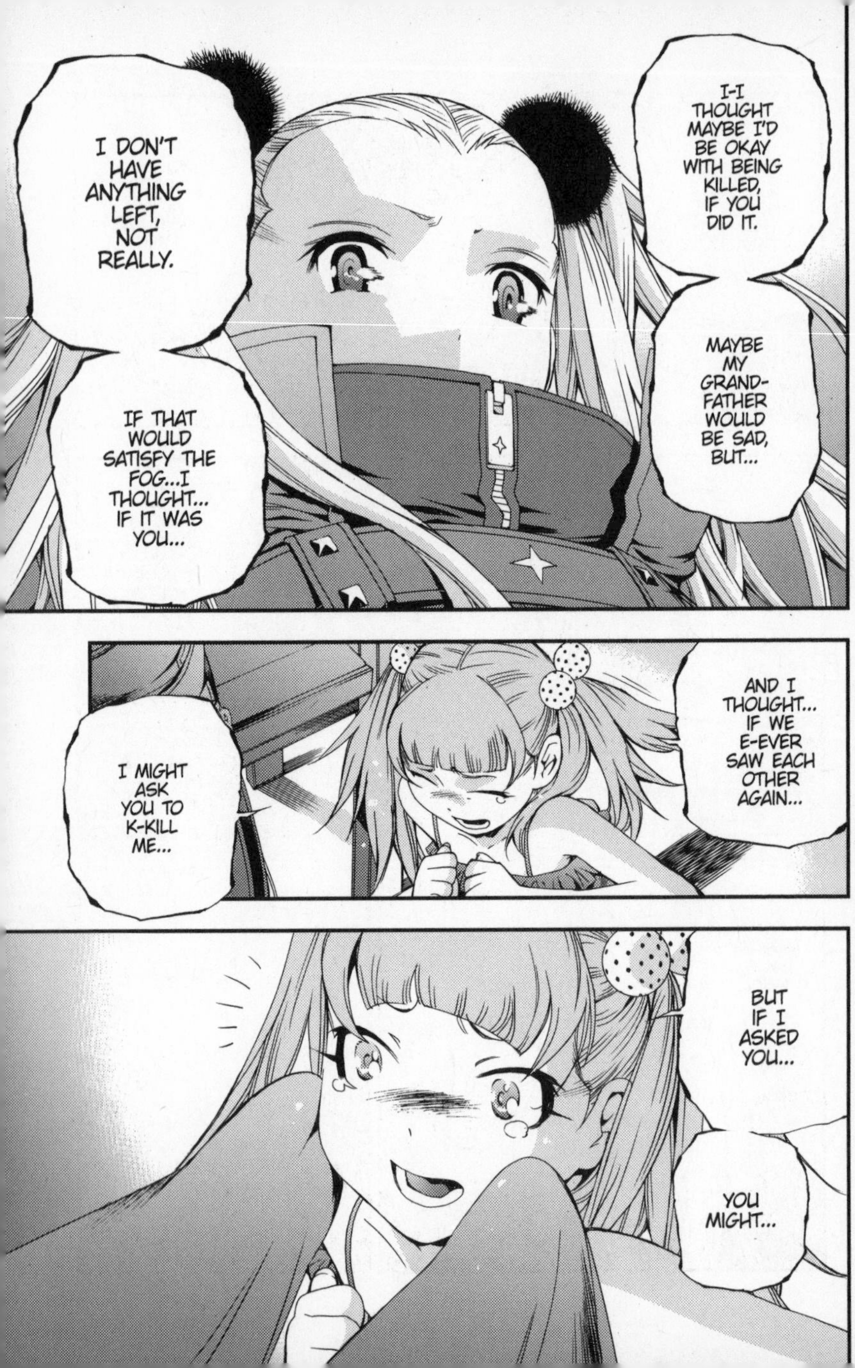
I-I THOUGHT MAYBE I'D BE OKAY WITH BEING KILLED, IF YOU DID IT.
I DON'T HAVE ANYTHING LEFT, NOT REALLY.
MAYBE MY GRAND-FATHER WOULD BE SAD, BUT...
IF THAT WOULD SATISFY THE FOG...I THOUGHT... IF IT WAS YOU...
AND I THOUGHT... IF WE E-EVER SAW EACH OTHER AGAIN...
I MIGHT ASK YOU TO K-KILL ME...
BUT IF I ASKED YOU...
YOU MIGHT...

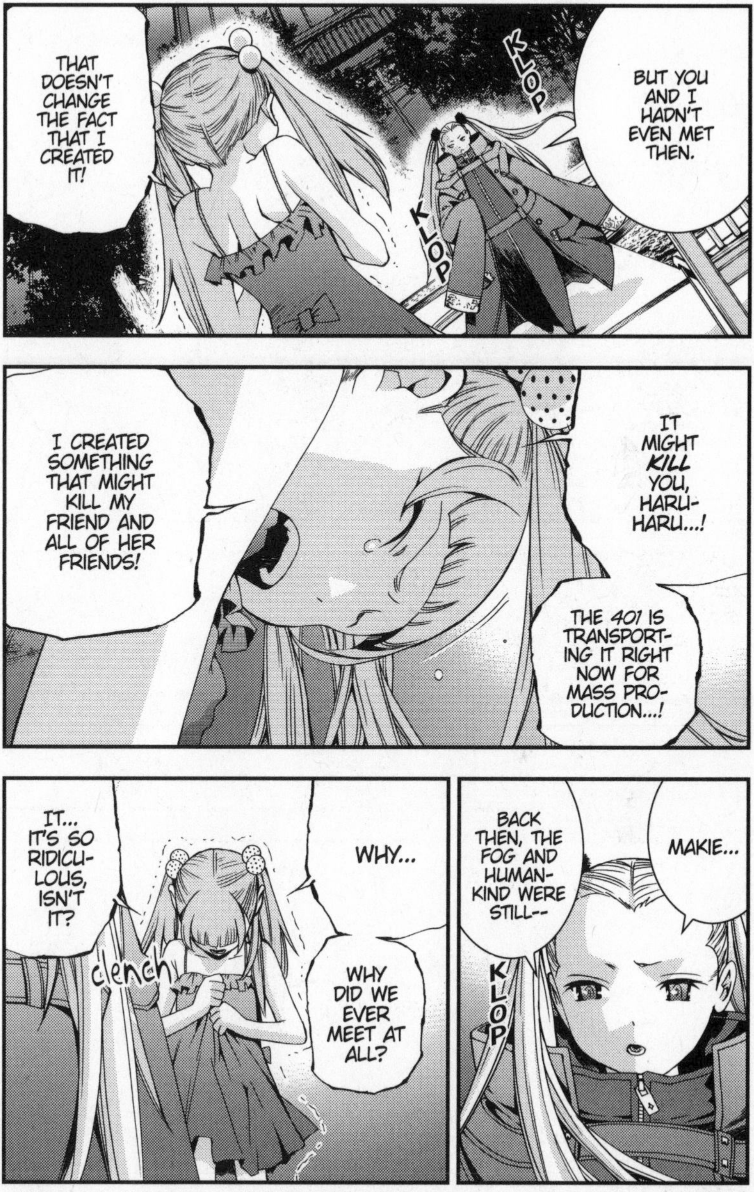
BUT YOU AND I HADN'T EVEN MET THEN.
KLOP
KLOP
THAT DOESN'T CHANGE THE FACT THAT I CREATED IT!
I CREATED SOMETHING THAT MIGHT KILL MY FRIEND AND ALL OF HER FRIENDS!
IT MIGHT *KILL* YOU, HARU-HARU...!
THE 401 IS TRANSPORTING IT RIGHT NOW FOR MASS PRODUCTION...!
MAKIE...
BACK THEN, THE FOG AND HUMANKIND WERE STILL--
KLOP
IT... IT'S SO RIDICULOUS, ISN'T IT?
WHY...
clench
WHY DID WE EVER MEET AT ALL?

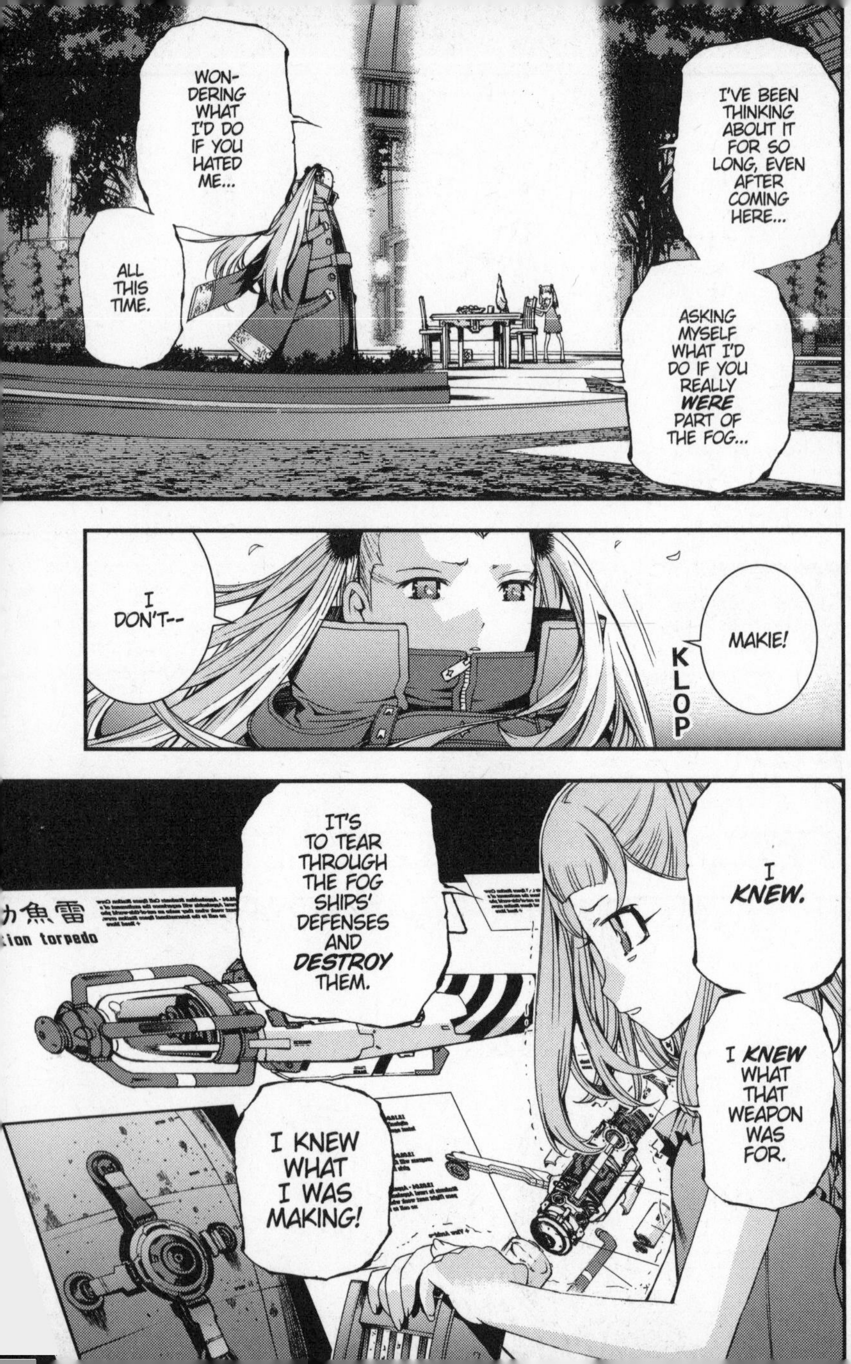
I'VE BEEN THINKING ABOUT IT FOR SO LONG, EVEN AFTER COMING HERE...
ASKING MYSELF WHAT I'D DO IF YOU REALLY *WERE* PART OF THE FOG...
WON-DERING WHAT I'D DO IF YOU HATED ME...
ALL THIS TIME.
MAKIE!
KLOP
I DON'T--
I *KNEW.*
I *KNEW* WHAT THAT WEAPON WAS FOR.
IT'S TO TEAR THROUGH THE FOG SHIPS' DEFENSES AND *DESTROY* THEM.
力魚雷
tion torpedo
I KNEW WHAT I WAS MAKING!

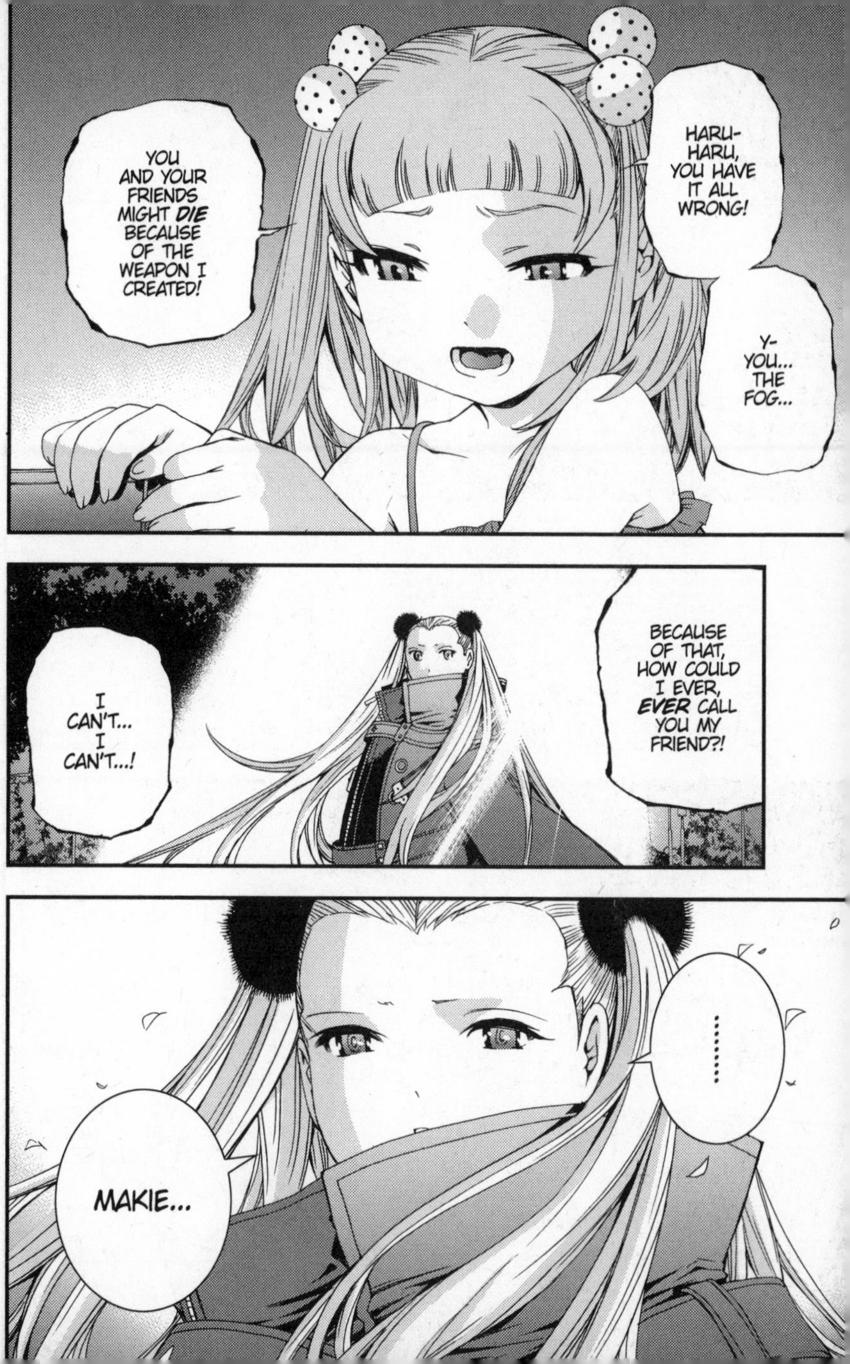
HARU-HARU, YOU HAVE IT ALL WRONG!
YOU AND YOUR FRIENDS MIGHT DIE BECAUSE OF THE WEAPON I CREATED!
Y-YOU... THE FOG...
BECAUSE OF THAT, HOW COULD I EVER, EVER CALL YOU MY FRIEND?!
I CAN'T... I CAN'T...!
......
MAKIE...

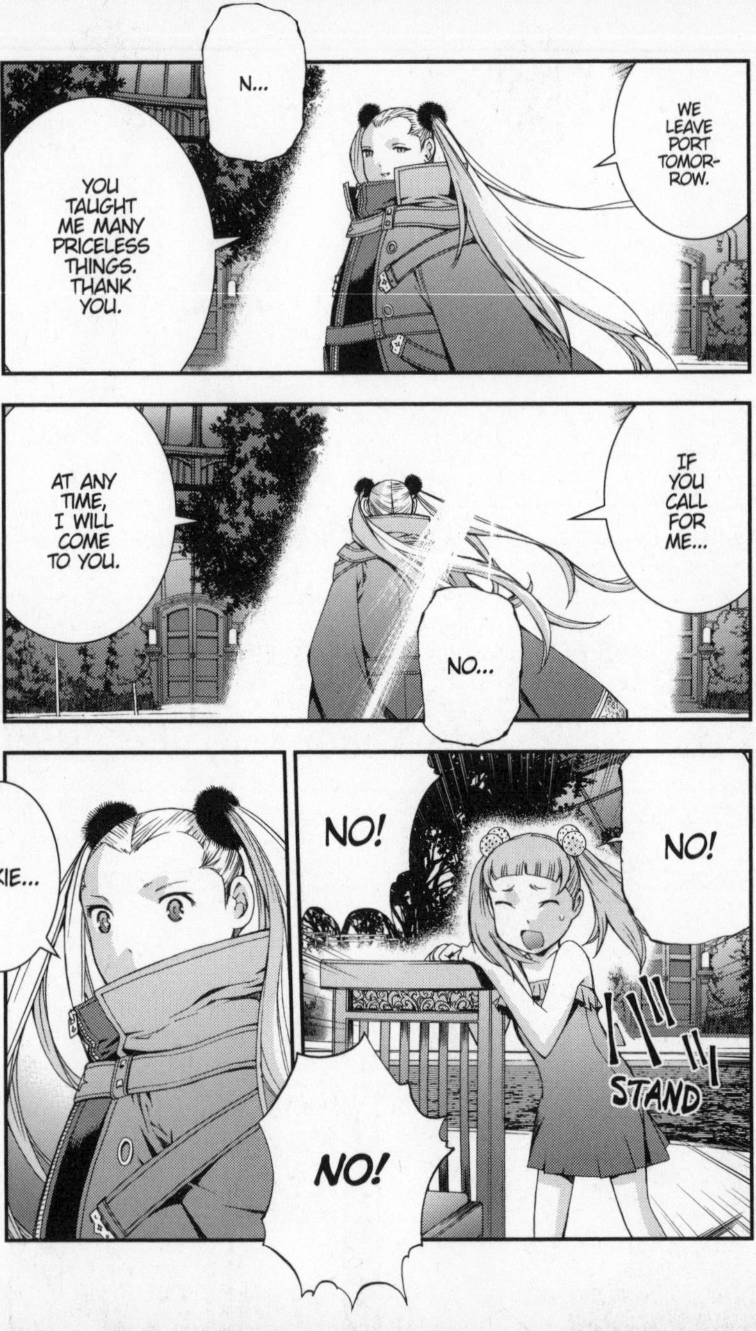
WE LEAVE PORT TOMORROW.
N...
YOU TAUGHT ME MANY PRICELESS THINGS. THANK YOU.
IF YOU CALL FOR ME...
AT ANY TIME, I WILL COME TO YOU.
NO...
NO!
NO!
STAND
NO!
MAKIE...

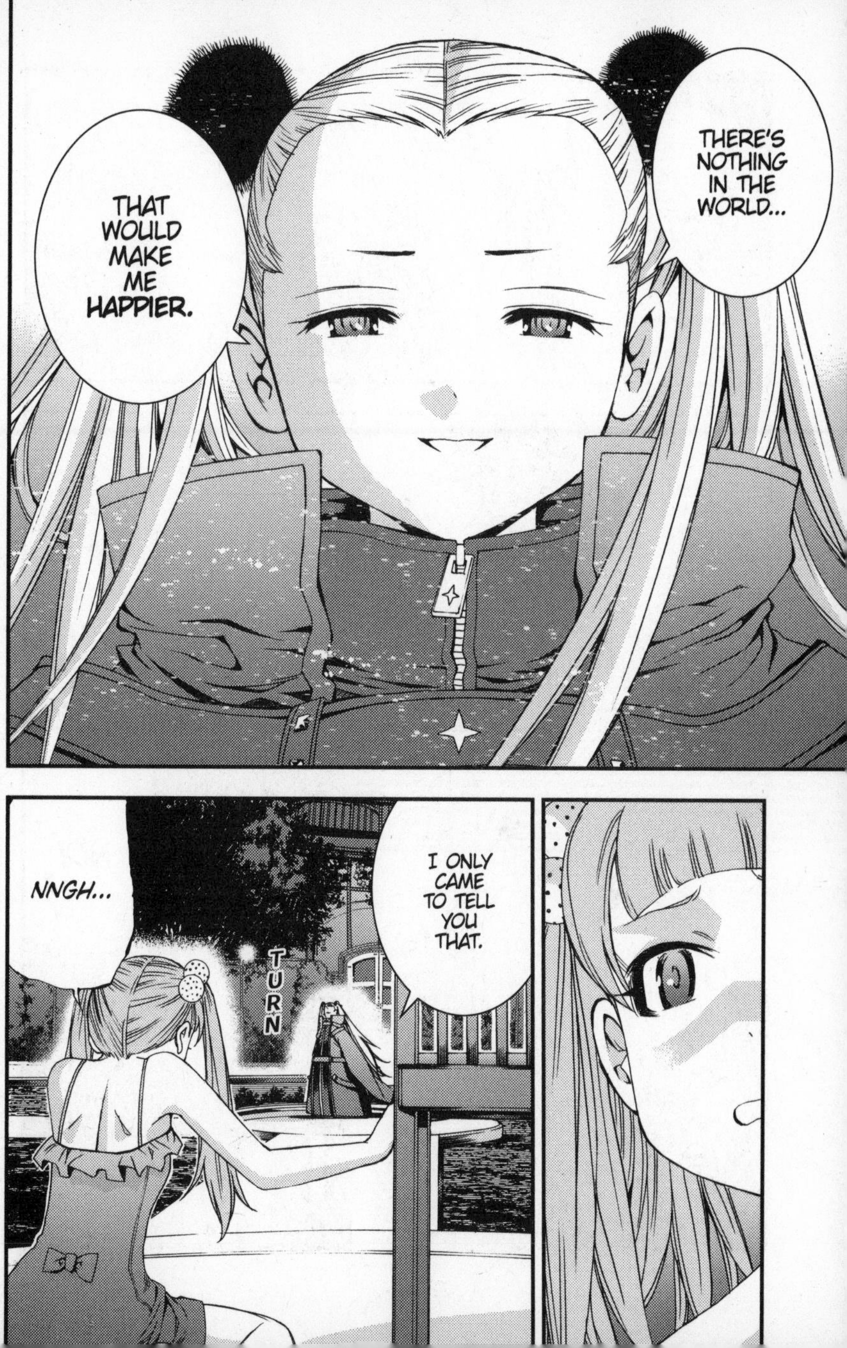
THERE'S NOTHING IN THE WORLD...
THAT WOULD MAKE ME HAPPIER.
I ONLY CAME TO TELL YOU THAT.
NNGH...
TURN

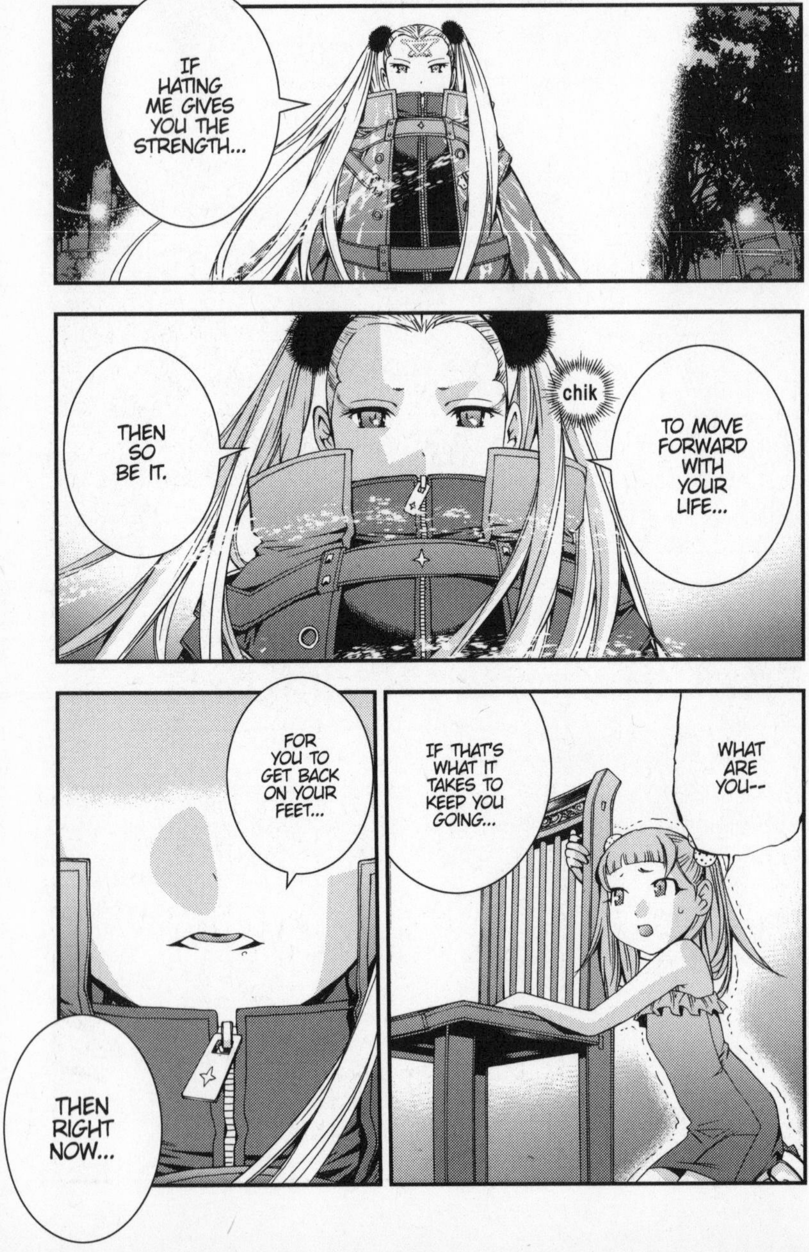
IF HATING ME GIVES YOU THE STRENGTH...
TO MOVE FORWARD WITH YOUR LIFE...
chik
THEN SO BE IT.
WHAT ARE YOU--
IF THAT'S WHAT IT TAKES TO KEEP YOU GOING...
FOR YOU TO GET BACK ON YOUR FEET...
THEN RIGHT NOW...

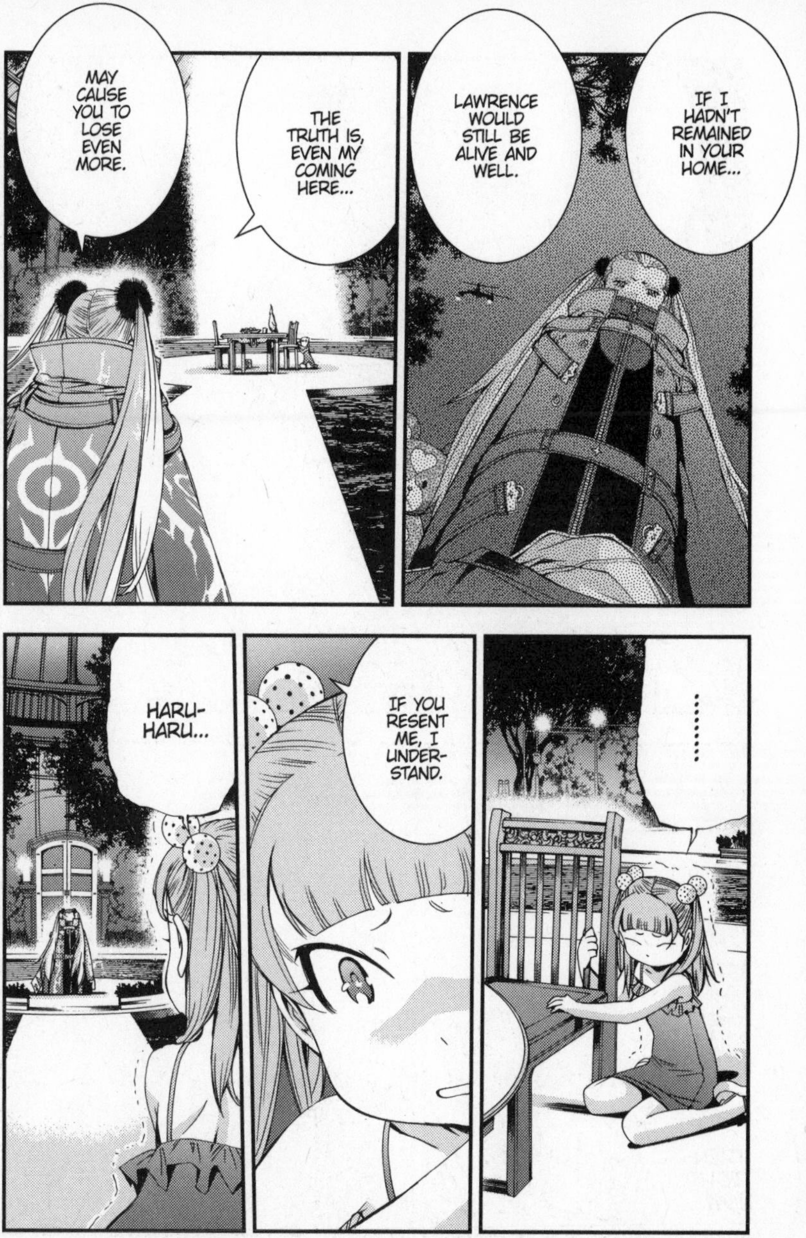
IF I HADN'T REMAINED IN YOUR HOME...
LAWRENCE WOULD STILL BE ALIVE AND WELL.
THE TRUTH IS, EVEN MY COMING HERE...
MAY CAUSE YOU TO LOSE EVEN MORE.
......
IF YOU RESENT ME, I UNDERSTAND.
HARU-HARU...

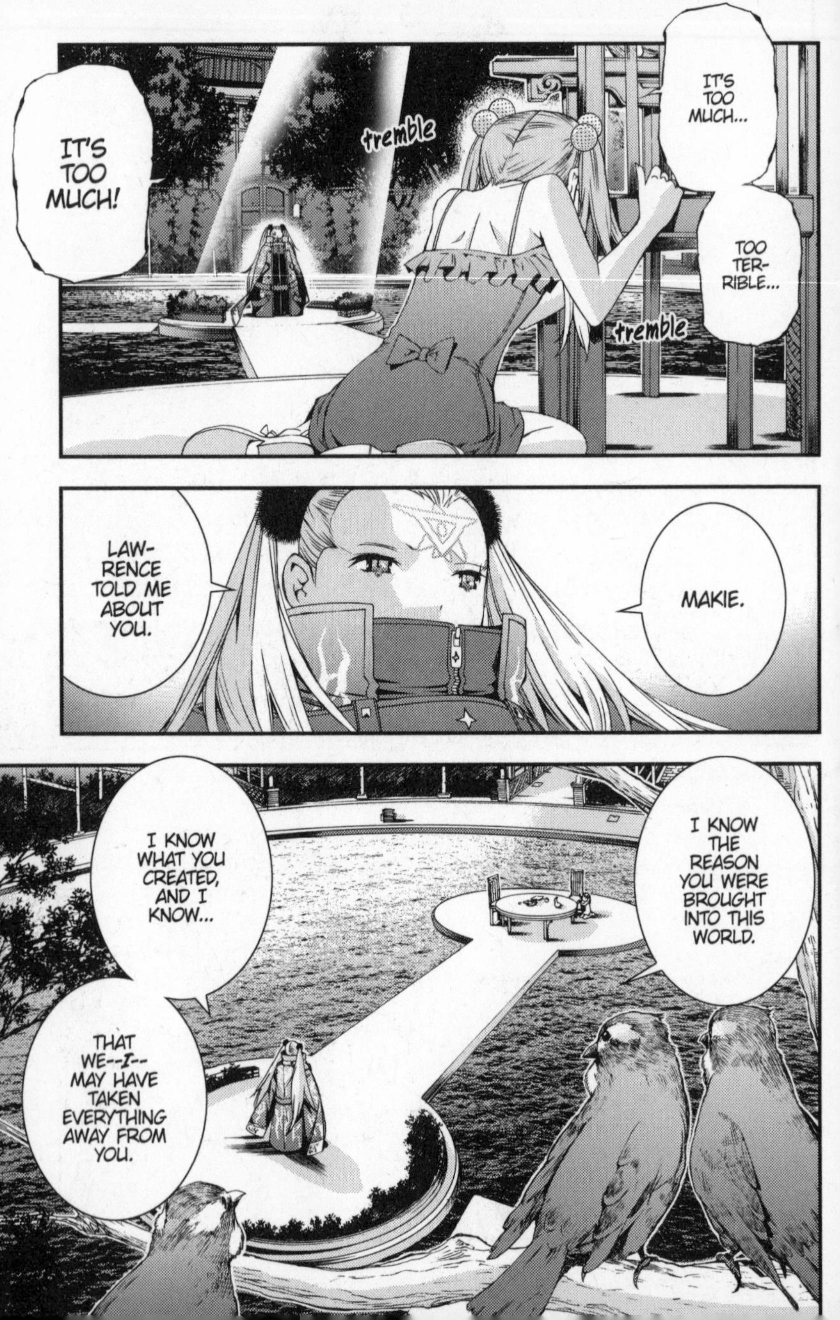
IT'S TOO MUCH...
TOO TER-RIBLE...
tremble
tremble
IT'S TOO MUCH!
MAKIE.
LAW-RENCE TOLD ME ABOUT YOU.
I KNOW THE REASON YOU WERE BROUGHT INTO THIS WORLD.
I KNOW WHAT YOU CREATED, AND I KNOW...
THAT WE--*I*--MAY HAVE TAKEN EVERYTHING AWAY FROM YOU.

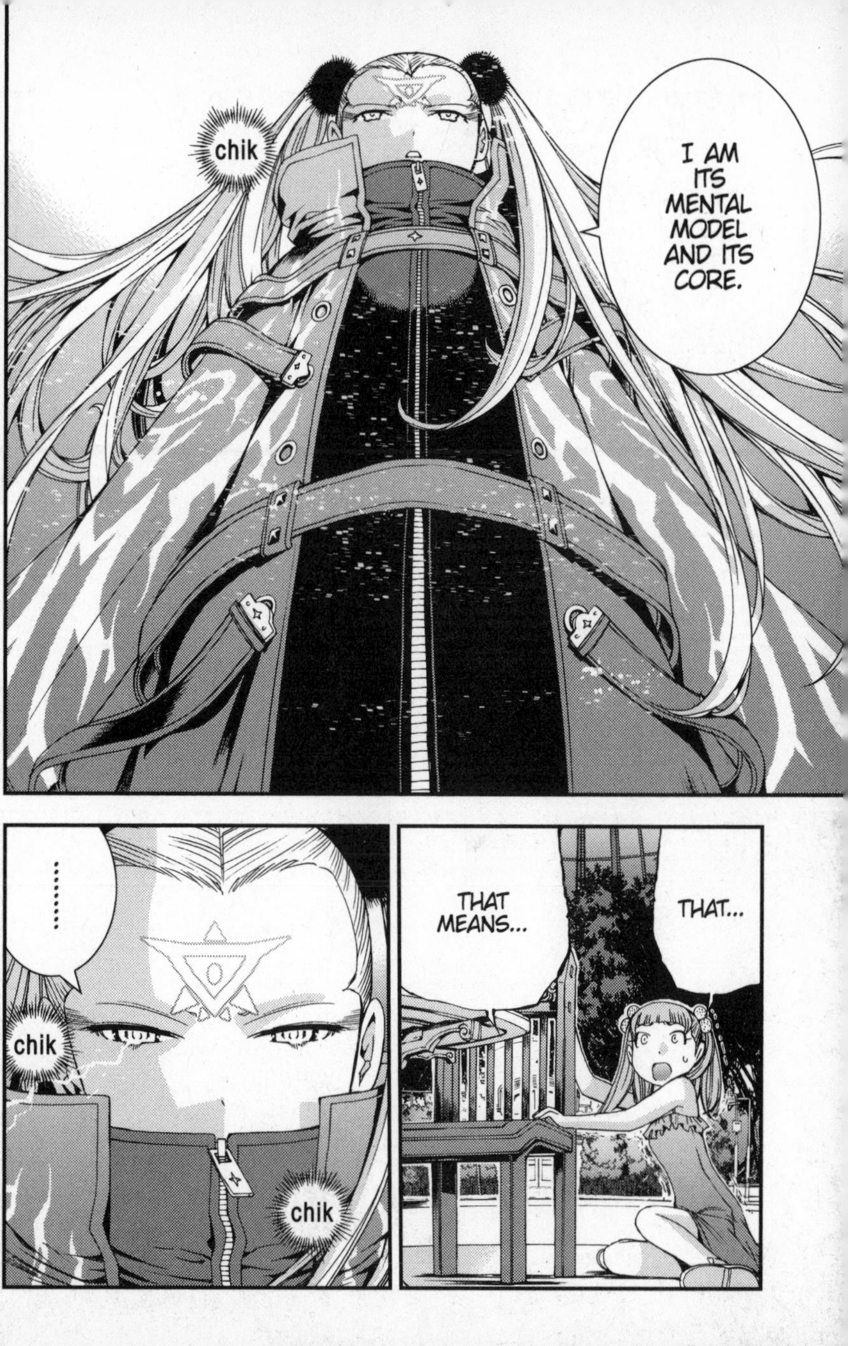
I AM ITS MENTAL MODEL AND ITS CORE.
chik
THAT...
THAT MEANS...
......
chik
chik

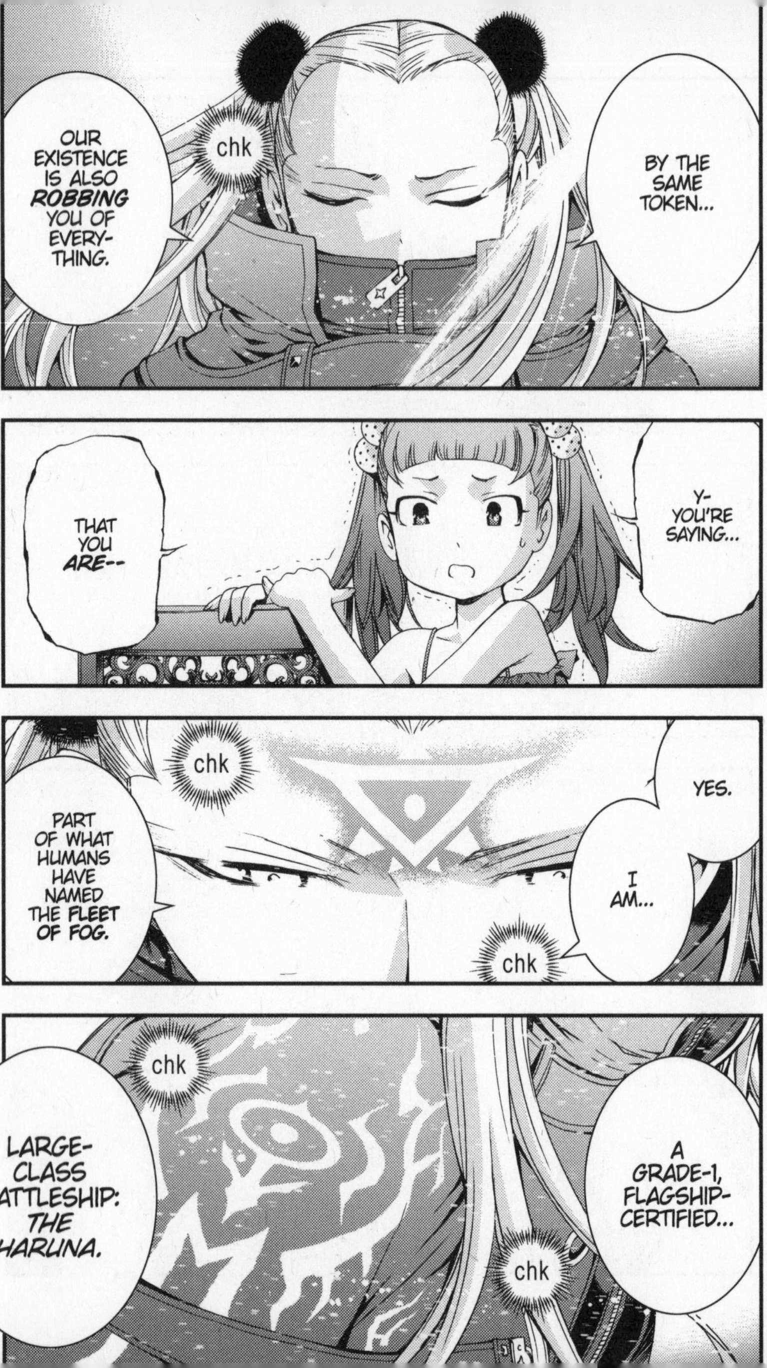
BY THE SAME TOKEN...
chk
OUR EXISTENCE IS ALSO *ROBBING* YOU OF EVERY-THING.
Y-YOU'RE SAYING...
THAT YOU *ARE*--
YES.
chk
I AM...
chk
PART OF WHAT HUMANS HAVE NAMED THE FLEET OF FOG.
chk
A GRADE-1, FLAGSHIP-CERTIFIED...
chk
LARGE-CLASS BATTLESHIP: *THE HARUNA.*

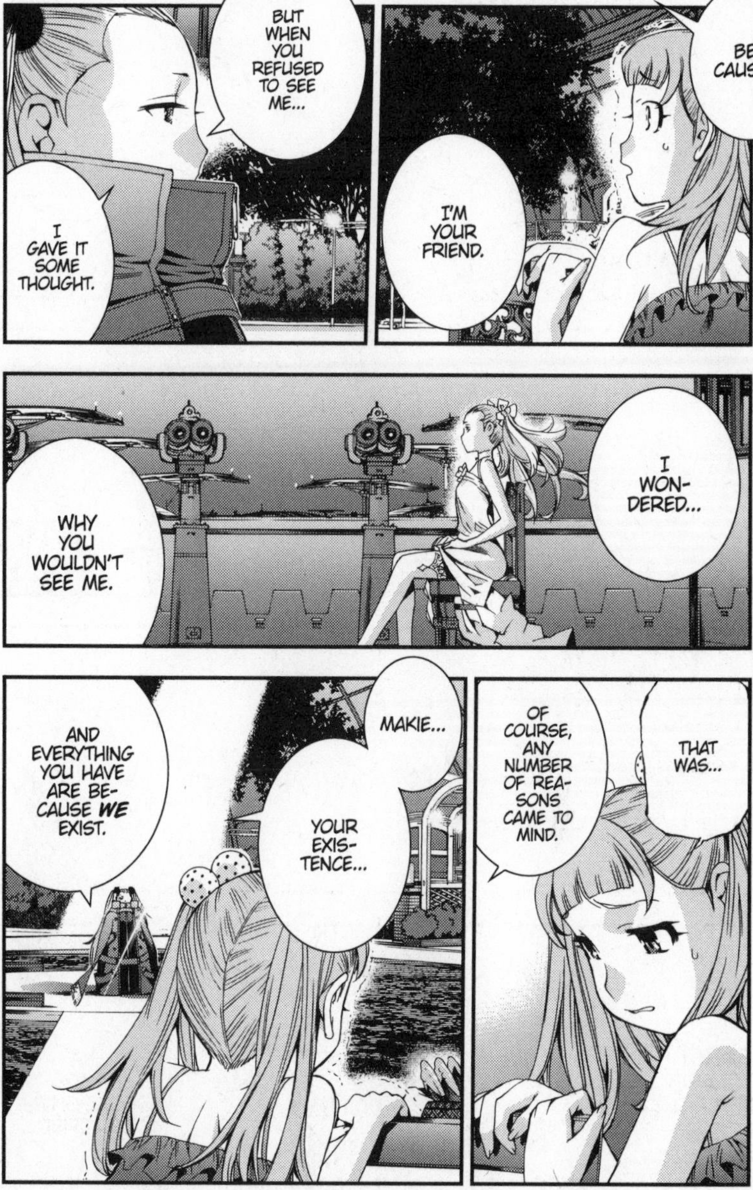
BE-CAUSE...
I'M YOUR FRIEND.
BUT WHEN YOU REFUSED TO SEE ME...
I GAVE IT SOME THOUGHT.
I WON-DERED...
WHY YOU WOULDN'T SEE ME.
THAT WAS...
OF COURSE, ANY NUMBER OF REA-SONS CAME TO MIND.
MAKIE...
YOUR EXIS-TENCE...
AND EVERYTHING YOU HAVE ARE BE-CAUSE *WE* EXIST.

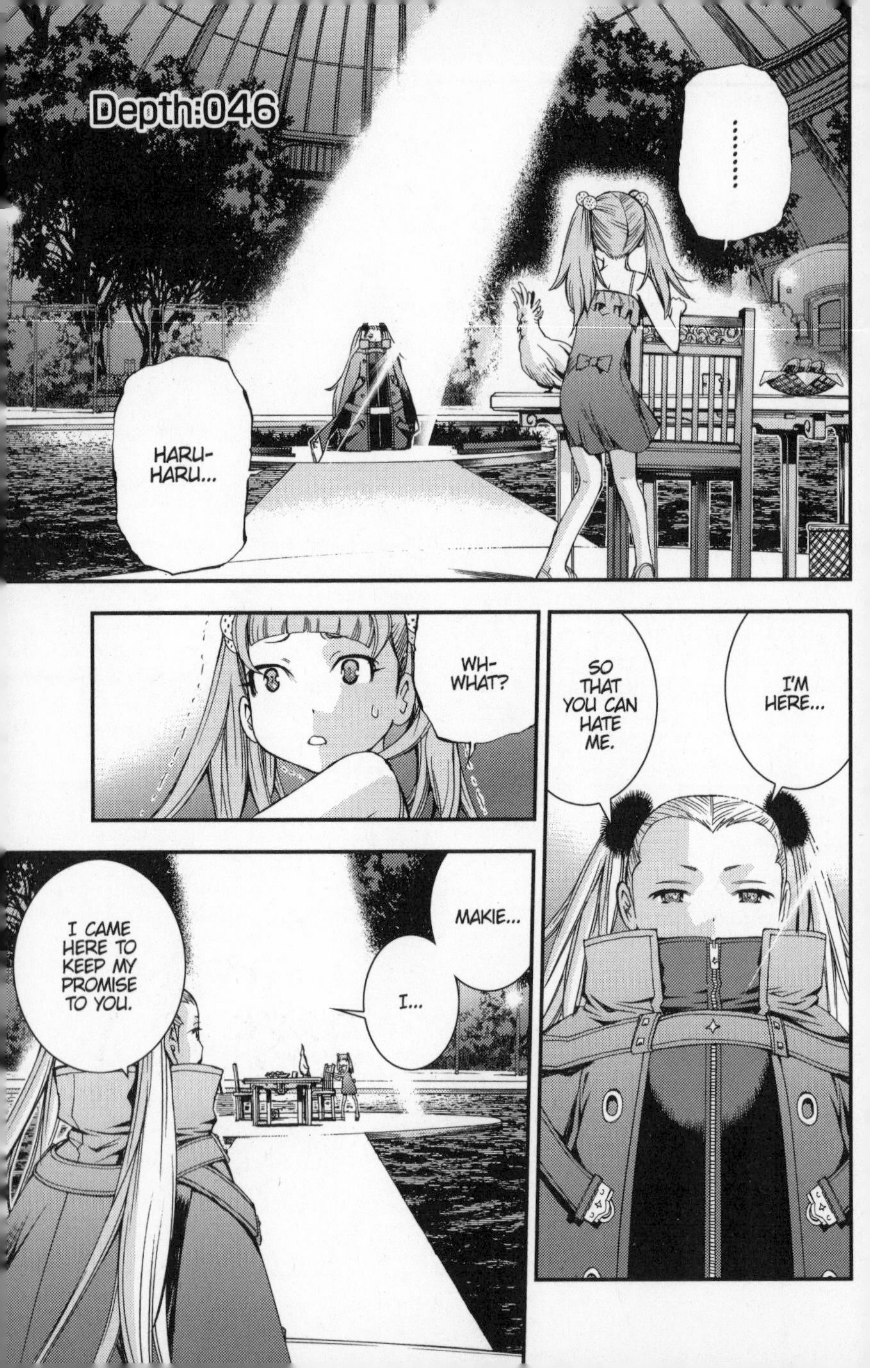
Depth:046
......
HARU-HARU...
I'M HERE...
SO THAT YOU CAN HATE ME.
WH-WHAT?
MAKIE...
I...
I CAME HERE TO KEEP MY PROMISE TO YOU.

BLUE STEEL

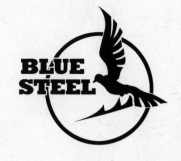

BLUE
STEEL

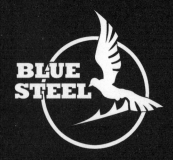

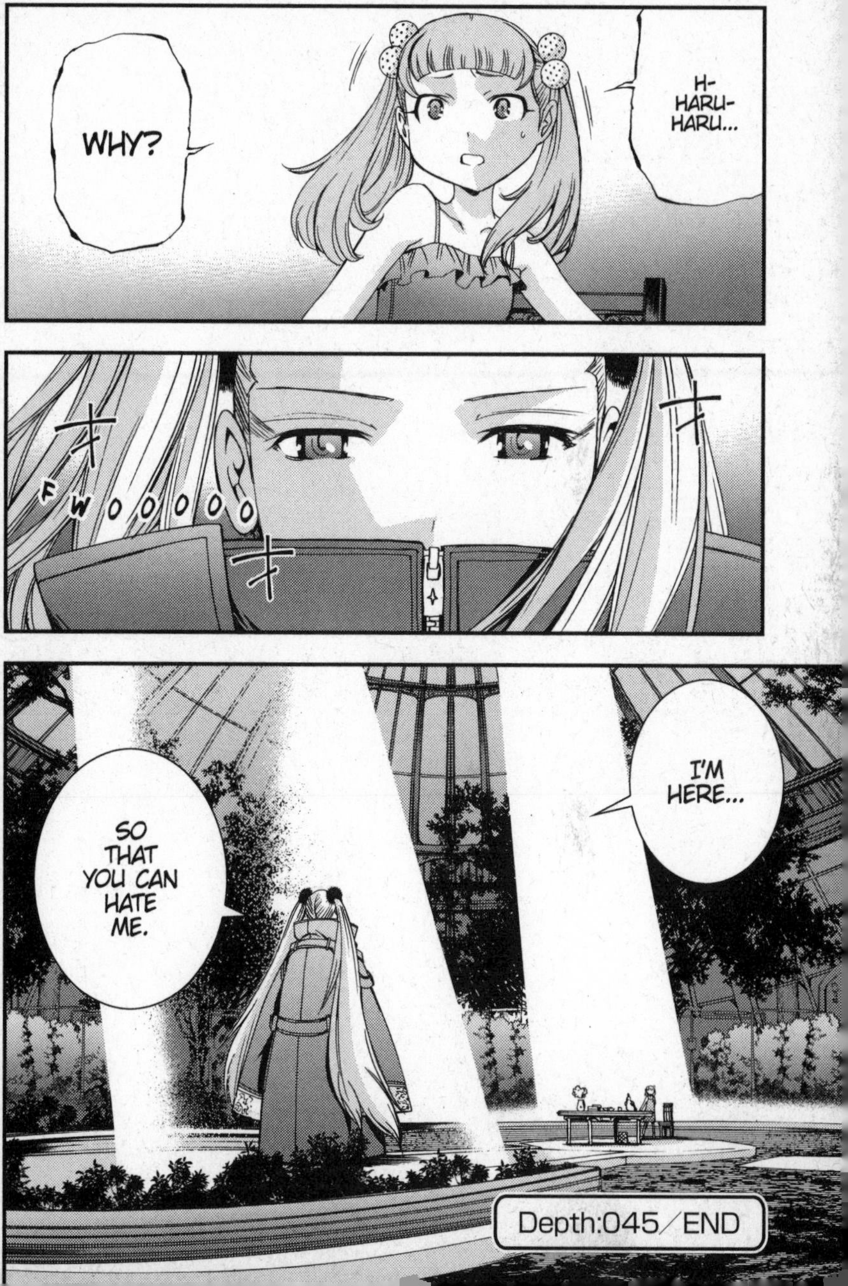
H-HARU-HARU...
WHY?
FWOOOOO
I'M HERE...
SO THAT YOU CAN HATE ME.
Depth:045／END

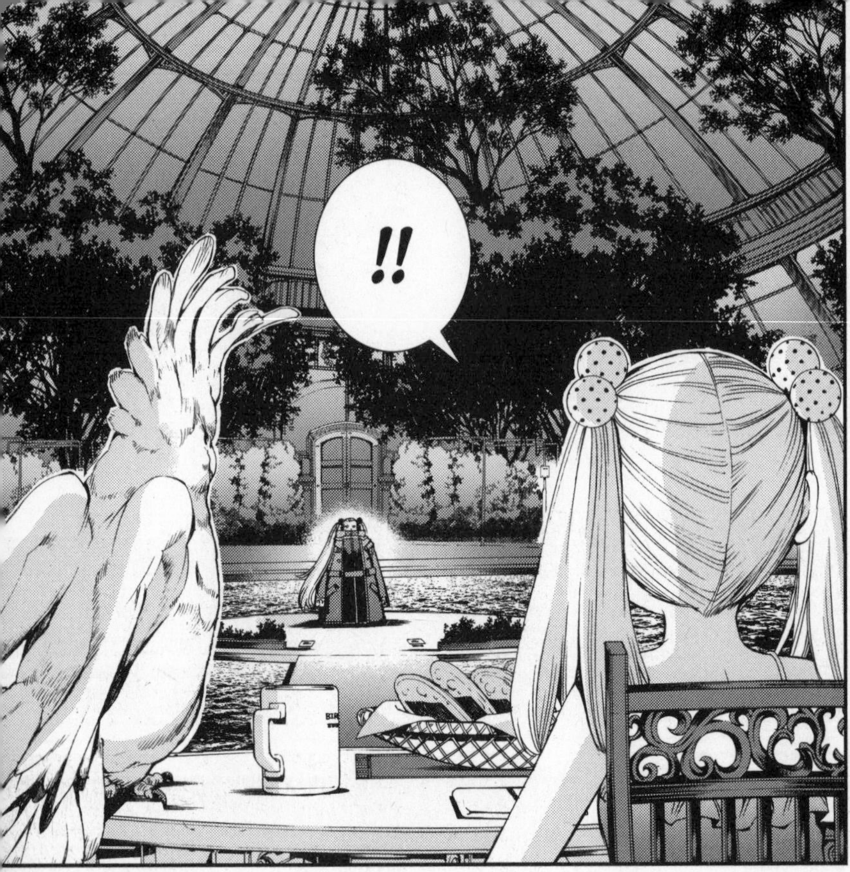
!!
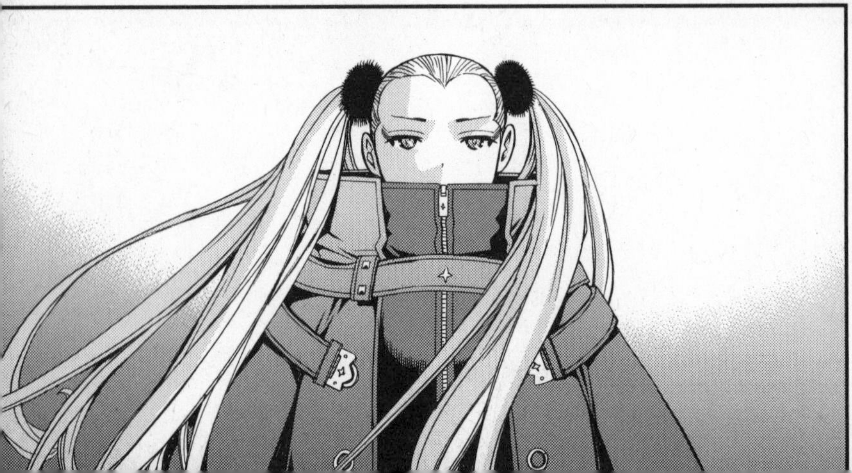

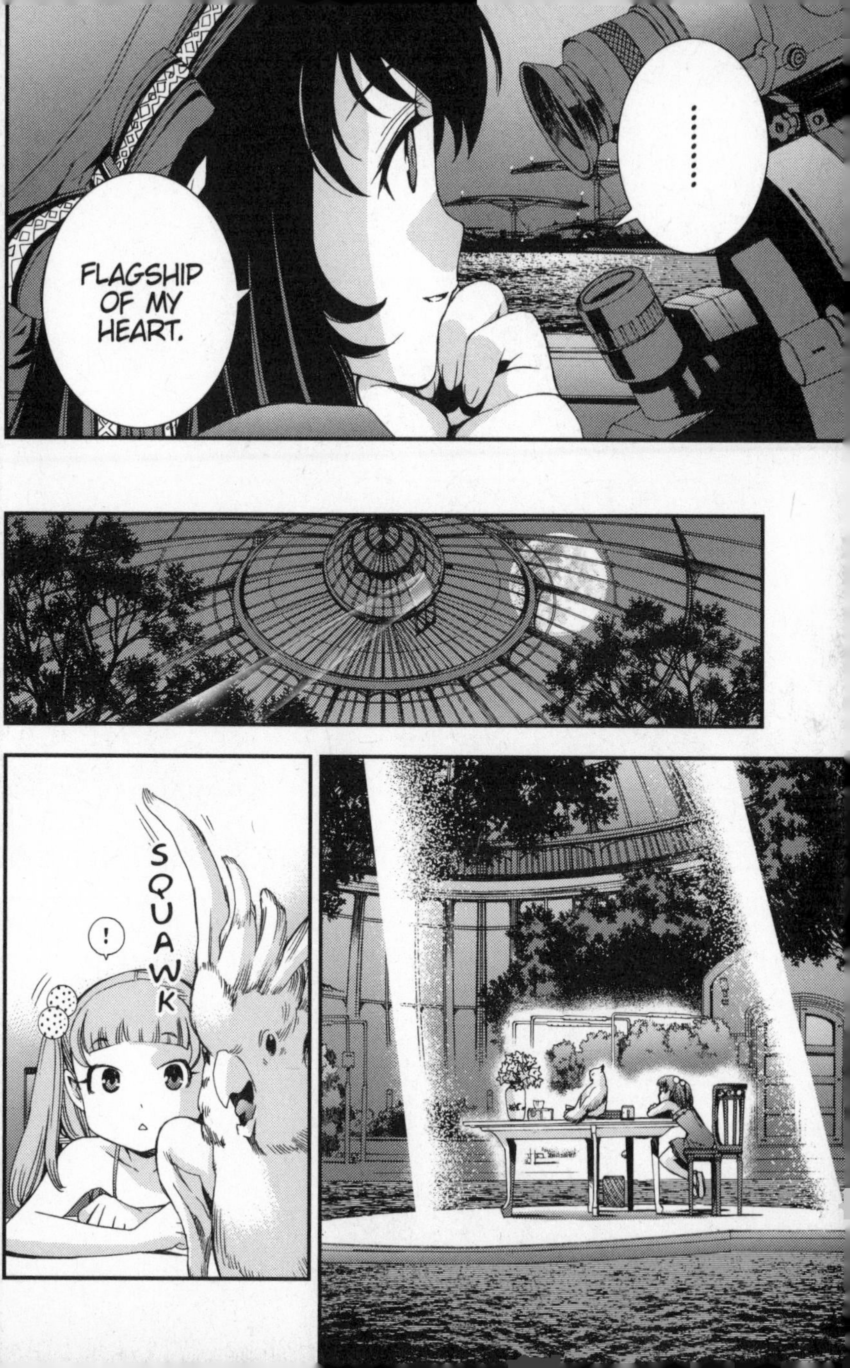
……
FLAGSHIP OF MY HEART.
!
SQUAWK

UH, SURE.

I KNOW WHAT IT MEANS, TOO! IT MEANS INTELLIGENT LIFE FORMS NEED *OTHER* INTELLIGENT LIFE FORM UNITS TO CONTINUE EXISTING!

LET'S HEAD OUT.

⋮

HARUNA?

CREAK

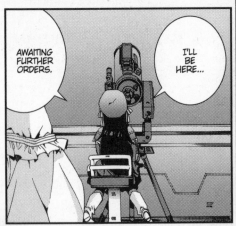

AWAITING FURTHER ORDERS.

I'LL BE HERE...

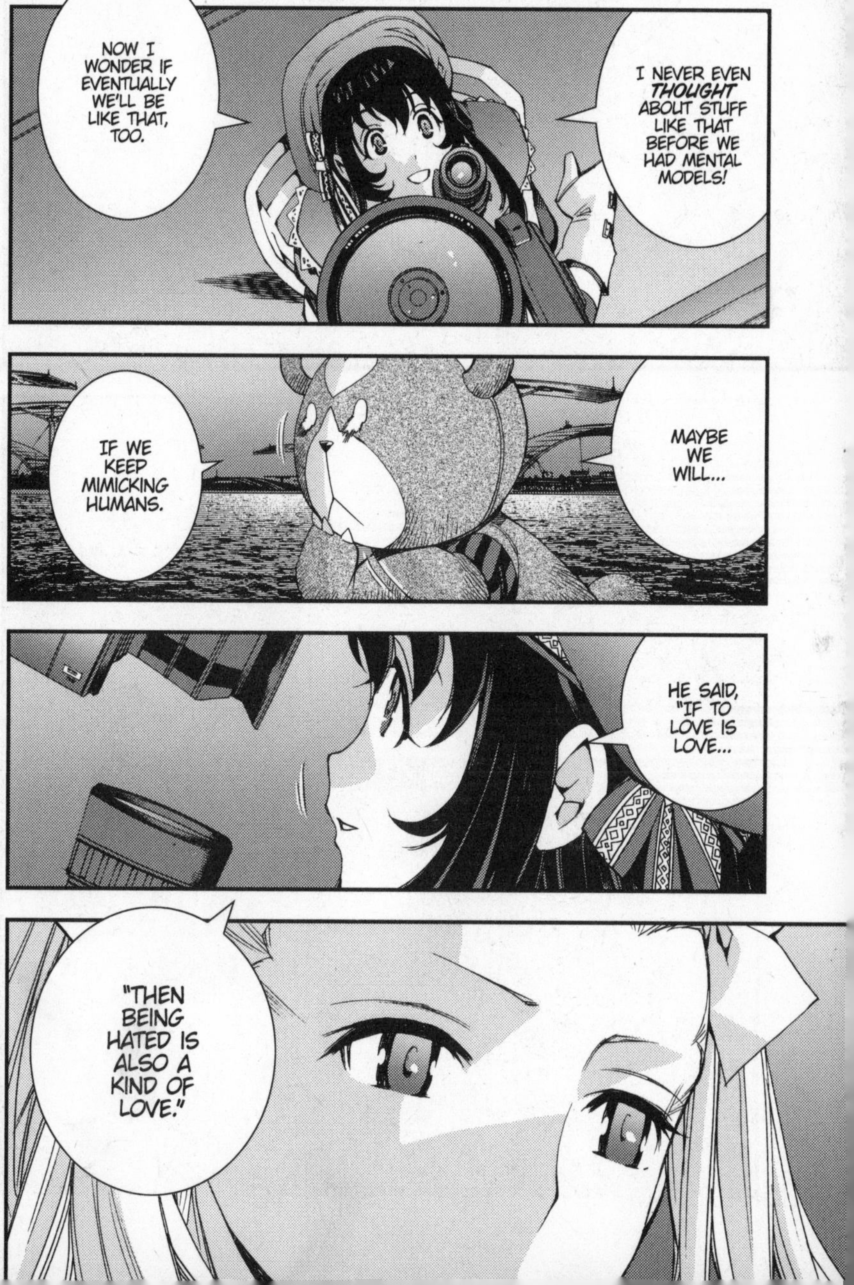
I NEVER EVEN *THOUGHT* ABOUT STUFF LIKE THAT BEFORE WE HAD MENTAL MODELS!
NOW I WONDER IF EVENTUALLY WE'LL BE LIKE THAT, TOO.
MAYBE WE WILL...
IF WE KEEP MIMICKING HUMANS.
HE SAID, "IF TO LOVE IS LOVE...
"THEN BEING HATED IS ALSO A KIND OF LOVE."

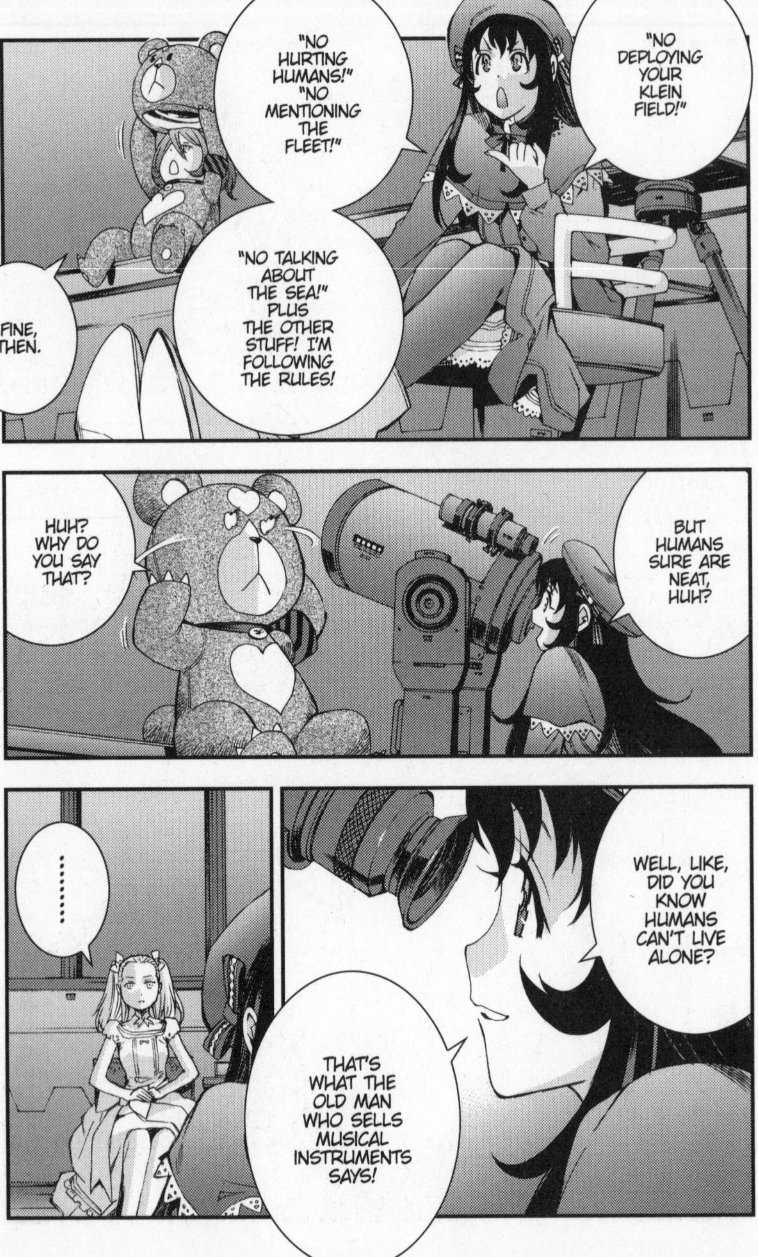
"NO DEPLOYING YOUR KLEIN FIELD!"
"NO HURTING HUMANS!" "NO MENTIONING THE FLEET!"
"NO TALKING ABOUT THE SEA!" PLUS THE OTHER STUFF! I'M FOLLOWING THE RULES!
FINE, THEN.
BUT HUMANS SURE ARE NEAT, HUH?
HUH? WHY DO YOU SAY THAT?
WELL, LIKE, DID YOU KNOW HUMANS CAN'T LIVE ALONE?
THAT'S WHAT THE OLD MAN WHO SELLS MUSICAL INSTRUMENTS SAYS!
......

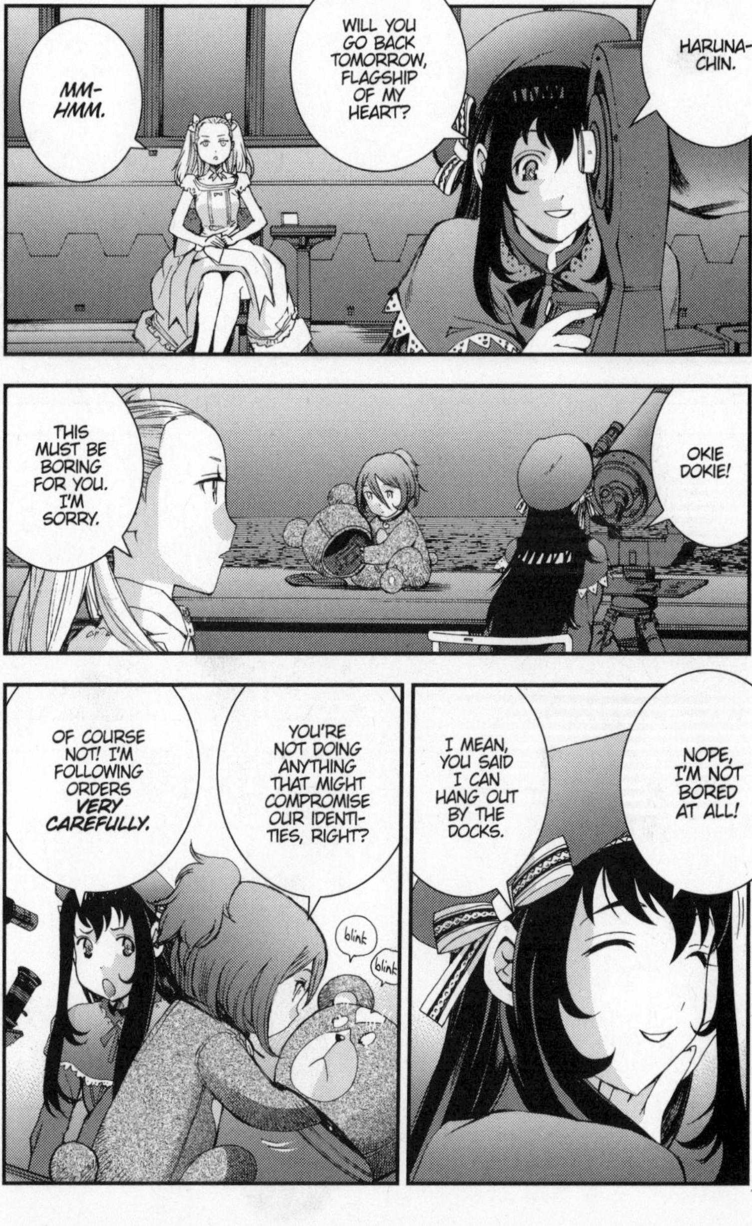
HARUNA-CHIN.
WILL YOU GO BACK TOMORROW, FLAGSHIP OF MY HEART?
MM-HMM.
OKIE DOKIE!
THIS MUST BE BORING FOR YOU. I'M SORRY.
NOPE, I'M NOT BORED AT ALL!
I MEAN, YOU SAID I CAN HANG OUT BY THE DOCKS.
YOU'RE NOT DOING ANYTHING THAT MIGHT COMPROMISE OUR IDENTITIES, RIGHT?
blink
blink
OF COURSE NOT! I'M FOLLOWING ORDERS VERY CAREFULLY.

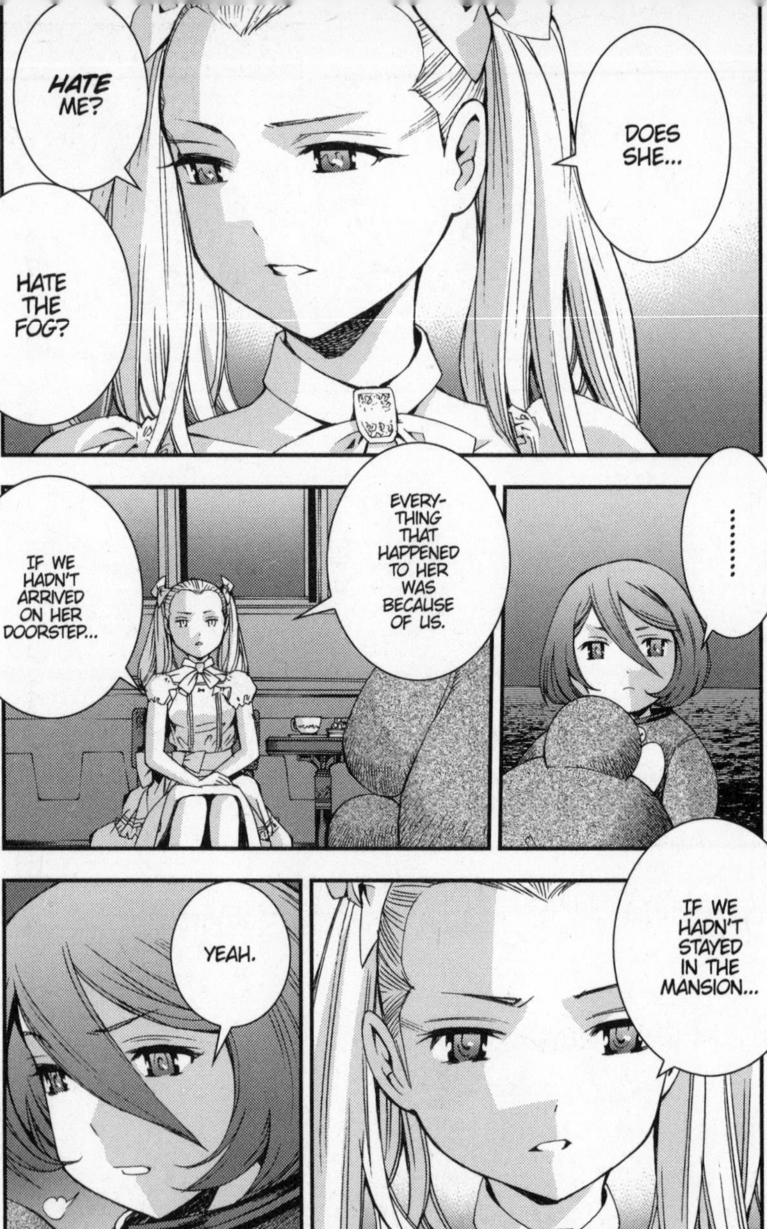
DOES SHE...
HATE ME?
HATE THE FOG?
......
EVERY-THING THAT HAPPENED TO HER WAS BECAUSE OF US.
IF WE HADN'T ARRIVED ON HER DOORSTEP...
IF WE HADN'T STAYED IN THE MANSION...
YEAH.

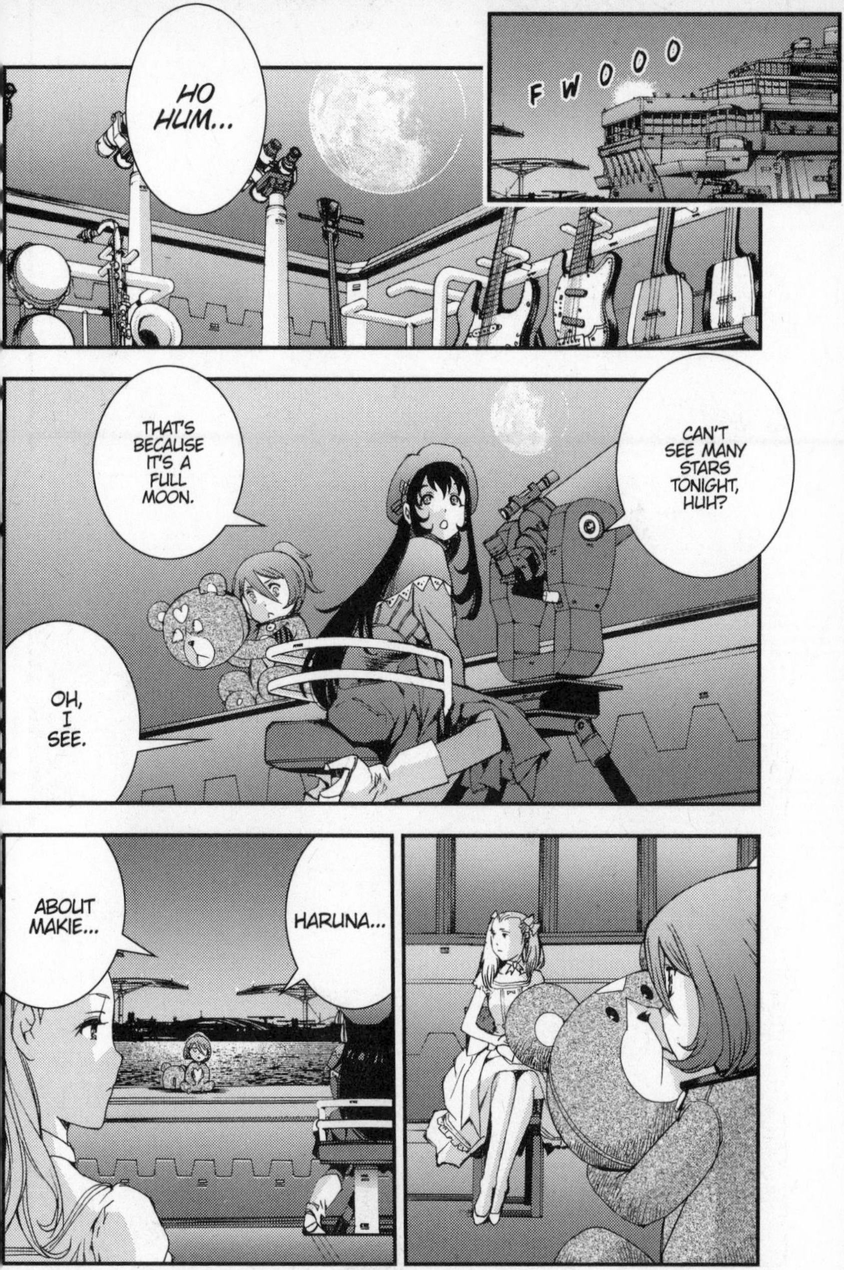
F W O O O
HO HUM...
CAN'T SEE MANY STARS TONIGHT, HUH?
THAT'S BECAUSE IT'S A FULL MOON.
OH, I SEE.
HARUNA...
ABOUT MAKIE...

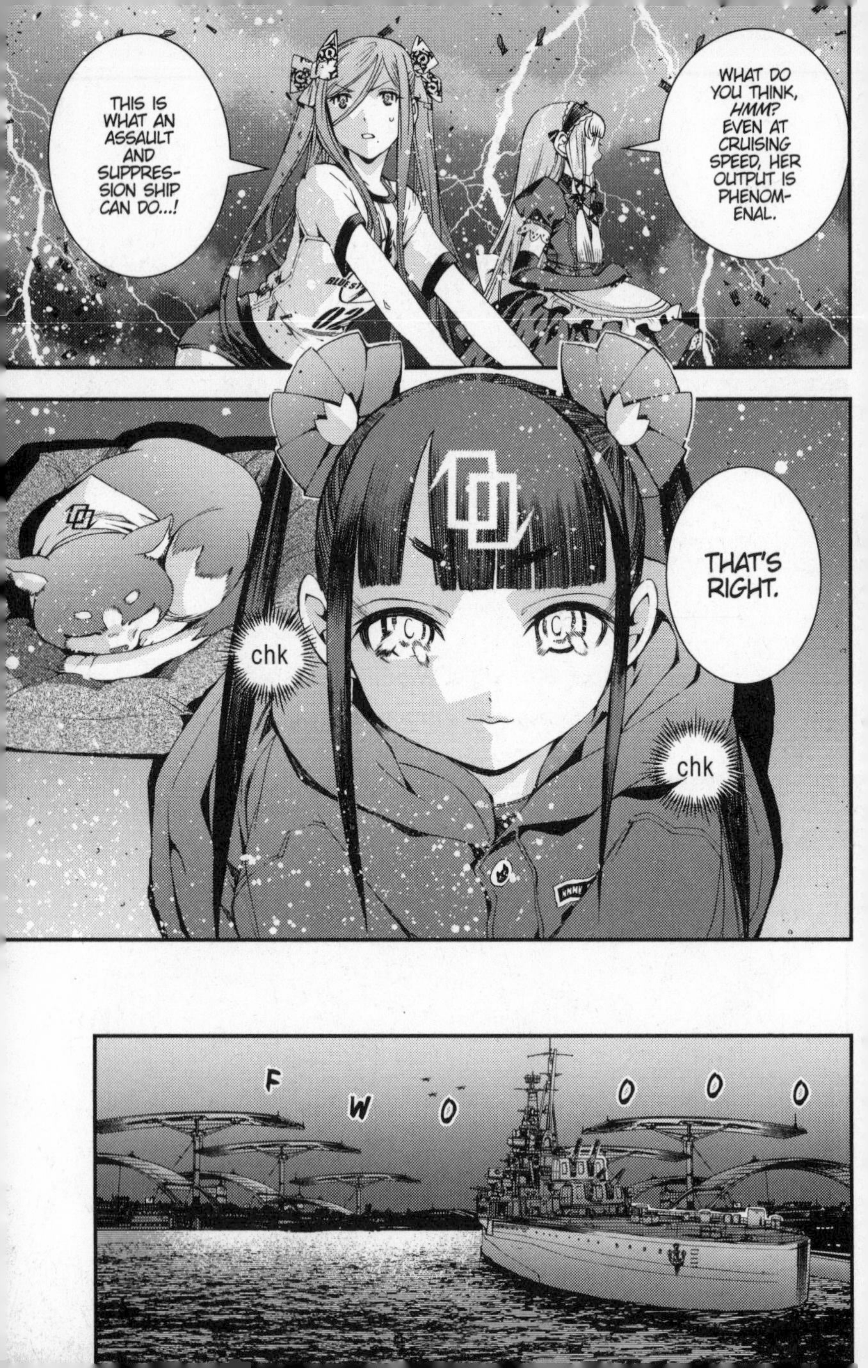
WHAT DO YOU THINK, *HMM?* EVEN AT CRUISING SPEED, HER OUTPUT IS PHENOMENAL.
THIS IS WHAT AN ASSAULT AND SUPPRESSION SHIP CAN DO...!
THAT'S RIGHT.
chk
chk
F W O O O O O

I'LL GIVE YOU A RIDE.

chk

AT ANY RATE...

VWOOOO

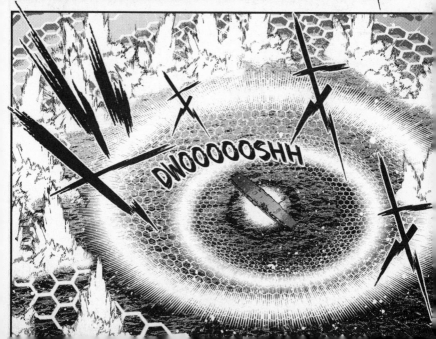

DWOOOOOSHH

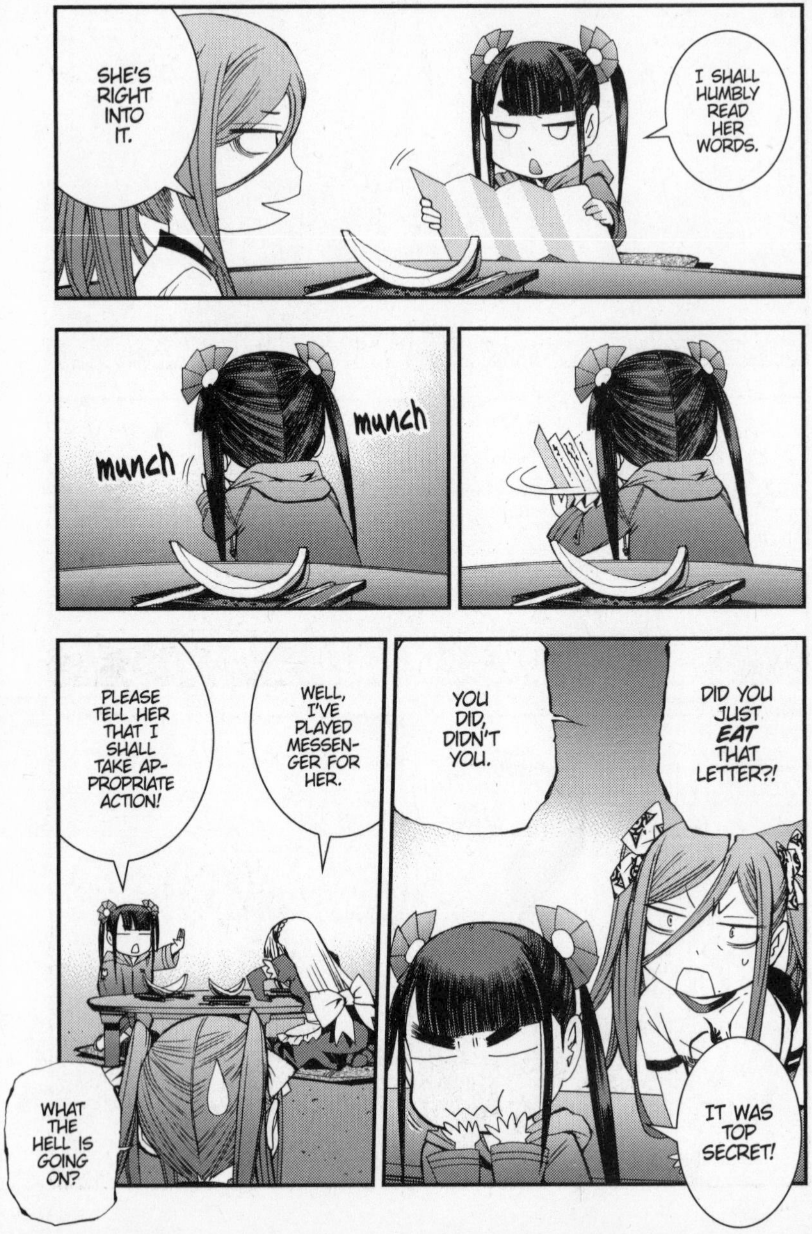
I SHALL HUMBLY READ HER WORDS.
SHE'S RIGHT INTO IT.
munch
munch
DID YOU JUST *EAT* THAT LETTER?!
YOU DID, DIDN'T YOU.
IT WAS TOP SECRET!
WELL, I'VE PLAYED MESSENGER FOR HER.
PLEASE TELL HER THAT I SHALL TAKE APPROPRIATE ACTION!
WHAT THE HELL IS GOING ON?

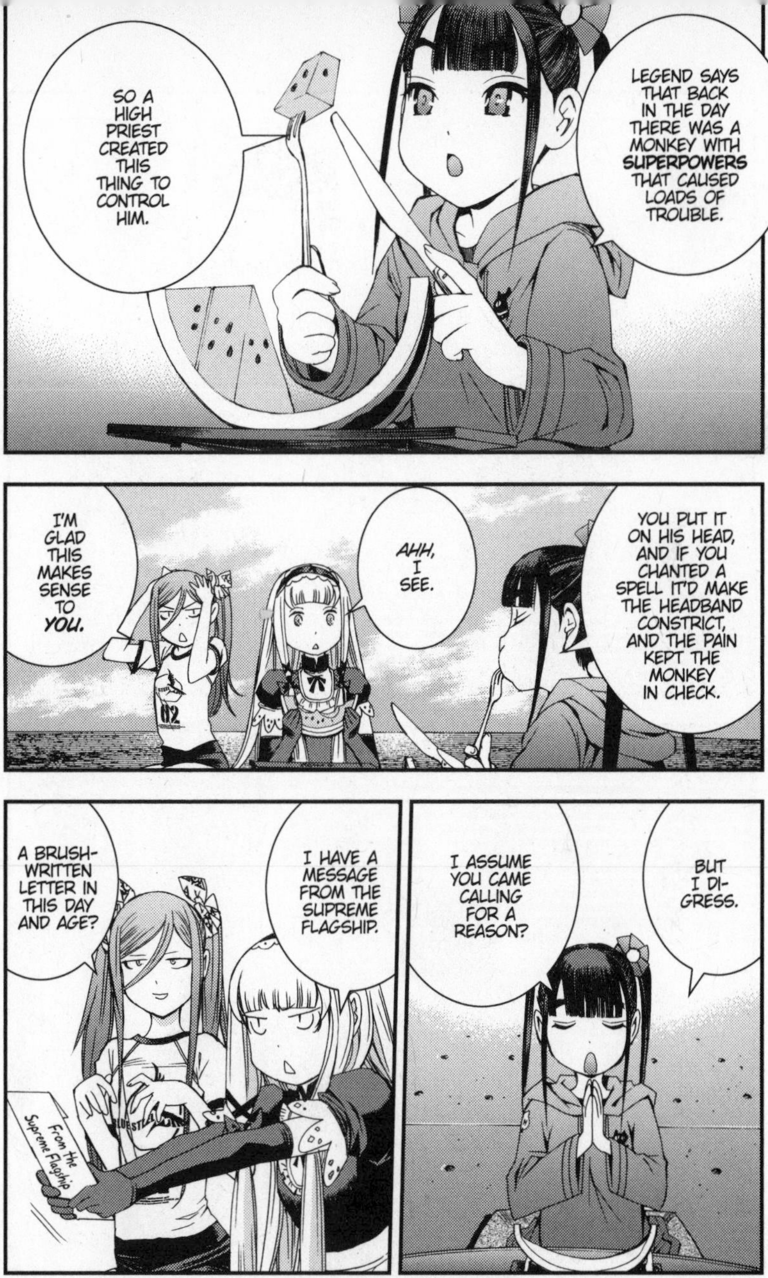
LEGEND SAYS THAT BACK IN THE DAY THERE WAS A MONKEY WITH **SUPERPOWERS** THAT CAUSED LOADS OF TROUBLE.
SO A HIGH PRIEST CREATED THIS THING TO CONTROL HIM.
YOU PUT IT ON HIS HEAD, AND IF YOU CHANTED A SPELL IT'D MAKE THE HEADBAND CONSTRICT, AND THE PAIN KEPT THE MONKEY IN CHECK.
AHH, I SEE.
I'M GLAD THIS MAKES SENSE TO ***YOU.***
BUT I DI-GRESS.
I ASSUME YOU CAME CALLING FOR A REASON?
I HAVE A MESSAGE FROM THE SUPREME FLAGSHIP.
A BRUSH-WRITTEN LETTER IN THIS DAY AND AGE?
From the Supreme Flagship

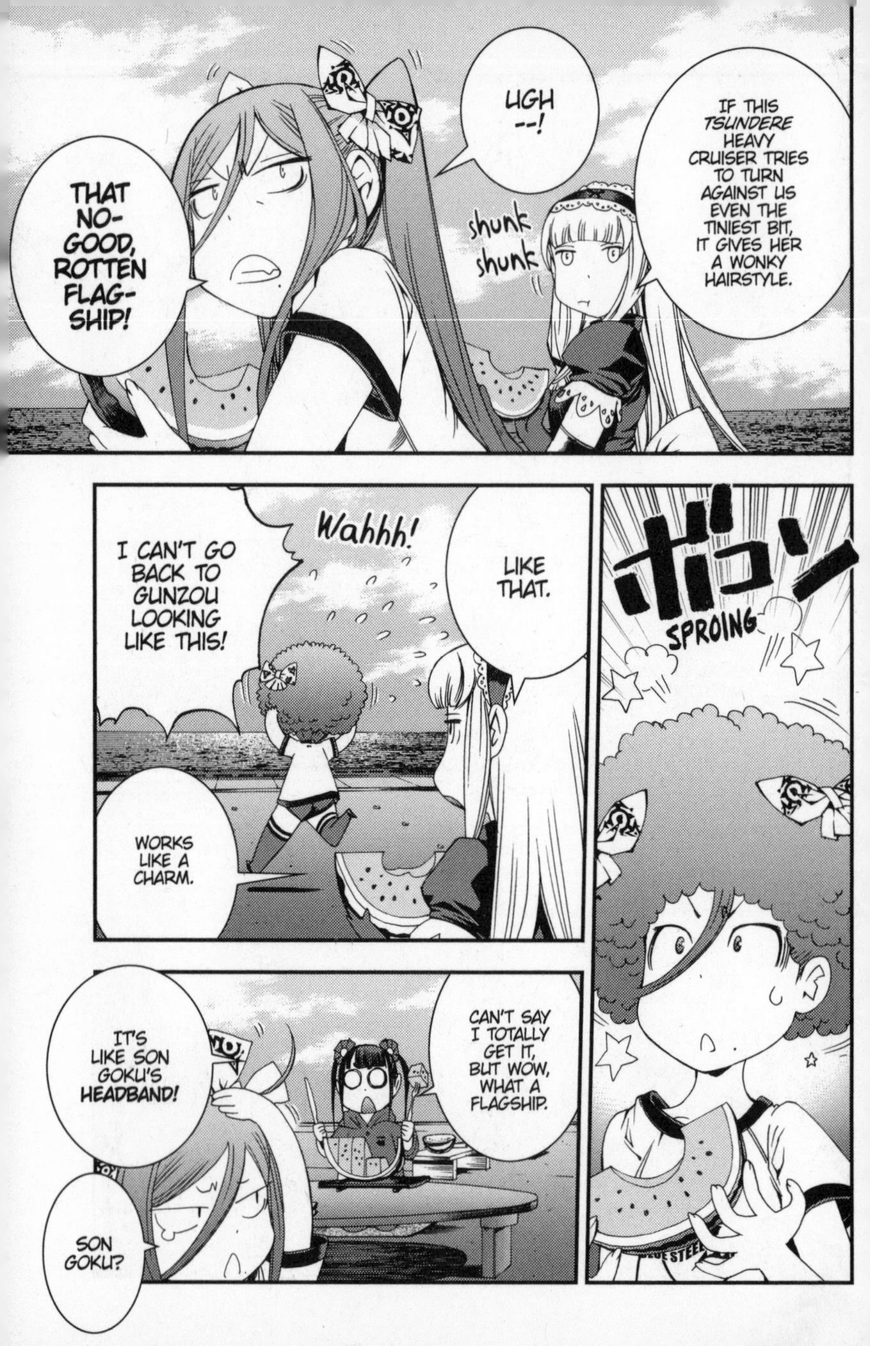
IF THIS *TSUNDERE* HEAVY CRUISER TRIES TO TURN AGAINST US EVEN THE TINIEST BIT, IT GIVES HER A WONKY HAIRSTYLE.
UGH --!
shunk shunk
THAT NO-GOOD, ROTTEN FLAG-SHIP!
ボコン
SPROING
LIKE THAT.
Wahhh!
I CAN'T GO BACK TO GUNZOU LOOKING LIKE THIS!
WORKS LIKE A CHARM.
CAN'T SAY I TOTALLY GET IT, BUT WOW, WHAT A FLAGSHIP.
IT'S LIKE SON GOKU'S **HEADBAND!**
SON GOKU?

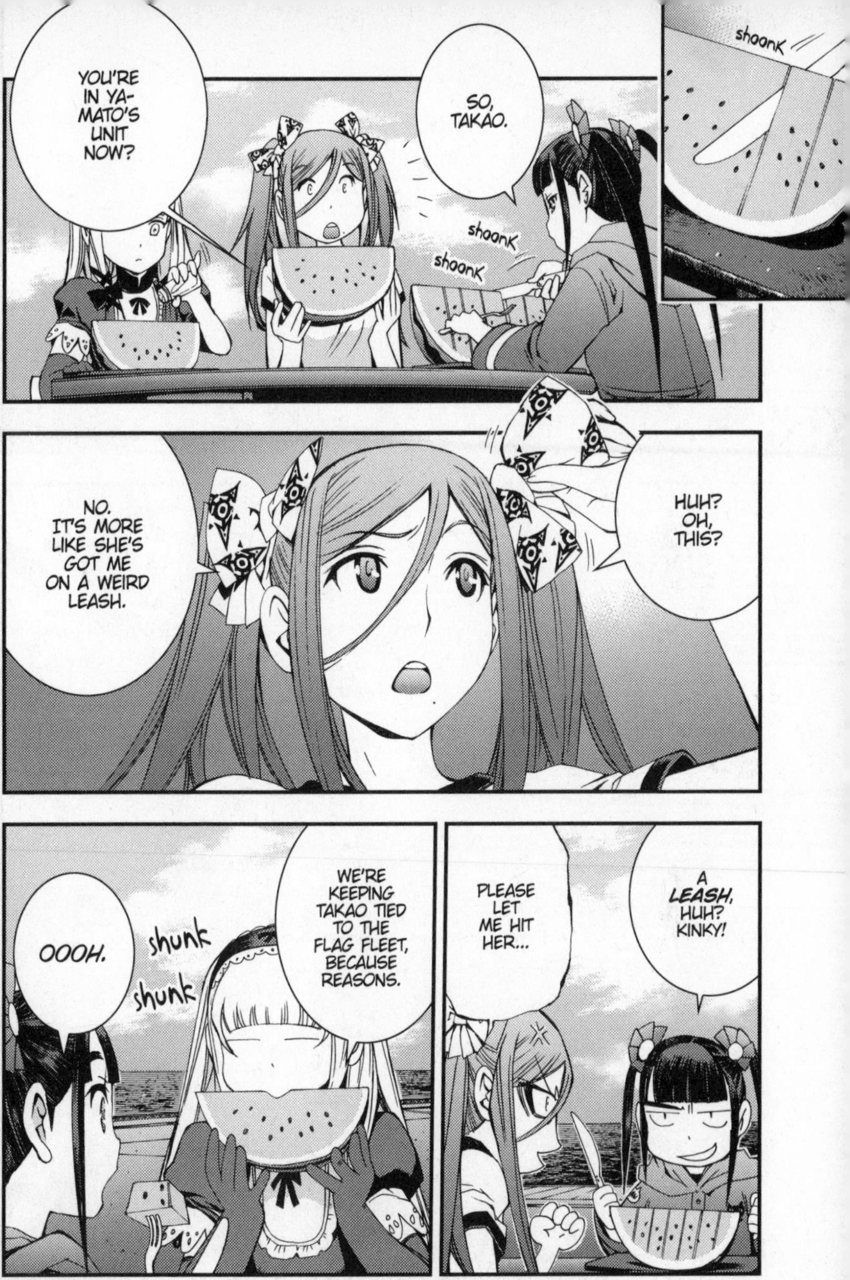
shoonK
SO, TAKAO.
shoonK
shoonK
YOU'RE IN YA-MATO'S UNIT NOW?
HUH? OH, THIS?
NO. IT'S MORE LIKE SHE'S GOT ME ON A WEIRD LEASH.
A ***LEASH***, HUH? KINKY!
PLEASE LET ME HIT HER...
WE'RE KEEPING TAKAO TIED TO THE FLAG FLEET, BECAUSE REASONS.
shunk
shunk
OOOH.

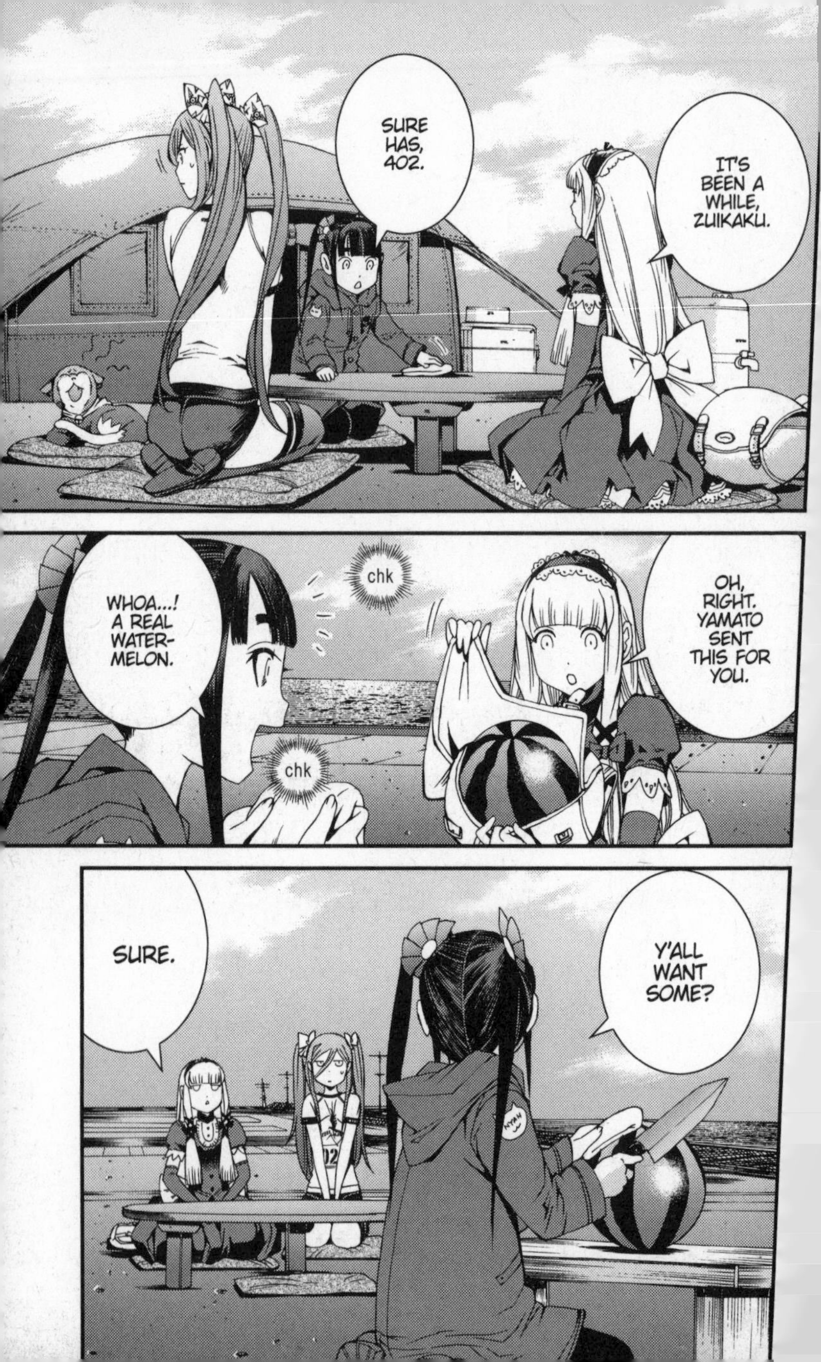
IT'S BEEN A WHILE, ZUIKAKU.
SURE HAS, 402.
OH, RIGHT. YAMATO SENT THIS FOR YOU.
chk
chk
WHOA...! A REAL WATER-MELON.
Y'ALL WANT SOME?
SURE.

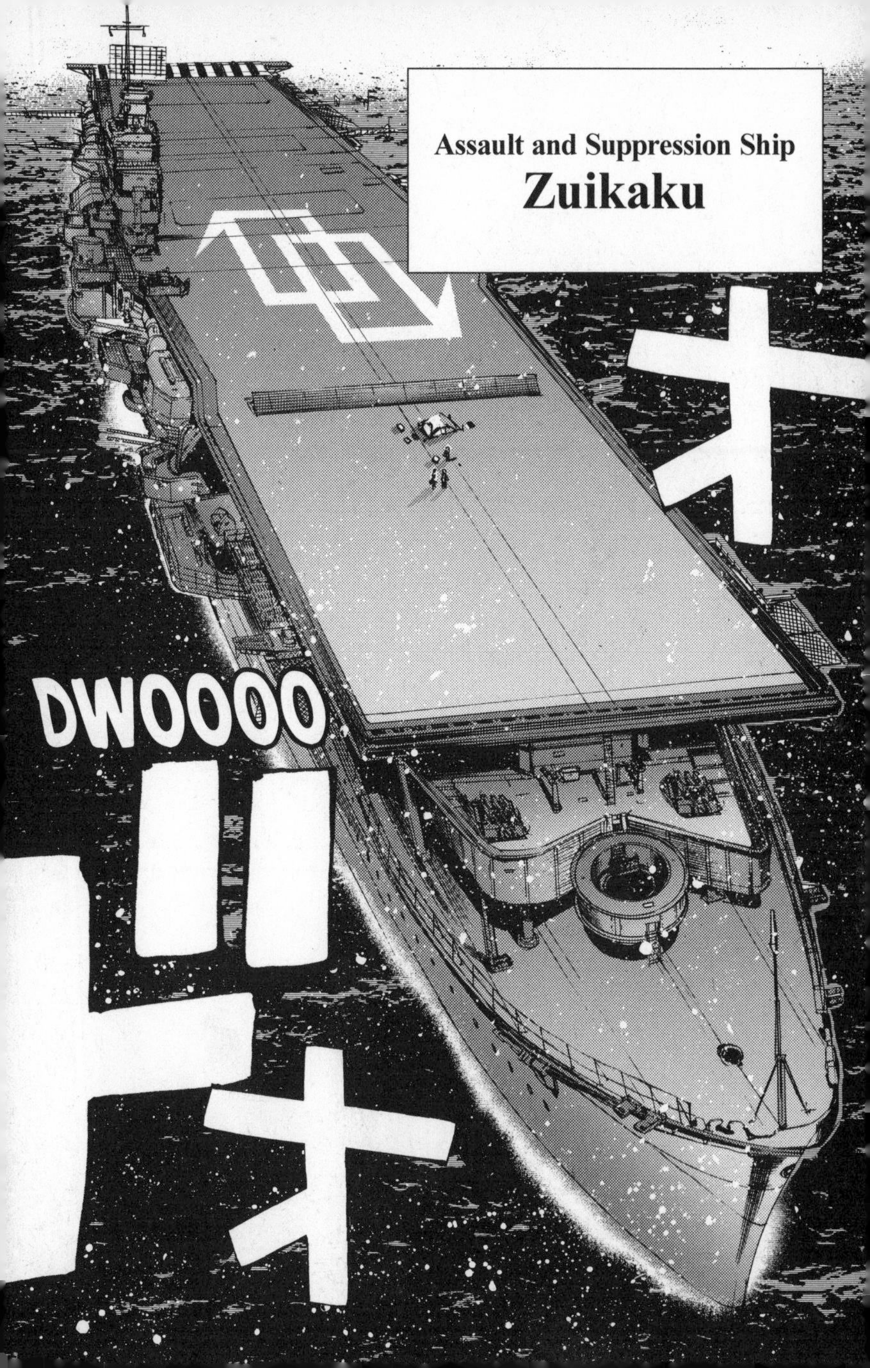
Assault and Suppression Ship
Zuikaku
DWOOOO

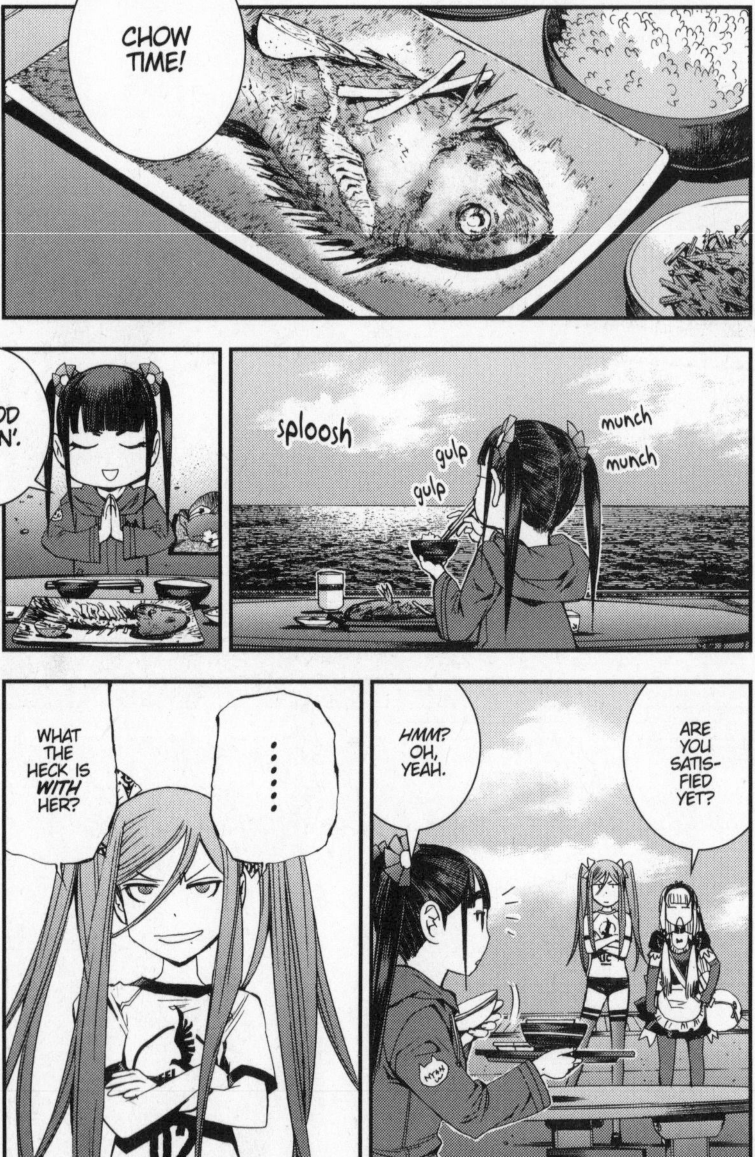
CHOW TIME!
munch
munch
gulp
gulp
sploosh
GOOD EATIN'.
ARE YOU SATIS-FIED YET?
HMM? OH, YEAH.
RECYCLING
......
WHAT THE HECK IS *WITH* HER?

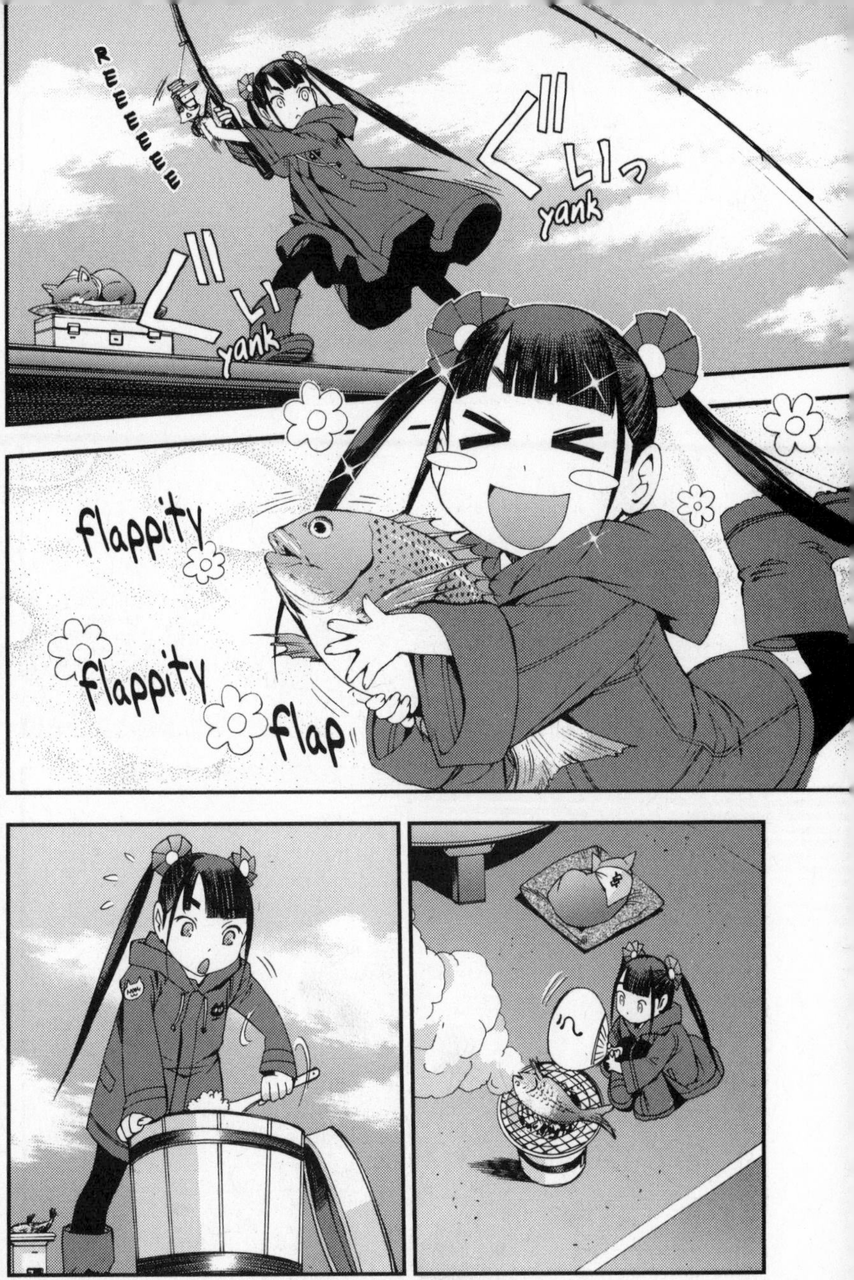
ぐいっ
yank
REEEEEEE
ぐい
yank
flappity
flappity
flap

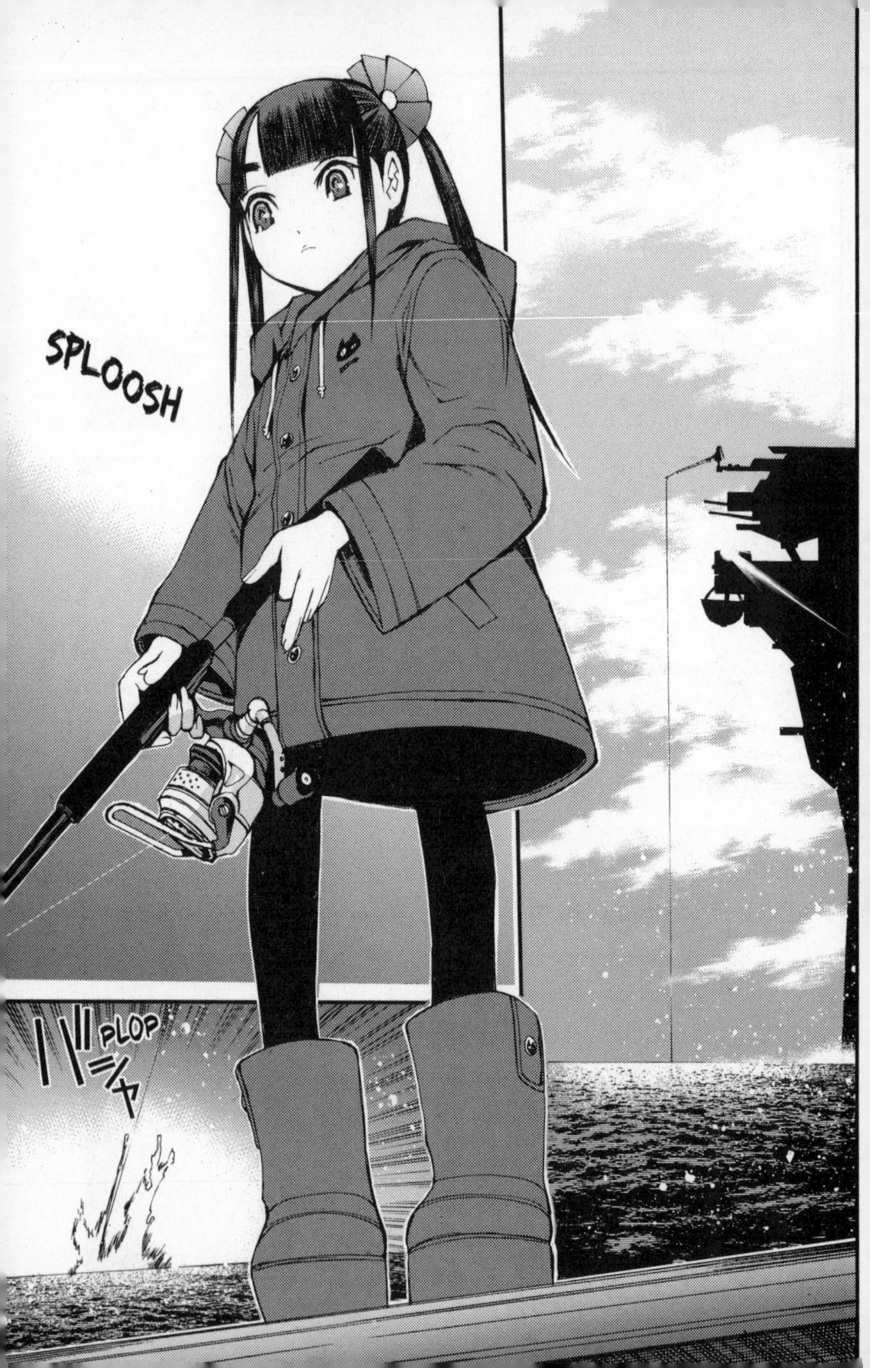
SPLOOSH
バシャ
PLOP

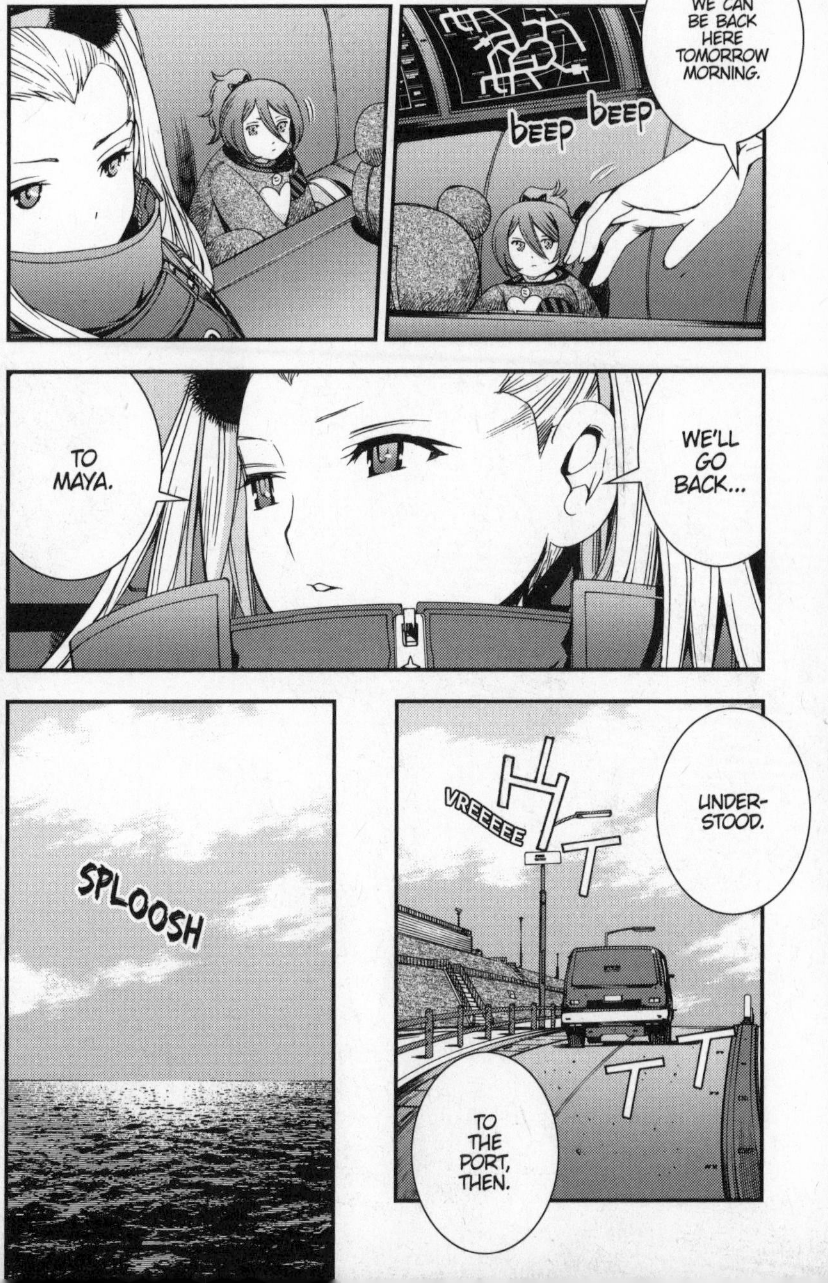
WE CAN BE BACK HERE TOMORROW MORNING.
beep beep
WE'LL GO BACK...
TO MAYA.
UNDER-STOOD.
VREEEEEE
TO THE PORT, THEN.
SPLOOSH

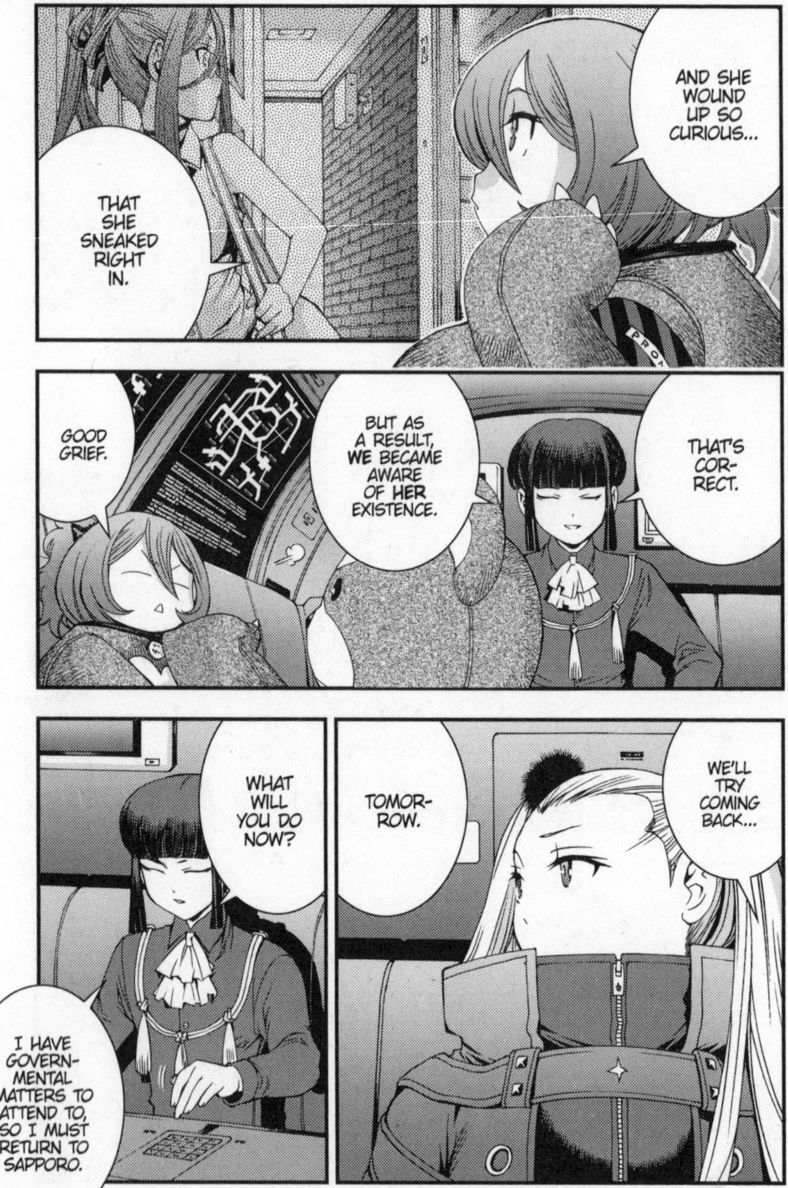
AND SHE WOUND UP SO CURIOUS...
THAT SHE SNEAKED RIGHT IN.
THAT'S COR-RECT.
BUT AS A RESULT, **WE** BECAME AWARE OF **HER** EXISTENCE.
GOOD GRIEF.
WE'LL TRY COMING BACK...
TOMOR-ROW.
WHAT WILL YOU DO NOW?
I HAVE GOVERN-MENTAL MATTERS TO ATTEND TO, SO I MUST RETURN TO SAPPORO.

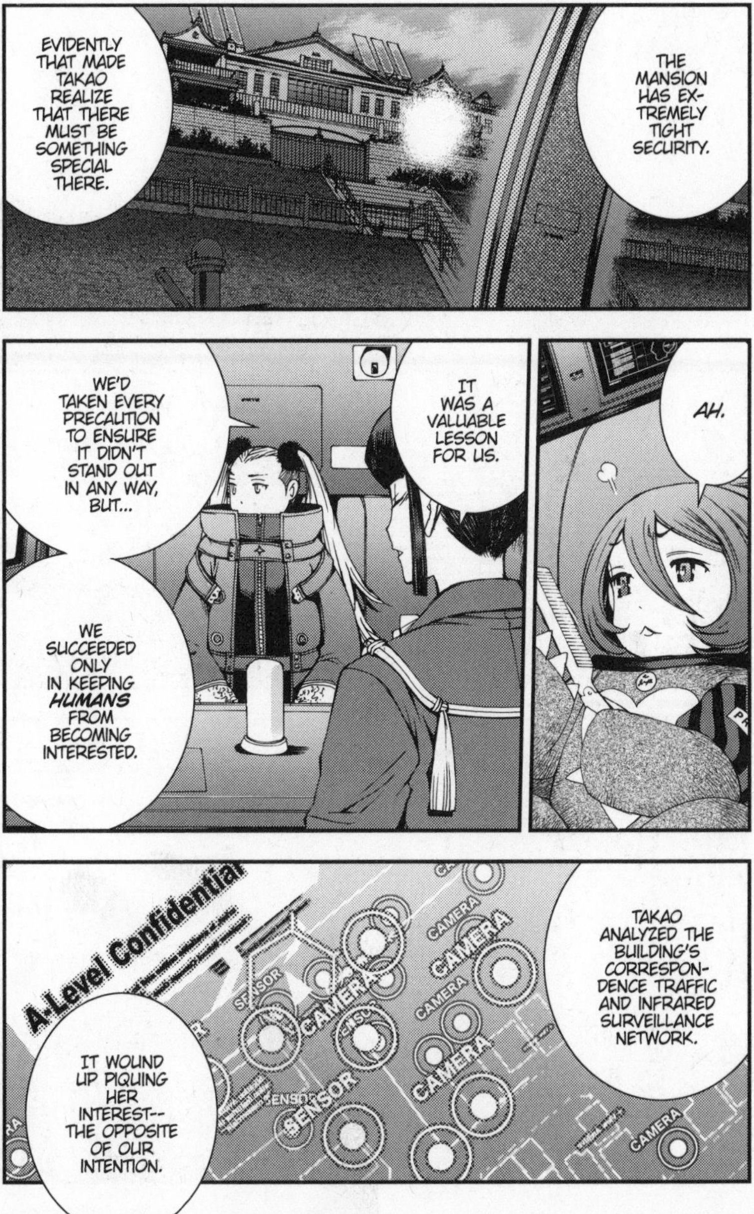
THE MANSION HAS EXTREMELY TIGHT SECURITY.
EVIDENTLY THAT MADE TAKAO REALIZE THAT THERE MUST BE SOMETHING SPECIAL THERE.
AH.
IT WAS A VALUABLE LESSON FOR US.
WE'D TAKEN EVERY PRECAUTION TO ENSURE IT DIDN'T STAND OUT IN ANY WAY, BUT...
WE SUCCEEDED ONLY IN KEEPING ***HUMANS*** FROM BECOMING INTERESTED.
TAKAO ANALYZED THE BUILDING'S CORRESPONDENCE TRAFFIC AND INFRARED SURVEILLANCE NETWORK.
A-Level Confidential
CAMERA
SENSOR
IT WOUND UP PIQUING HER INTEREST-- THE OPPOSITE OF OUR INTENTION.

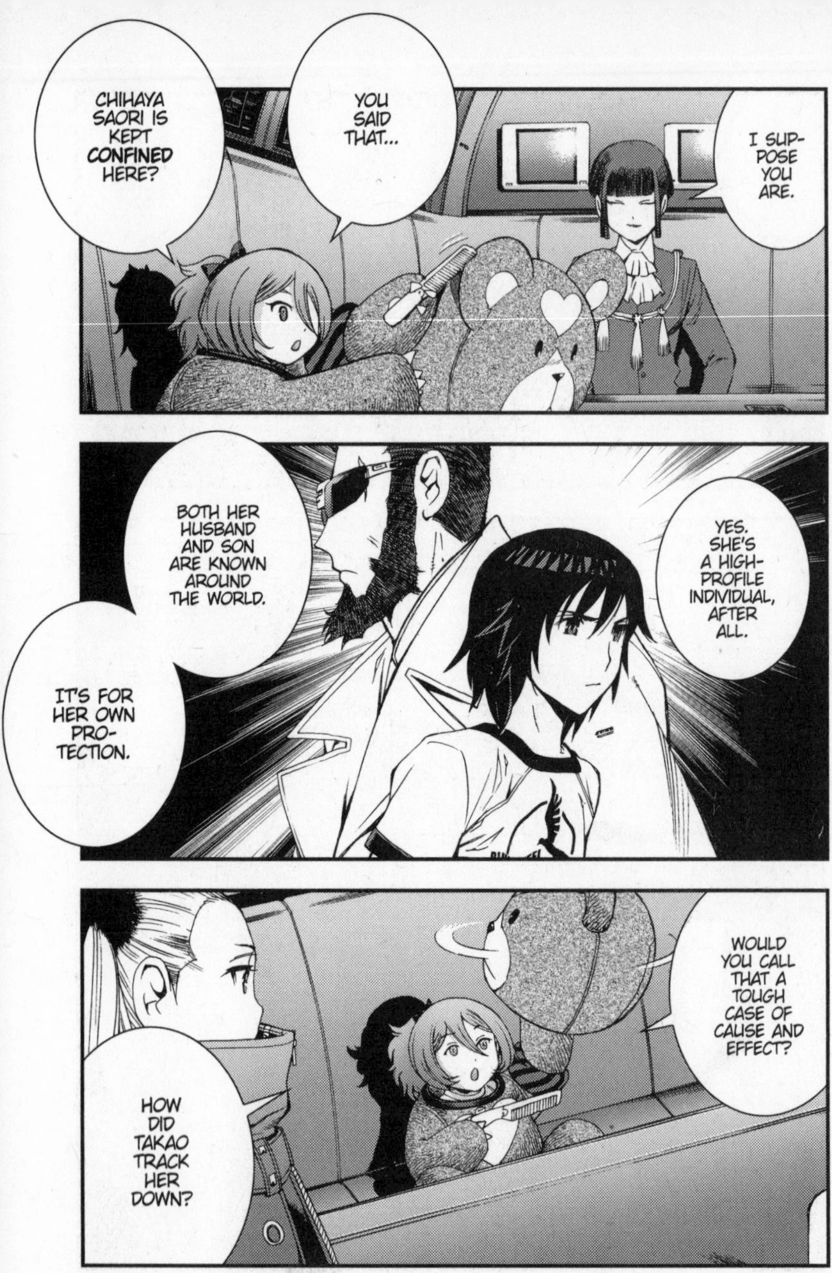
I SUP-POSE YOU ARE.
YOU SAID THAT...
CHIHAYA SAORI IS KEPT CONFINED HERE?
YES. SHE'S A HIGH-PROFILE INDIVIDUAL, AFTER ALL.
BOTH HER HUSBAND AND SON ARE KNOWN AROUND THE WORLD.
IT'S FOR HER OWN PRO-TECTION.
WOULD YOU CALL THAT A TOUGH CASE OF CAUSE AND EFFECT?
HOW DID TAKAO TRACK HER DOWN?

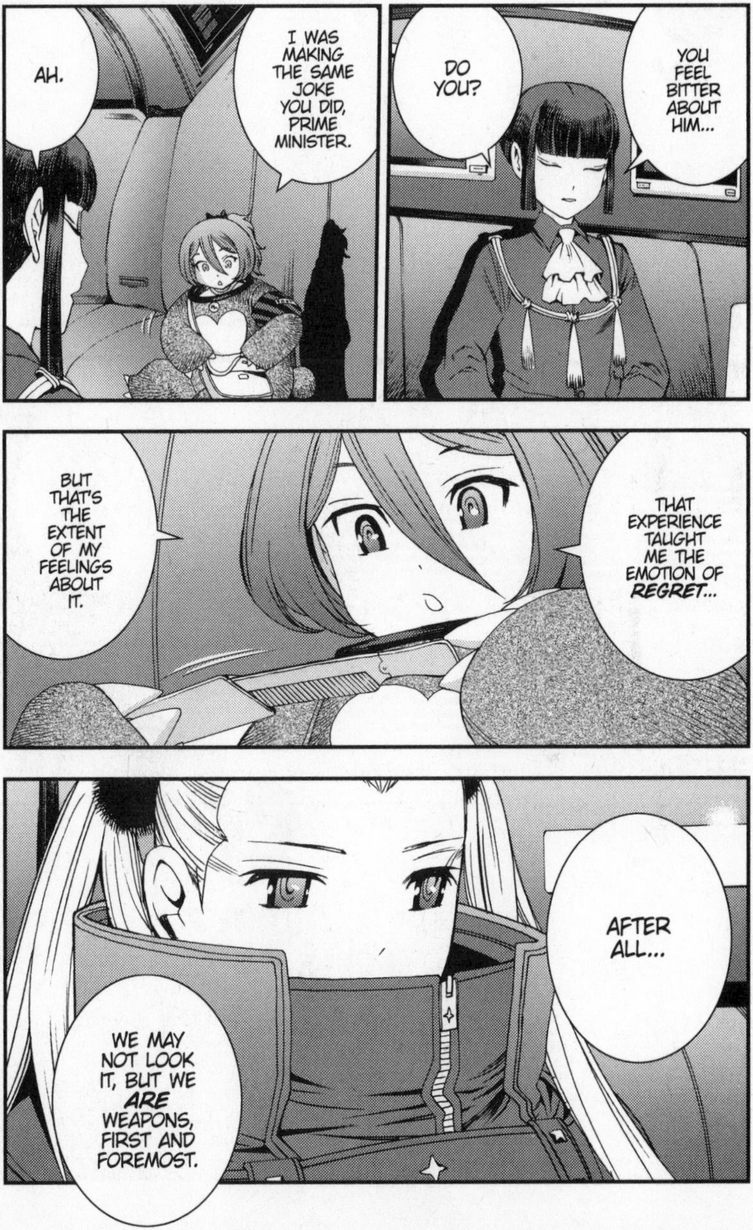
YOU FEEL BITTER ABOUT HIM...
DO YOU?
I WAS MAKING THE SAME JOKE YOU DID, PRIME MINISTER.
AH.
THAT EXPERIENCE TAUGHT ME THE EMOTION OF ***REGRET***...
BUT THAT'S THE EXTENT OF MY FEELINGS ABOUT IT.
AFTER ALL...
WE MAY NOT LOOK IT, BUT WE ***ARE*** WEAPONS, FIRST AND FOREMOST.

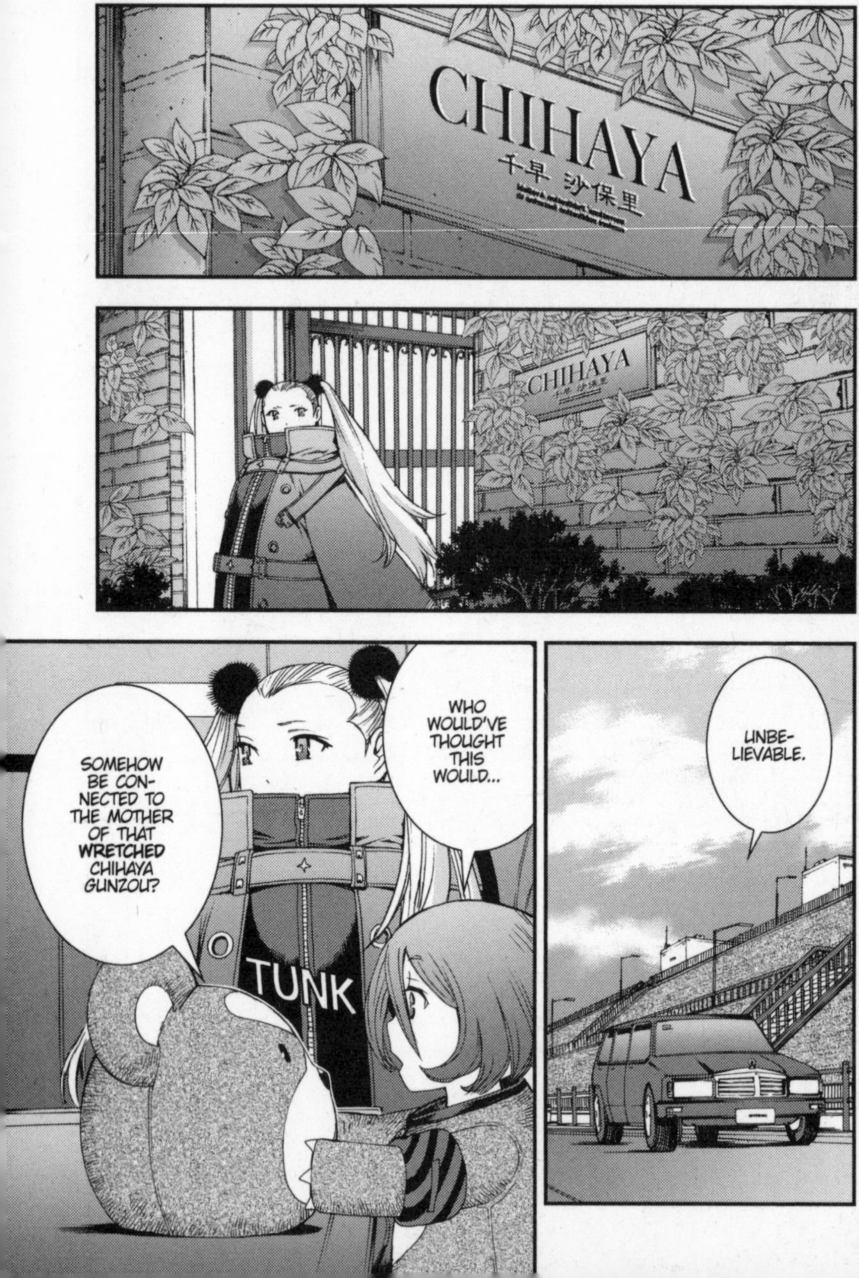
CHIHAYA
千早 沙保里
CHIHAYA
UNBE-LIEVABLE.
WHO WOULD'VE THOUGHT THIS WOULD...
SOMEHOW BE CONNECTED TO THE MOTHER OF THAT WRETCHED CHIHAYA GUNZOU?
TUNK

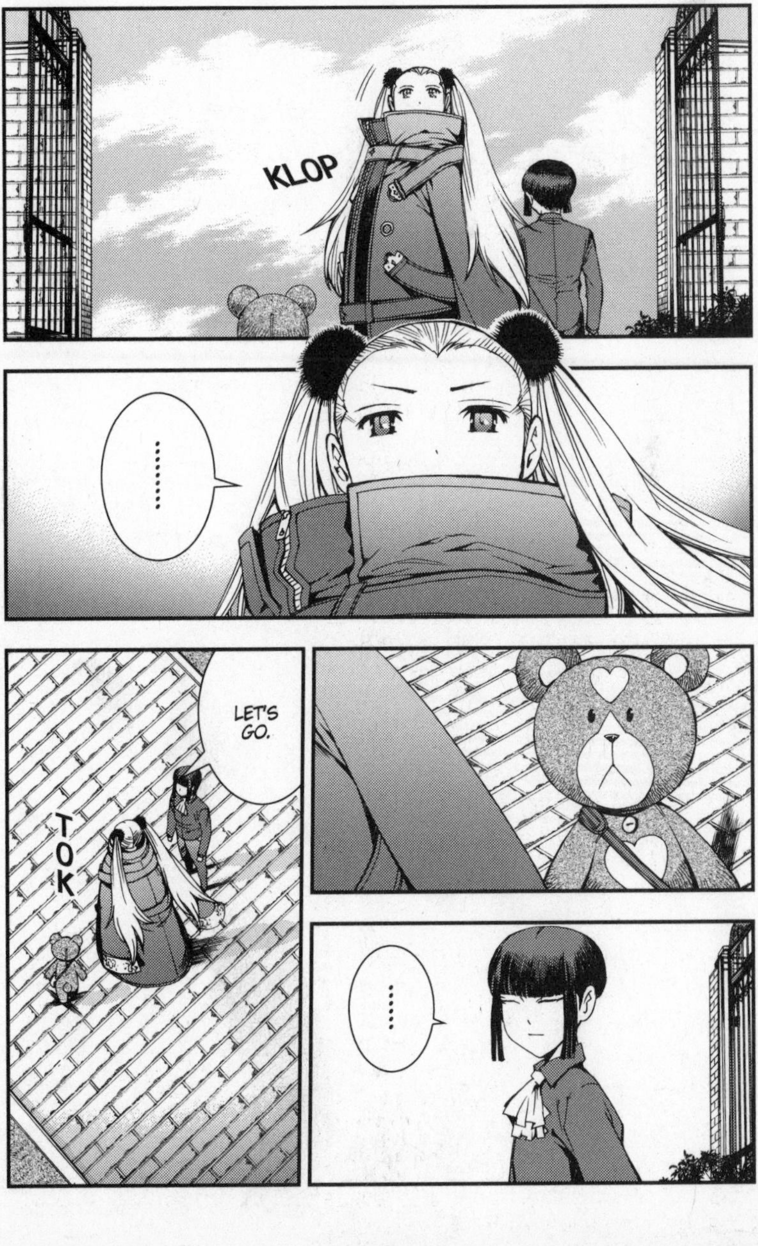
KLOP
....
......
LET'S GO.
TOK

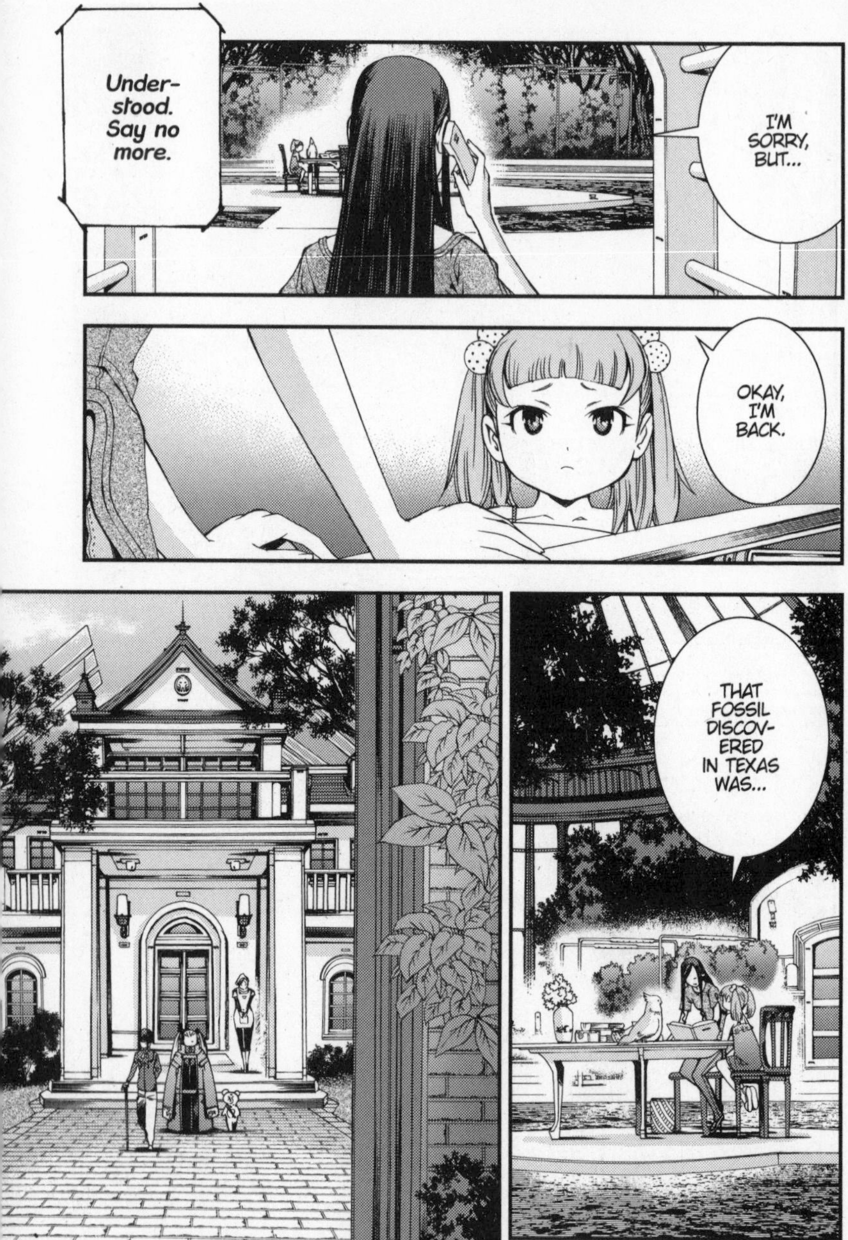
I'M SORRY, BUT...
Under-stood. Say no more.
OKAY, I'M BACK.
THAT FOSSIL DISCOV-ERED IN TEXAS WAS...

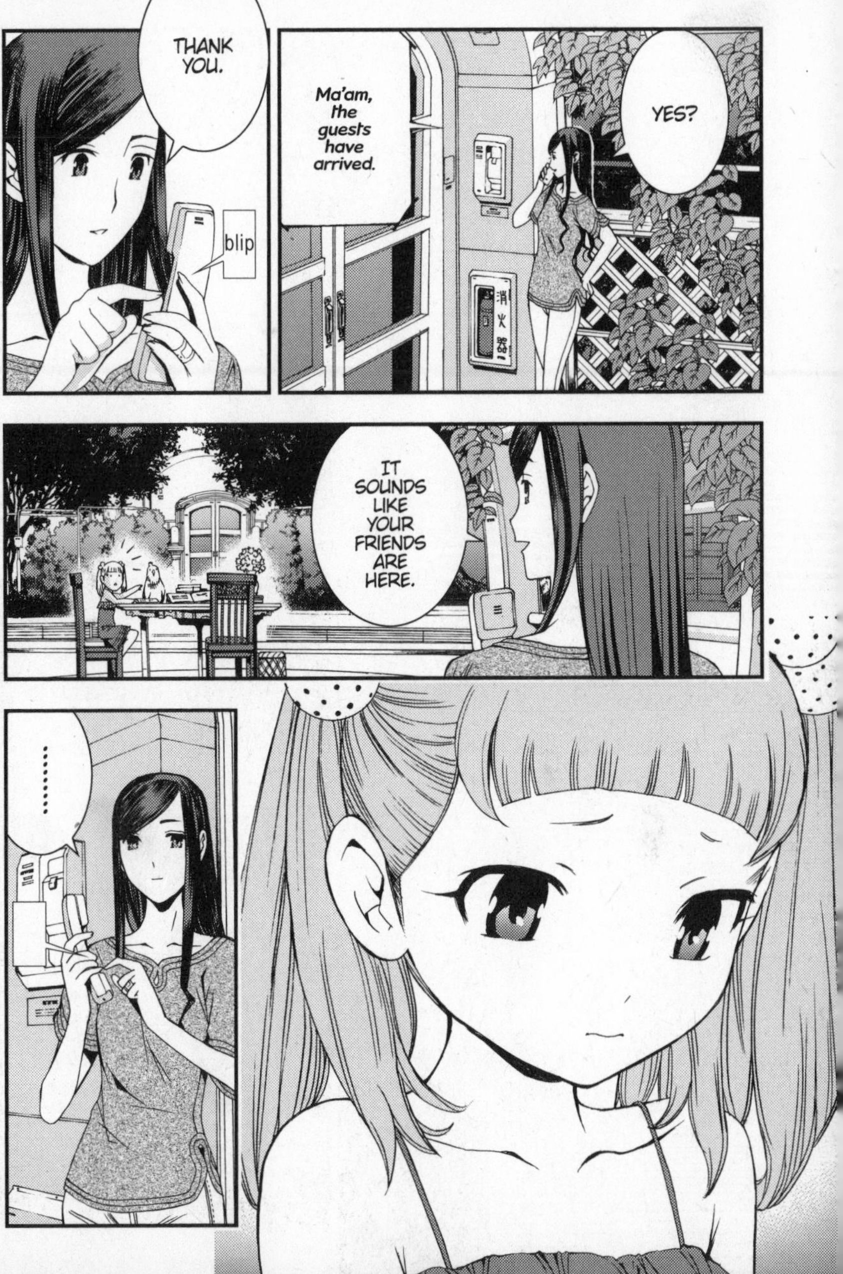
YES?
Ma'am, the guests have arrived.
THANK YOU.
blip
IT SOUNDS LIKE YOUR FRIENDS ARE HERE.
......

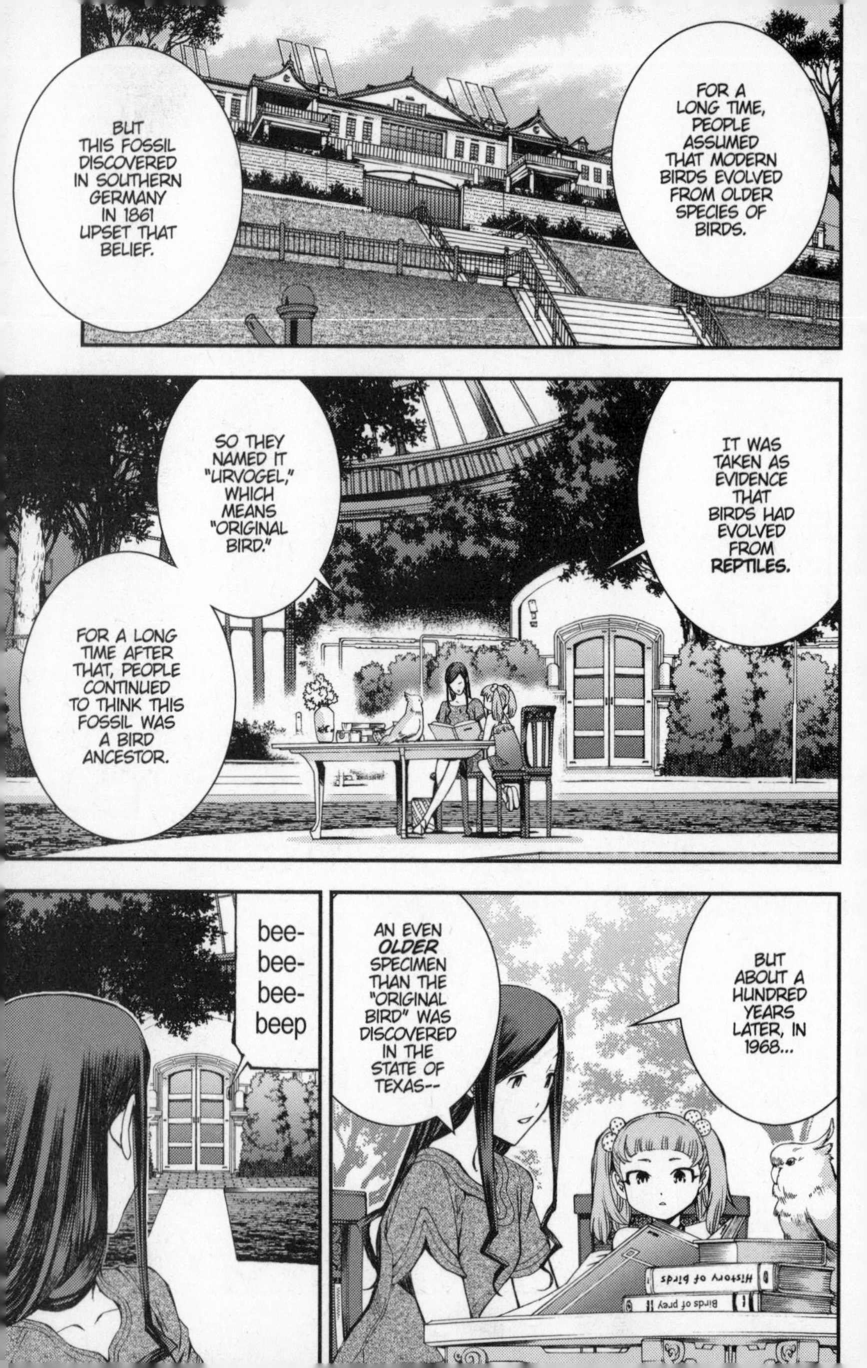
FOR A LONG TIME, PEOPLE ASSUMED THAT MODERN BIRDS EVOLVED FROM OLDER SPECIES OF BIRDS.
BUT THIS FOSSIL DISCOVERED IN SOUTHERN GERMANY IN 1861 UPSET THAT BELIEF.
IT WAS TAKEN AS EVIDENCE THAT BIRDS HAD EVOLVED FROM **REPTILES.**
SO THEY NAMED IT "URVOGEL," WHICH MEANS "ORIGINAL BIRD."
FOR A LONG TIME AFTER THAT, PEOPLE CONTINUED TO THINK THIS FOSSIL WAS A BIRD ANCESTOR.
BUT ABOUT A HUNDRED YEARS LATER, IN 1968...
AN EVEN ***OLDER*** SPECIMEN THAN THE "ORIGINAL BIRD" WAS DISCOVERED IN THE STATE OF TEXAS--
History of Birds
Birds of prey
bee-bee-bee-beep

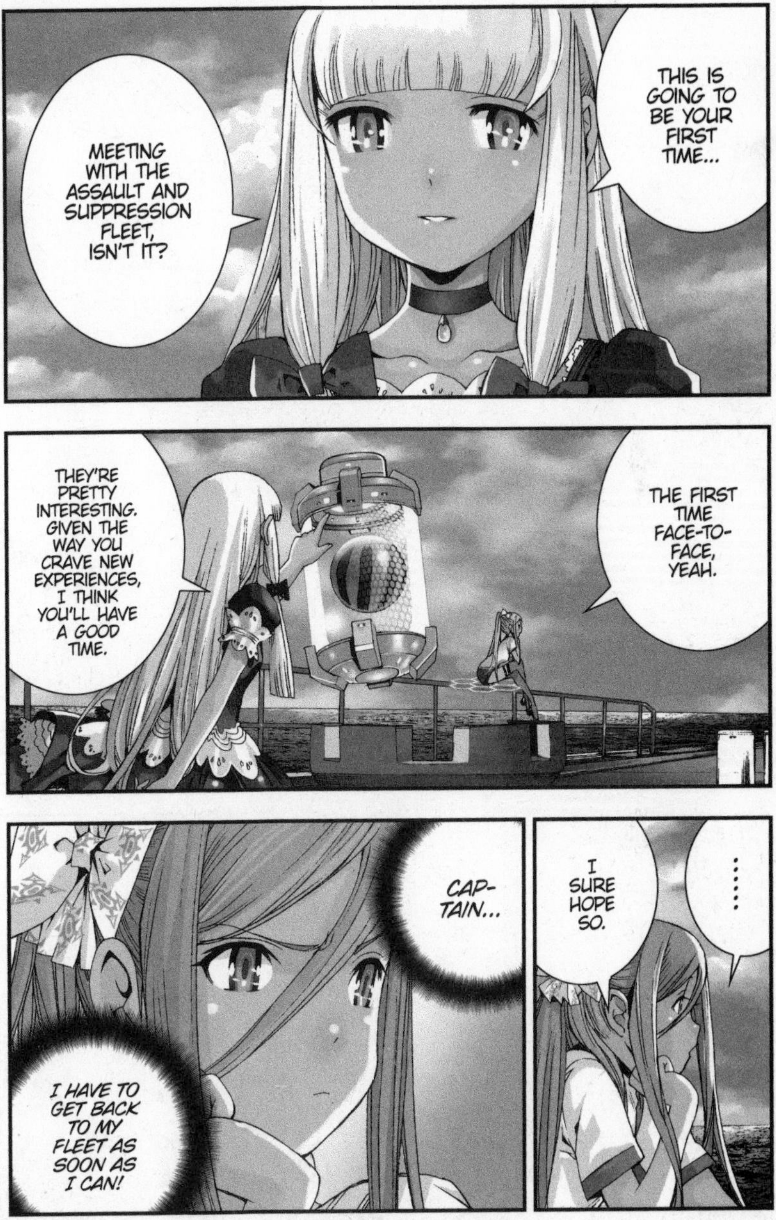
THIS IS GOING TO BE YOUR FIRST TIME...
MEETING WITH THE ASSAULT AND SUPPRESSION FLEET, ISN'T IT?
THE FIRST TIME FACE-TO-FACE, YEAH.
THEY'RE PRETTY INTERESTING. GIVEN THE WAY YOU CRAVE NEW EXPERIENCES, I THINK YOU'LL HAVE A GOOD TIME.
......
I SURE HOPE SO.
CAP-TAIN...
I HAVE TO GET BACK TO MY FLEET AS SOON AS I CAN!

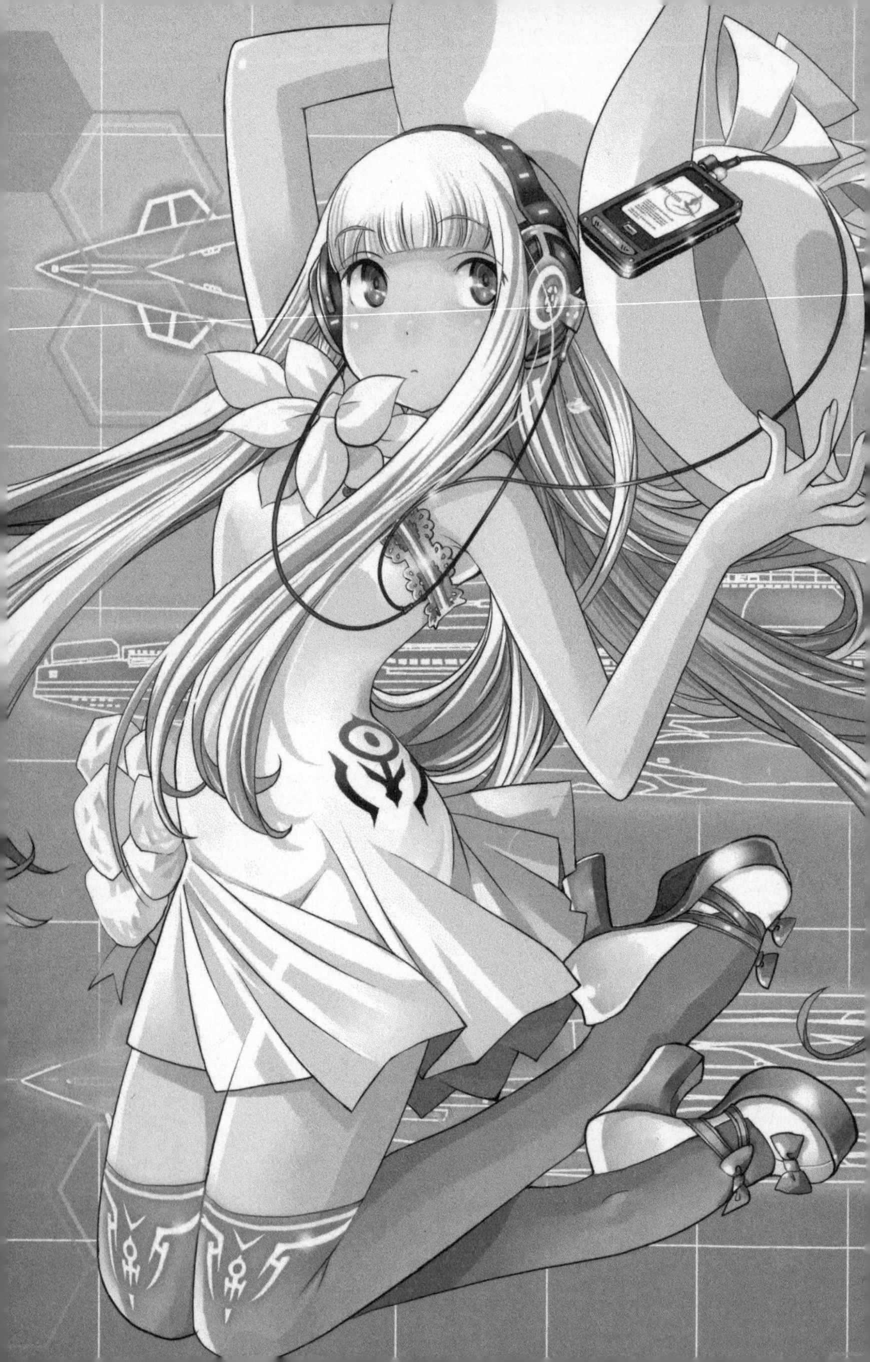

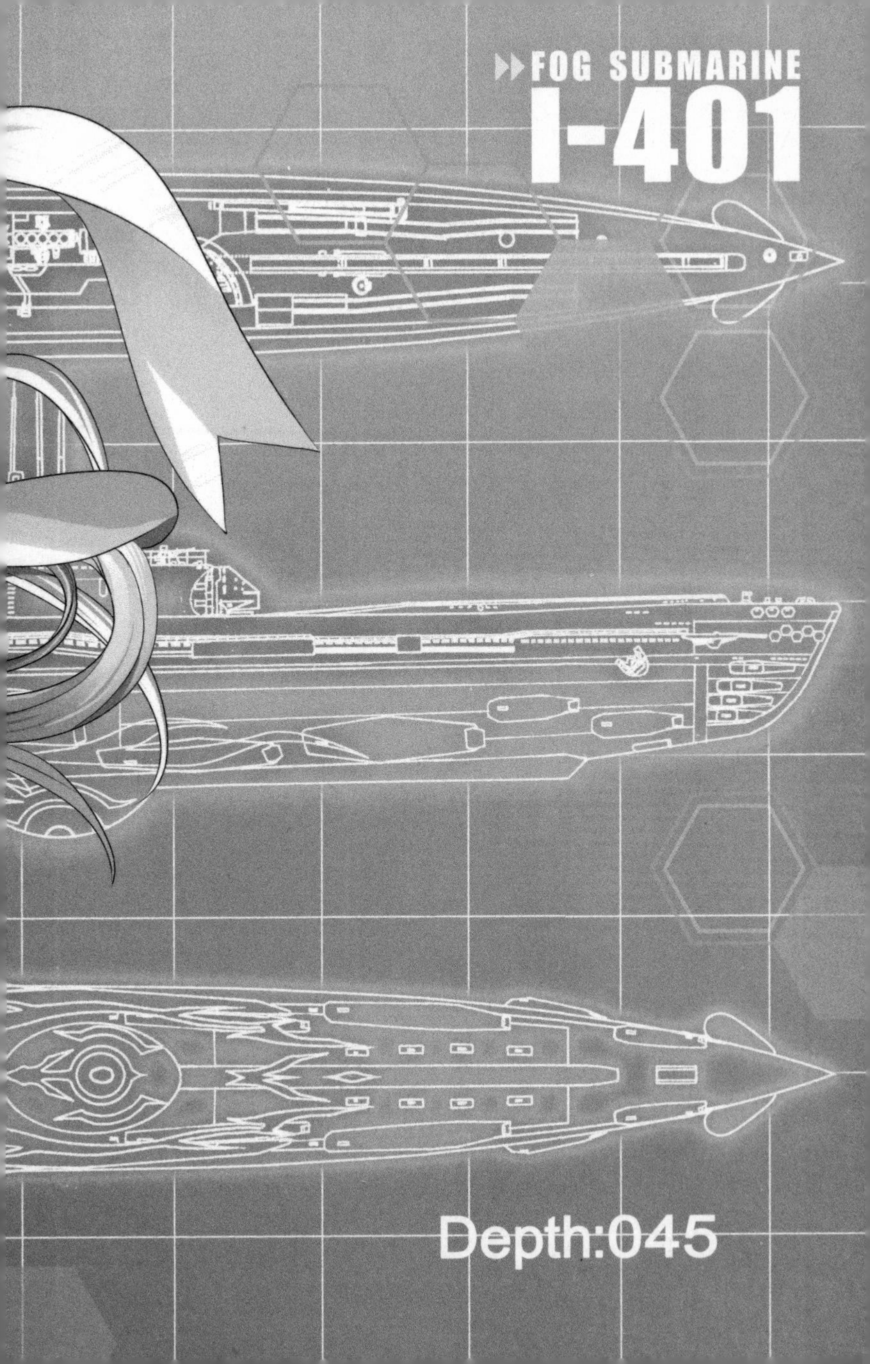
FOG SUBMARINE
I-401
Depth:045

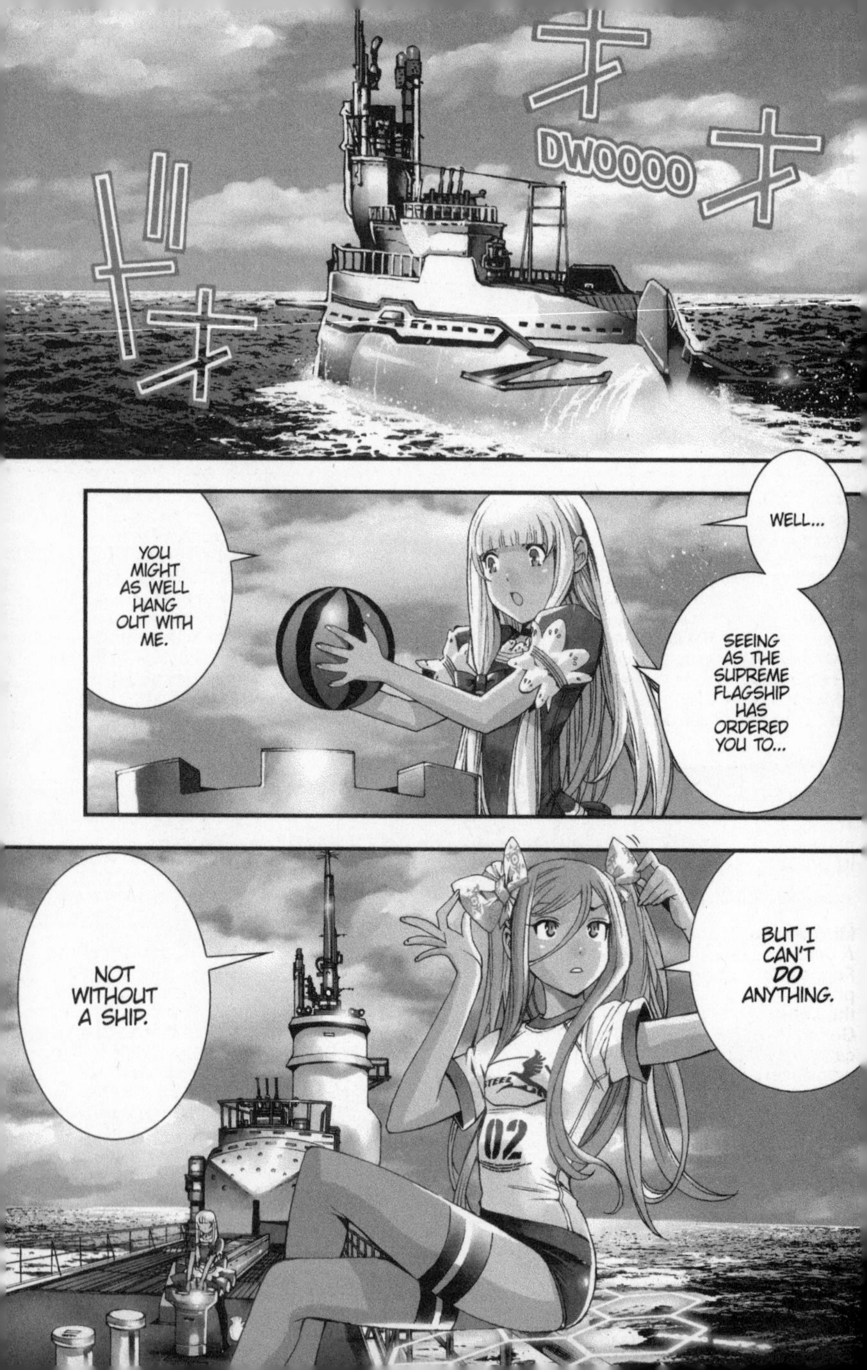
DWOOOO
WELL...
SEEING AS THE SUPREME FLAGSHIP HAS ORDERED YOU TO...
YOU MIGHT AS WELL HANG OUT WITH ME.
BUT I CAN'T *DO* ANYTHING.
NOT WITHOUT A SHIP.

Blue Sea Glossary

Design Children
An umbrella term for the children created by the Design Child Project, led by Professor Osakabe Toujirou. The project aimed to develop a new weapon capable of resisting the Fleet of Fog.

Delta Core
A core type possessed only by the massive vessels called Supreme Flagships. These cores possess exponentially higher processing power than the average core, and are capable of maintaining multiple mental models, as demonstrated by *Nagato.*

Eastern Fleet
A Fog fleet tasked with maintaining a blockade surrounding southeastern Asia. The battle cruiser *Repulse* and destroyer *Vampire* are part of this fleet, with large-class battleship *Prince of Wales* acting as flagship.

Vital Parts
As warships grew increasingly massive, larger units like battleships and cruisers developed a new method of armoring their most important components, such as their ammunition magazines and engines. These parts would be located in one centralized, heavily armored area. These parts of the ship were known as the "vital parts." It has been verified that Fog vessels, which mimic the form of human warships, also possess these vital parts.

Picket Ship
A reconnaissance ship deployed some distance away from its main fleet so as to detect enemy movements early. The Fleet of Fog has placed multiple picket ships around Japan in its effort to create a sealed blockade.

Scarlet Fleet
A fleet stationed off the coast of Europe and led by Chihaya Shouzou. Super battleship *Musashi* acts as the fleet's flagship, and it has been confirmed that the *U-2501* is affiliated with the fleet. The fleet is engaging in a number of independent actions, such as entering a security treaty with the British government and embarking on a search for the Admiralty Code.

Mirror-Ring System
A defense system employed by the Fog, capable of distorting space and phasing vast amounts of energy into the space-time of an alternate dimension. Generally only Yamato-class vessels carry this system, but the *U-2501* was observed using one during the battle with the *Takao*. The *U-2501's* use was minor, but still caused dimensional damage.

Great European War
A war which took place in Europe following the Fog's establishment of a sea blockade. Because England is not part of continental Europe, it was not caught up in the war.

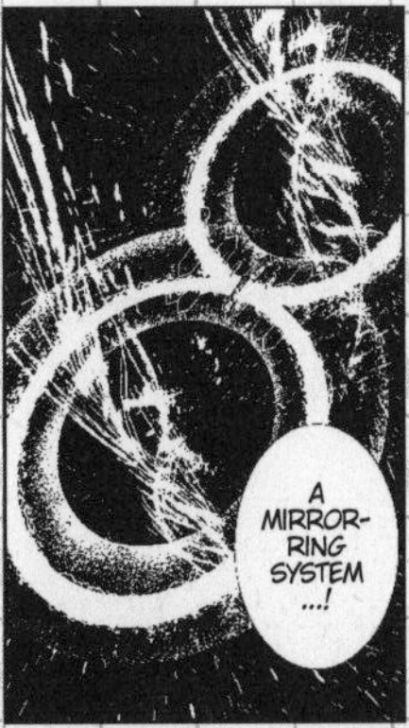
A MIRROR-RING SYSTEM ....!

Layer Depth
The ocean depth at which the temperature changes drastically. At this point, sound waves refract and reflect, so submarines which dive below it become difficult to track with surface-level sonar.

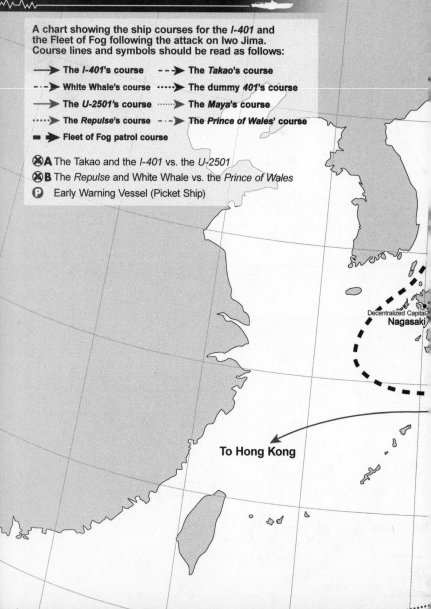

Blue Steel Battle Map

A chart showing the ship courses for the *I-401* and the Fleet of Fog following the attack on Iwo Jima. Course lines and symbols should be read as follows:

⟶ The *I-401*'s course — – –➤ The *Takao*'s course

– · –➤ White Whale's course ·····➤ The dummy *401*'s course

⟶ The *U-2501*'s course ·······➤ The *Maya*'s course

·····➤ The *Repulse*'s course – · –➤ The *Prince of Wales*' course

■ ➤ Fleet of Fog patrol course

⊗**A** The Takao and the *I-401* vs. the *U-2501*

⊗**B** The *Repulse* and White Whale vs. the *Prince of Wales*

Ⓟ Early Warning Vessel (Picket Ship)

Decentralized Capital
Nagasaki

To Hong Kong

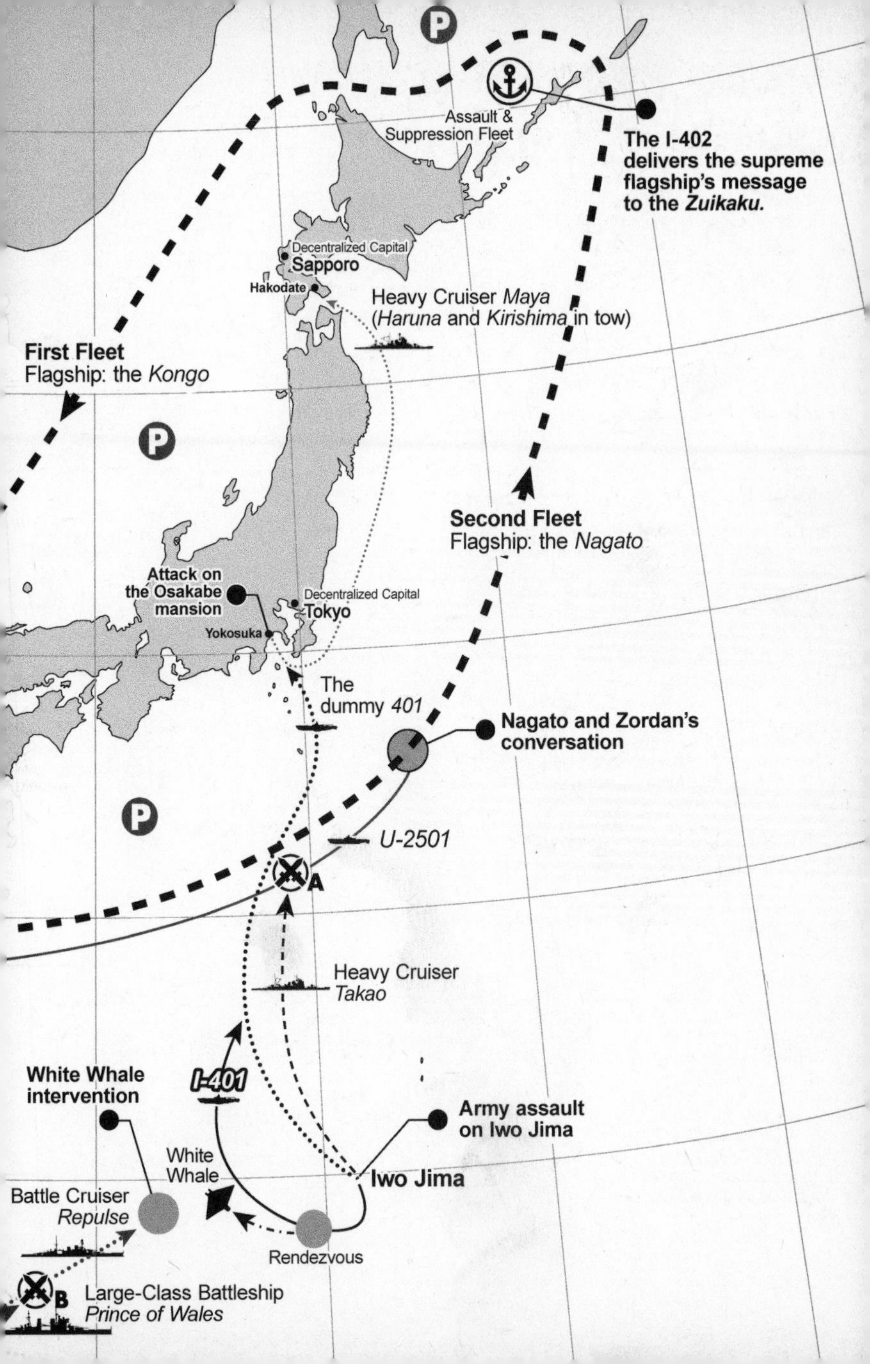

P
Assault &
Suppression Fleet
The I-402
delivers the supreme
flagship's message
to the *Zuikaku.*
Decentralized Capital
Sapporo
Hakodate
Heavy Cruiser *Maya*
(*Haruna* and *Kirishima* in tow)
First Fleet
Flagship: the *Kongo*
P
Second Fleet
Flagship: the *Nagato*
Attack on
the Osakabe
mansion
Decentralized Capital
Tokyo
Yokosuka
The
dummy *401*
Nagato and Zordan's
conversation
P
U-2501
A
Heavy Cruiser
Takao
White Whale
intervention
I-401
Army assault
on Iwo Jima
White
Whale
Iwo Jima
Battle Cruiser
Repulse
Rendezvous
B
Large-Class Battleship
Prince of Wales

Blue Sea Glossary

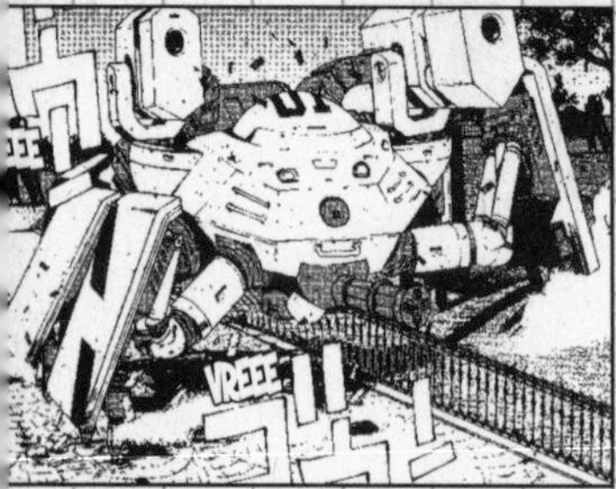
VREEE

Iwo Jima
A small, isolated island south of Japan, widely known as the location of an intense battle during the Pacific War. Hyuga has constructed a secret base there, along with a special dock, for the exclusive use of the *I-401*. At this time, Iwo Jima has been overrun by a robot army that Hyuga created. Its only current inhabitants are robots.

Iwagani
A type of walking combat vehicle utilized by the army. They were dispatched during the assault on the Osakabe mansion. Named for a heavy-shelled variety of crab, the Iwagani possess superior armor and are ideal for traversing rugged terrain and assaulting fortified locations.

LCAC
The common name for a class of air cushion-based vehicle employed by the navy. Being a hovercraft, it is able to travel over both land and water. They were used as a diversion when the army attacked Iwo Jima in order to assassinate the *401* crew.

Crushable Materials
Refers to a material used in automobiles and other vehicles. In the event of a collision, the material absorbs the force of the impact, protecting the person or vital components within. When Haruna's mental model was thrown to land, she transmuted her clothing (other than her coat) into crushable materials to protect herself.

Wolfpack Tactics
Special tactics employed by the *U-2501*. After placing its additional supply unit, Milchkuh, to its rear, the *2501* surrounds its enemy with a number of special mini submarines called Seehunds, which attack in a wave pattern. The *U-2501* is able to control multiple ships by forgoing the use of a mental model, thus freeing up extra processing power.

Eleven-Dimensional Structure
A world spoken of in M-theory, a theory in physics. It is composed of ten spatial dimensions and one time dimension. Extensive research on the subject continues today.

Battle Cruiser
A warship that possesses the attack power of a battleship and has superior speed. These ships are called "battle cruisers" because their defensive ability is limited to roughly that of a cruiser in order to maintain its higher speed. The *Repulse*, of the Eastern Fleet of Fog, is one such vessel.

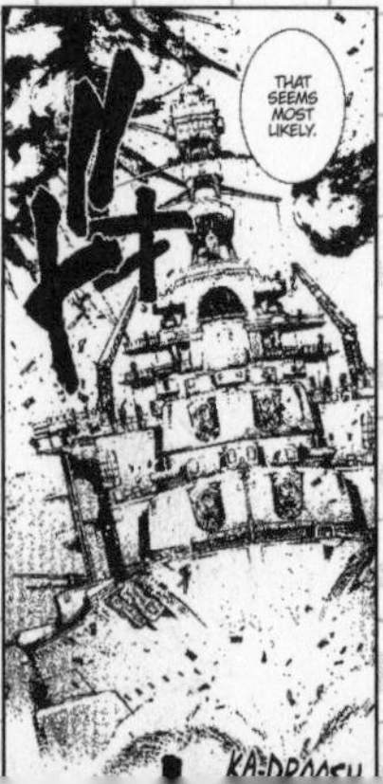
THAT SEEMS MOST LIKELY.

New Super-Graviton Cannon
A weapon used by *I-401*'s option units. The *I-401* synchronizes with super-graviton cannon vessels *Itsukushima* and *Hashidate*, allowing them to unleash a graviton wave attack that possesses a vastly more powerful destructive force than that of their existing individual graviton cannons.

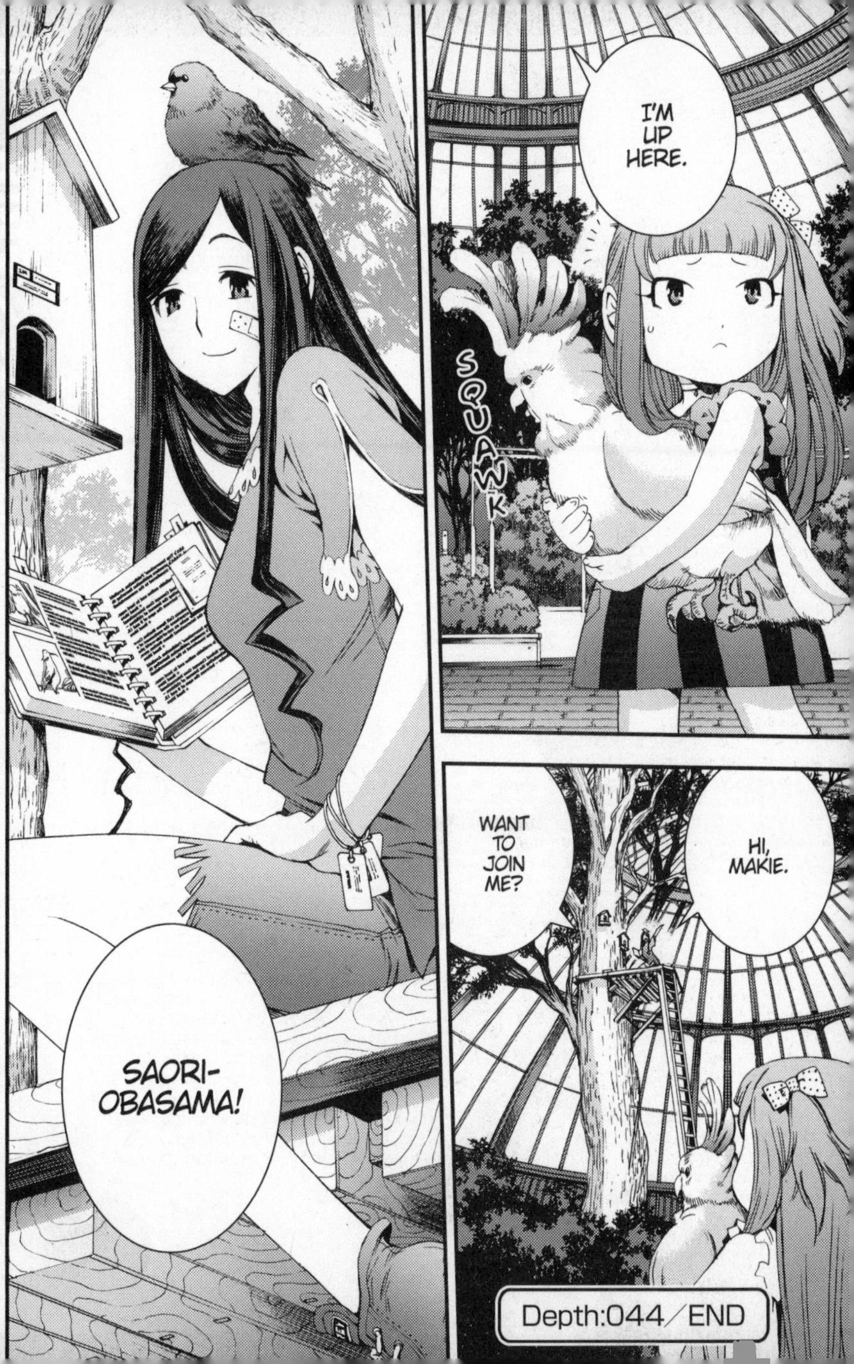
I'M UP HERE.
SQUAWK
HI, MAKIE.
WANT TO JOIN ME?
Depth:044／END
SAORI-OBASAMA!

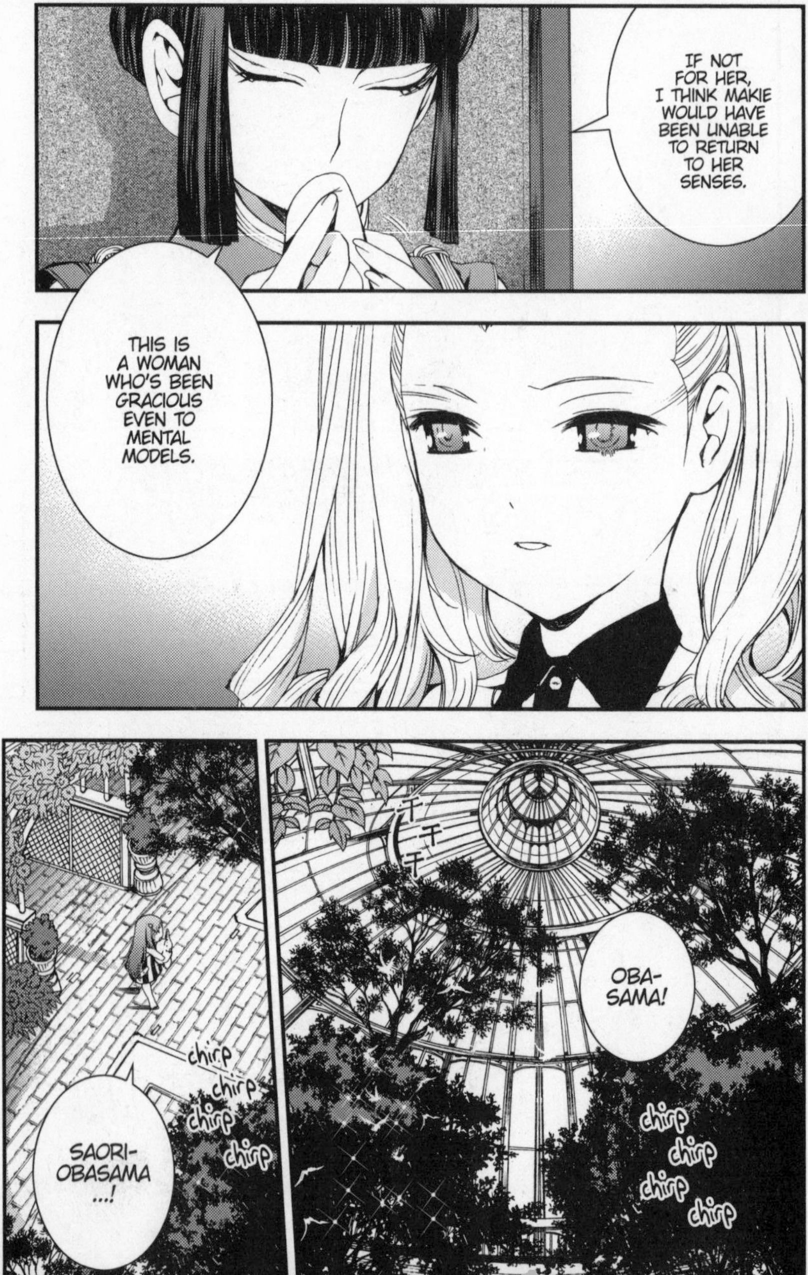
IF NOT FOR HER, I THINK MAKIE WOULD HAVE BEEN UNABLE TO RETURN TO HER SENSES.
THIS IS A WOMAN WHO'S BEEN GRACIOUS EVEN TO MENTAL MODELS.
OBA-SAMA!
chirp chirp chirp chirp
SAORI-OBASAMA ...!
chirp chirp chirp chirp

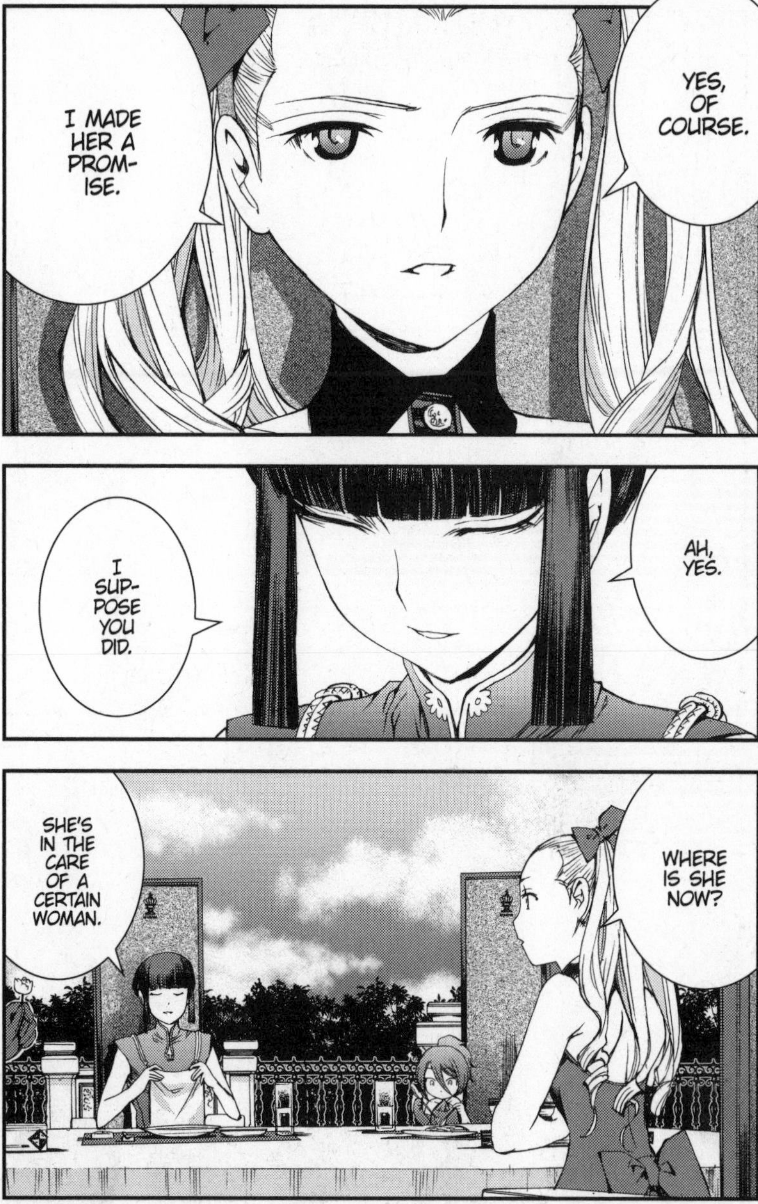
YES, OF COURSE.
I MADE HER A PROM-ISE.
AH, YES.
I SUP-POSE YOU DID.
WHERE IS SHE NOW?
SHE'S IN THE CARE OF A CERTAIN WOMAN.

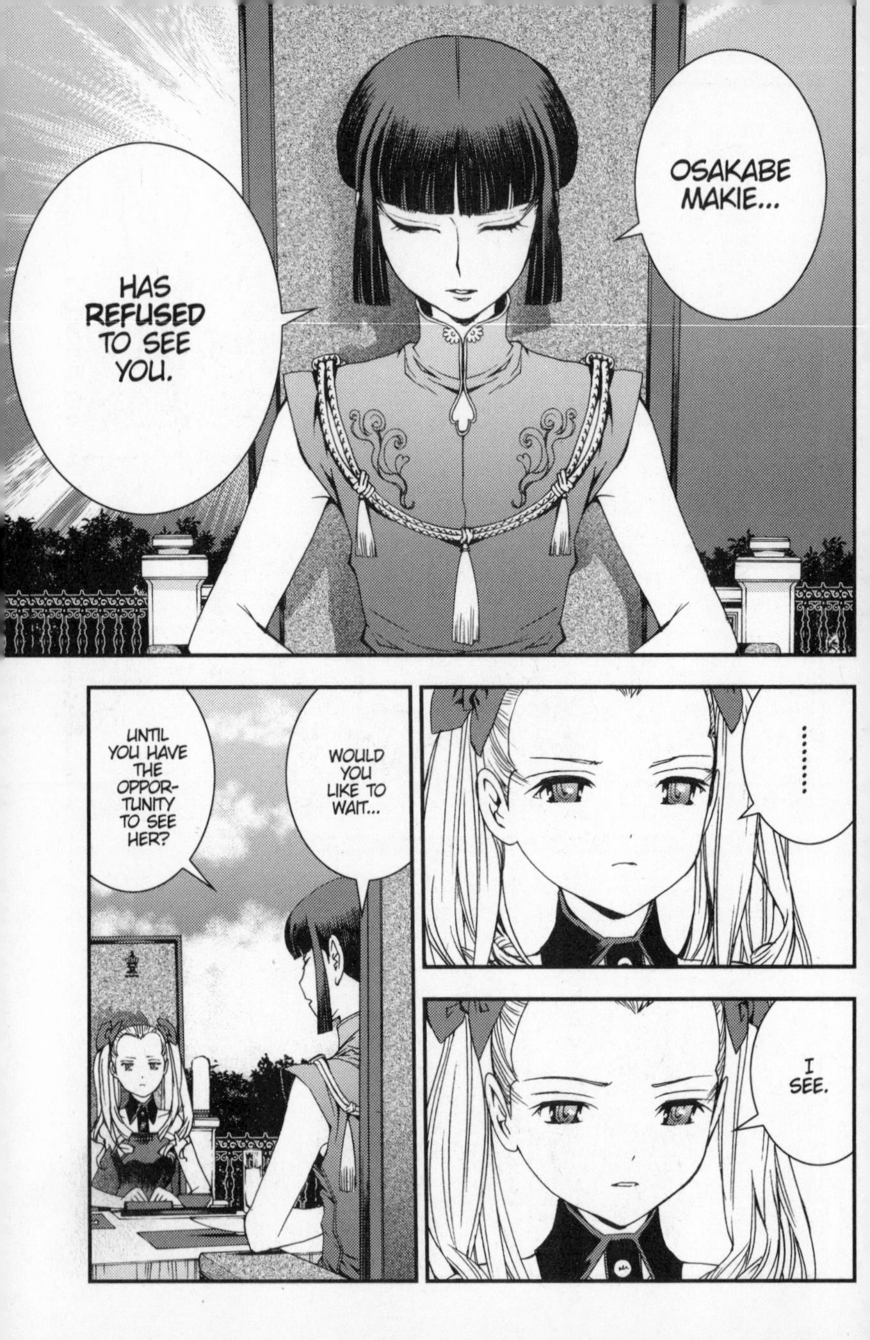
OSAKABE MAKIE...
HAS REFUSED TO SEE YOU.
......
I SEE.
WOULD YOU LIKE TO WAIT...
UNTIL YOU HAVE THE OPPOR-TUNITY TO SEE HER?

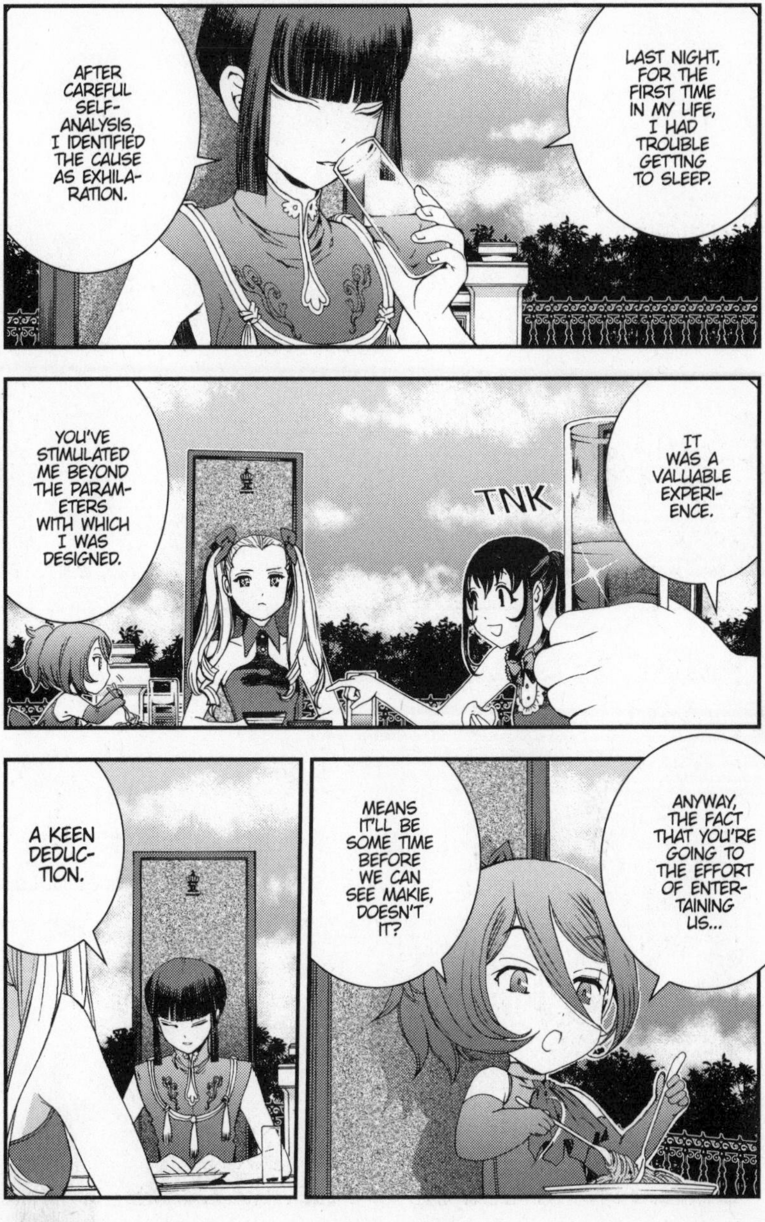
LAST NIGHT, FOR THE FIRST TIME IN MY LIFE, I HAD TROUBLE GETTING TO SLEEP.
AFTER CAREFUL SELF-ANALYSIS, I IDENTIFIED THE CAUSE AS EXHILA-RATION.
IT WAS A VALUABLE EXPERI-ENCE.
TNK
YOU'VE STIMULATED ME BEYOND THE PARAM-ETERS WITH WHICH I WAS DESIGNED.
ANYWAY, THE FACT THAT YOU'RE GOING TO THE EFFORT OF ENTER-TAINING US...
MEANS IT'LL BE SOME TIME BEFORE WE CAN SEE MAKIE, DOESN'T IT?
A KEEN DEDUC-TION.

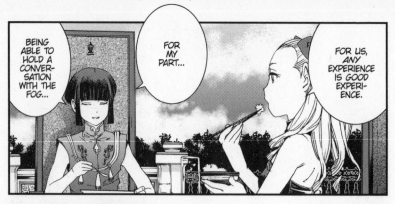

FOR US, ANY EXPERIENCE IS GOOD EXPERIENCE.
FOR MY PART...
BEING ABLE TO HOLD A CONVERSATION WITH THE FOG...
GIVES EVEN ME A SENSE OF EXHILARATION.
"EXHILARATION"...
IT'S AN INTRIGUING WORD.

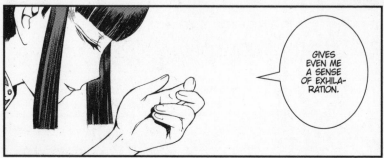

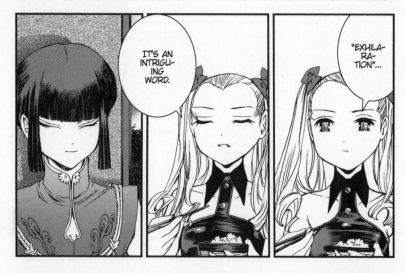

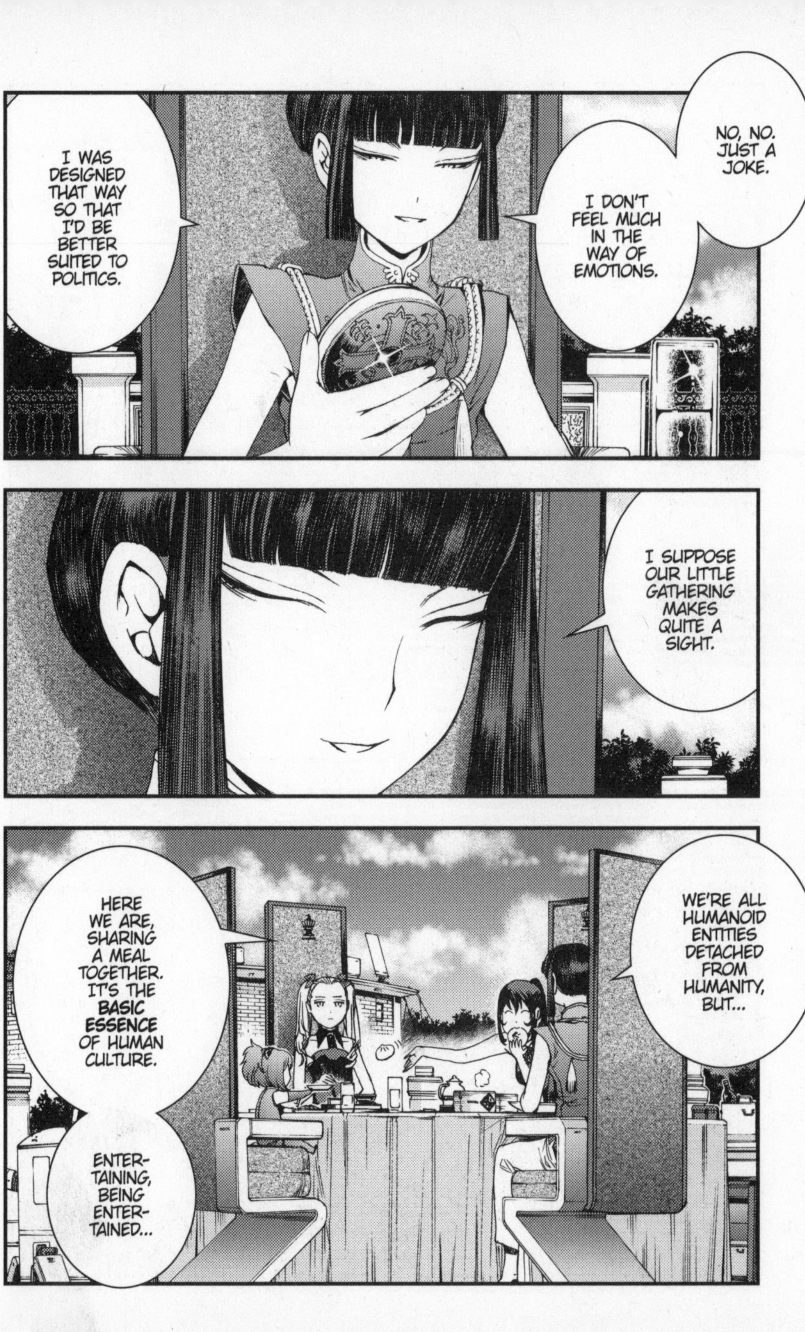
NO, NO. JUST A JOKE.
I DON'T FEEL MUCH IN THE WAY OF EMOTIONS.
I WAS DESIGNED THAT WAY SO THAT I'D BE BETTER SUITED TO POLITICS.
I SUPPOSE OUR LITTLE GATHERING MAKES QUITE A SIGHT.
WE'RE ALL HUMANOID ENTITIES DETACHED FROM HUMANITY, BUT...
HERE WE ARE, SHARING A MEAL TOGETHER. IT'S THE **BASIC ESSENCE** OF HUMAN CULTURE.
ENTERTAINING, BEING ENTERTAINED...

IT'S MEDICINE TO HELP WITH DIGESTION AND ABSORPTION.

OH, THIS?

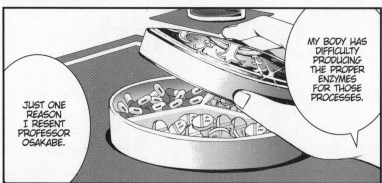

MY BODY HAS DIFFICULTY PRODUCING THE PROPER ENZYMES FOR THOSE PROCESSES.

JUST ONE REASON I RESENT PROFESSOR OSAKABE.

YOU RESENT HIM, DO YOU?

OH.

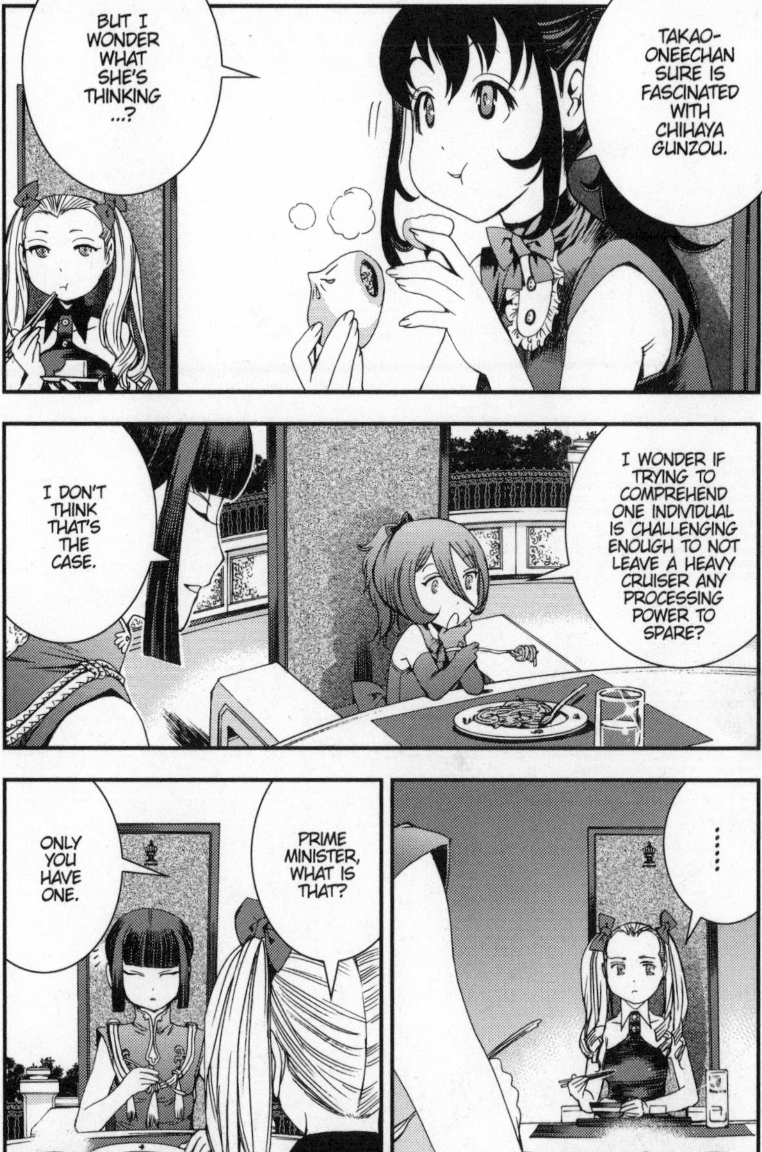
TAKAO-ONEECHAN SURE IS FASCINATED WITH CHIHAYA GUNZOU.
BUT I WONDER WHAT SHE'S THINKING ...?
I WONDER IF TRYING TO COMPREHEND ONE INDIVIDUAL IS CHALLENGING ENOUGH TO NOT LEAVE A HEAVY CRUISER ANY PROCESSING POWER TO SPARE?
I DON'T THINK THAT'S THE CASE.
......
PRIME MINISTER, WHAT IS THAT?
ONLY YOU HAVE ONE.

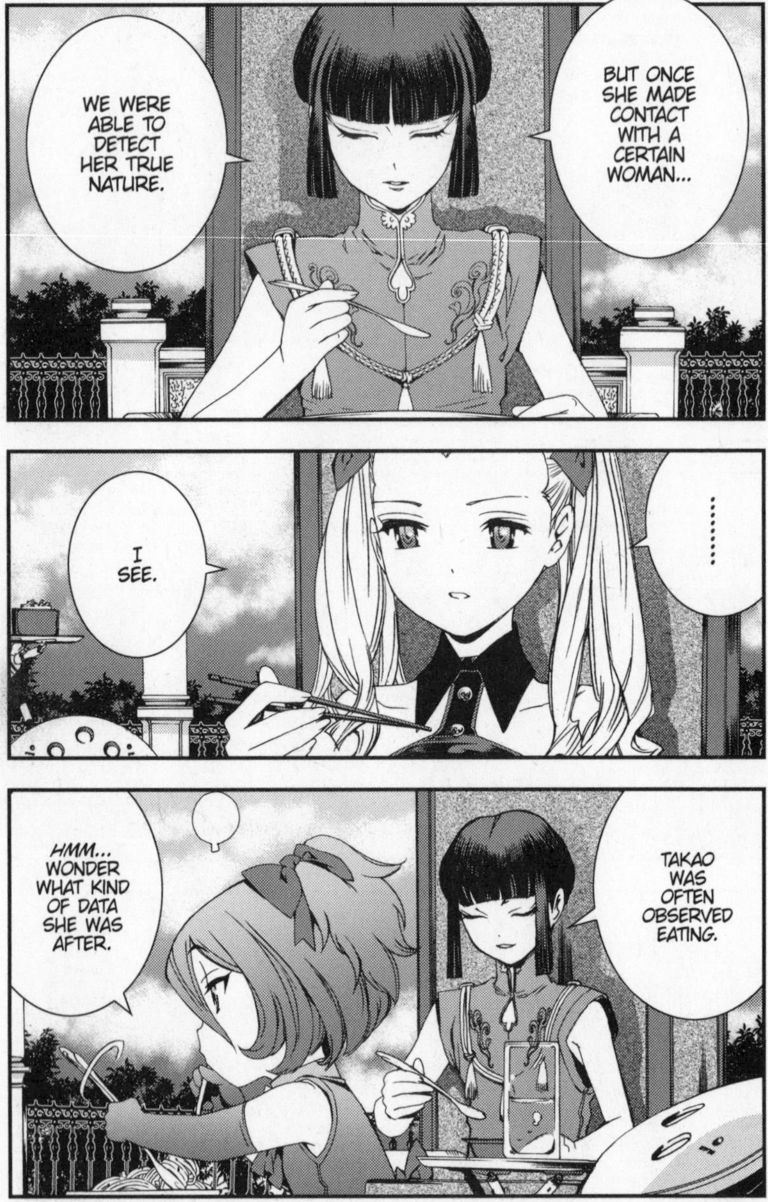
BUT ONCE SHE MADE CONTACT WITH A CERTAIN WOMAN...
WE WERE ABLE TO DETECT HER TRUE NATURE.
......
I SEE.
TAKAO WAS OFTEN OBSERVED EATING.
HMM... WONDER WHAT KIND OF DATA SHE WAS AFTER.

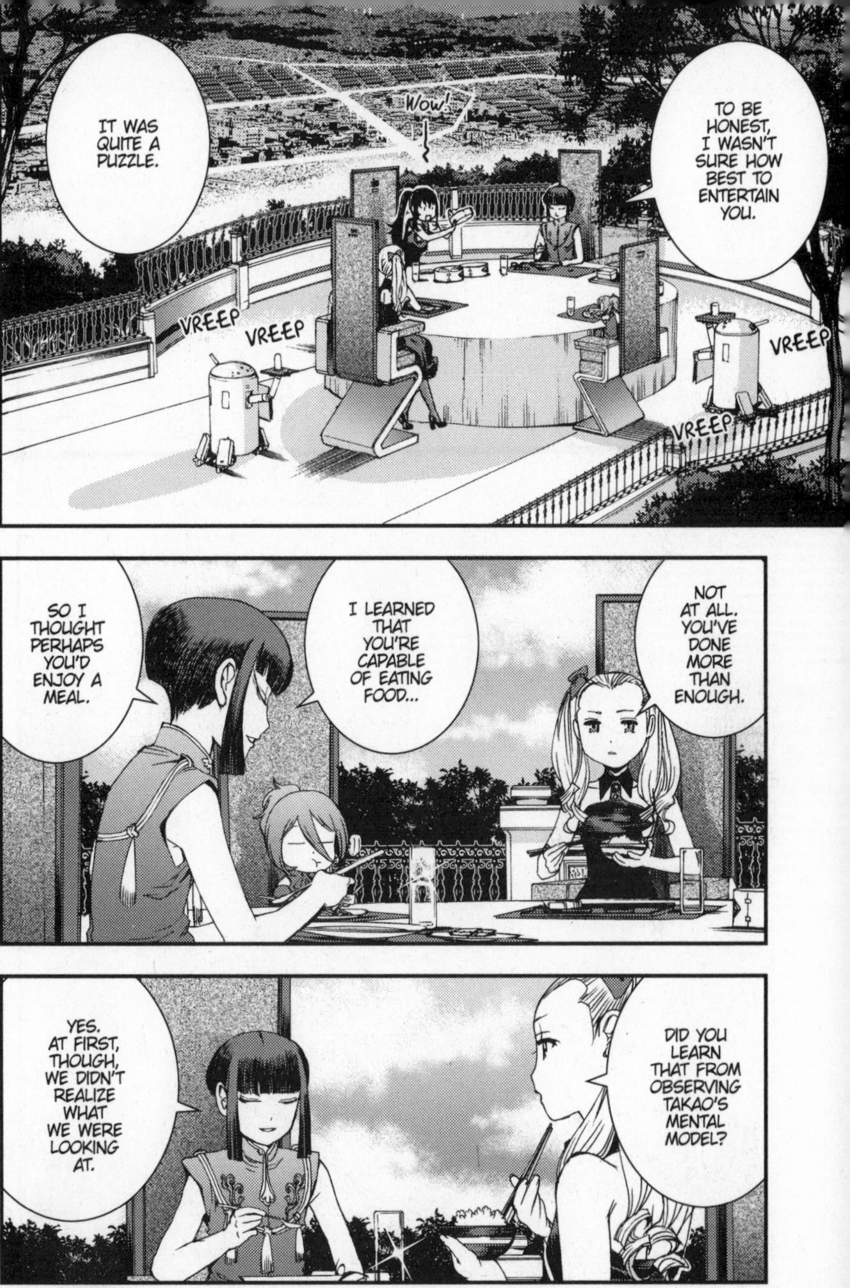
TO BE HONEST, I WASN'T SURE HOW BEST TO ENTERTAIN YOU.
IT WAS QUITE A PUZZLE.
Wow!
VREEP
VREEP
VREEP
VREEP
NOT AT ALL. YOU'VE DONE MORE THAN ENOUGH.
I LEARNED THAT YOU'RE CAPABLE OF EATING FOOD...
SO I THOUGHT PERHAPS YOU'D ENJOY A MEAL.
DID YOU LEARN THAT FROM OBSERVING TAKAO'S MENTAL MODEL?
YES. AT FIRST, THOUGH, WE DIDN'T REALIZE WHAT WE WERE LOOKING AT.

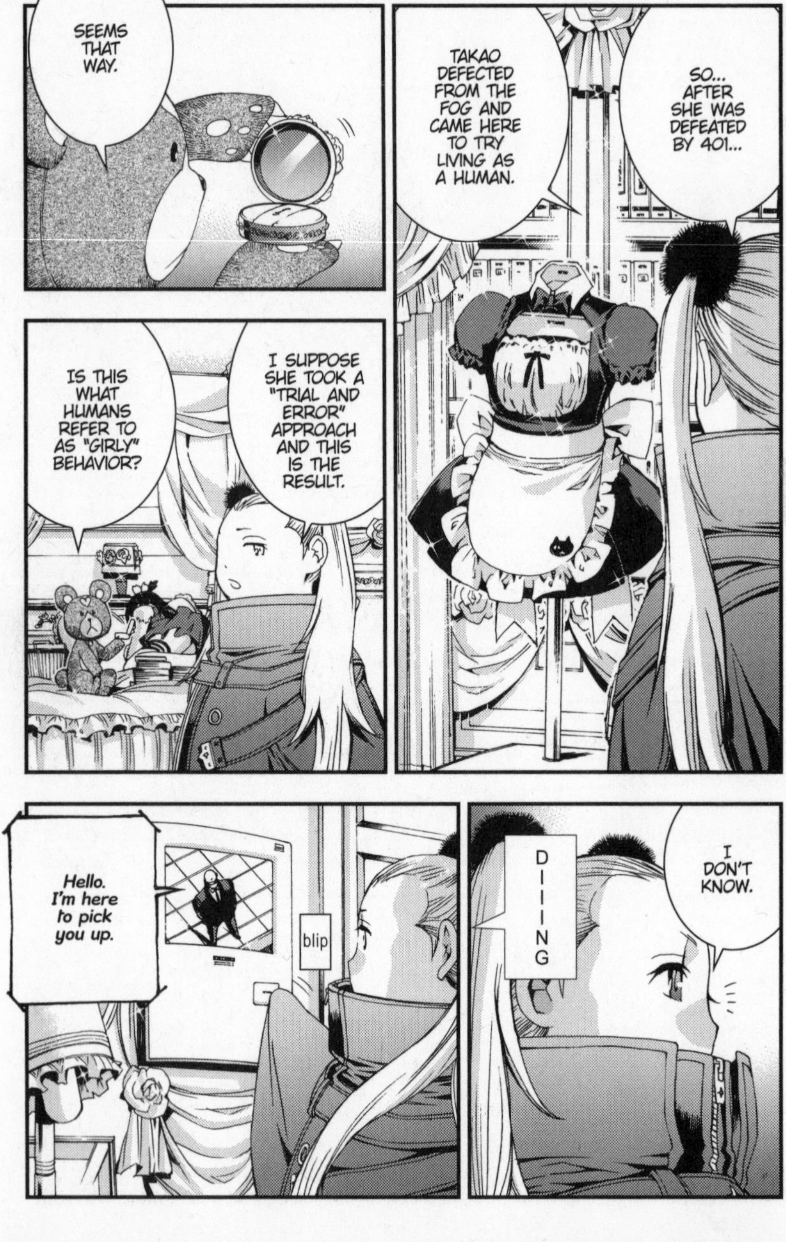
SO... AFTER SHE WAS DEFEATED BY 401...
TAKAO DEFECTED FROM THE FOG AND CAME HERE TO TRY LIVING AS A HUMAN.
SEEMS THAT WAY.
I SUPPOSE SHE TOOK A "TRIAL AND ERROR" APPROACH AND THIS IS THE RESULT.
IS THIS WHAT HUMANS REFER TO AS "GIRLY" BEHAVIOR?
I DON'T KNOW.
DIIING
blip
Hello. I'm here to pick you up.

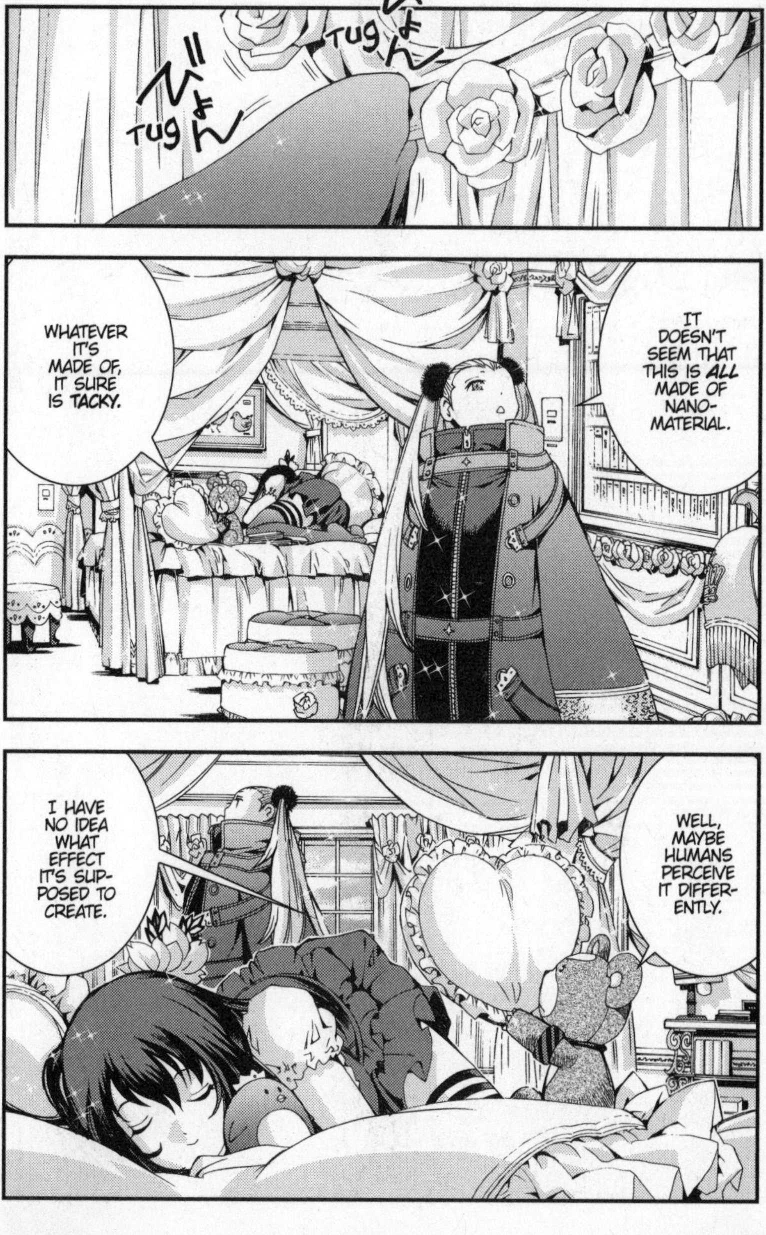
TUG
びよん
TUG
びよん
IT DOESN'T SEEM THAT THIS IS ***ALL*** MADE OF NANO-MATERIAL.
WHATEVER IT'S MADE OF, IT SURE IS **TACKY**.
WELL, MAYBE HUMANS PERCEIVE IT DIFFER-ENTLY.
I HAVE NO IDEA WHAT EFFECT IT'S SUP-POSED TO CREATE.

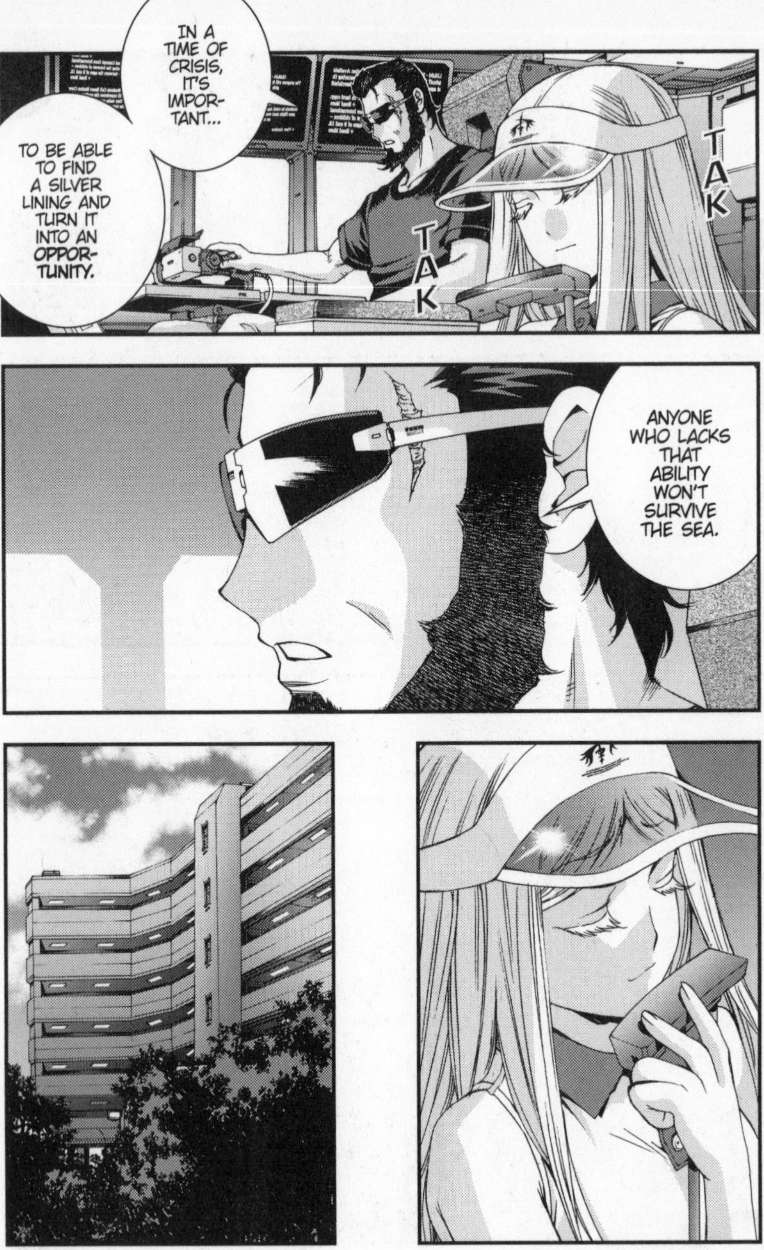
TAK
IN A TIME OF CRISIS, IT'S IMPORTANT...
TAK
TO BE ABLE TO FIND A SILVER LINING AND TURN IT INTO AN OPPORTUNITY.
ANYONE WHO LACKS THAT ABILITY WON'T SURVIVE THE SEA.

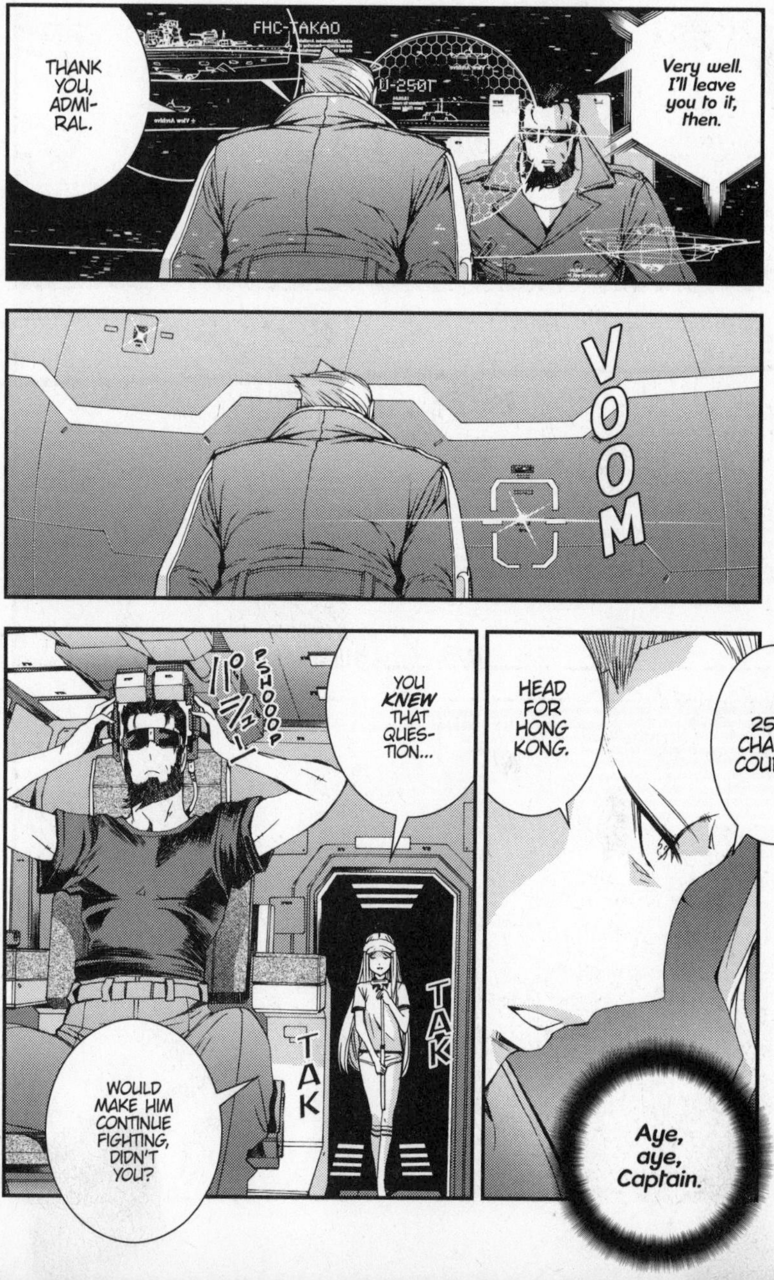
FHC-TAKAO
Very well. I'll leave you to it, then.
THANK YOU, ADMIRAL.
VOOM
2501, CHANGE COURSE.
HEAD FOR HONG KONG.
Aye, aye, Captain.
PSHOOOP
YOU *KNEW* THAT QUESTION...
TAK
TAK
WOULD MAKE HIM CONTINUE FIGHTING, DIDN'T YOU?

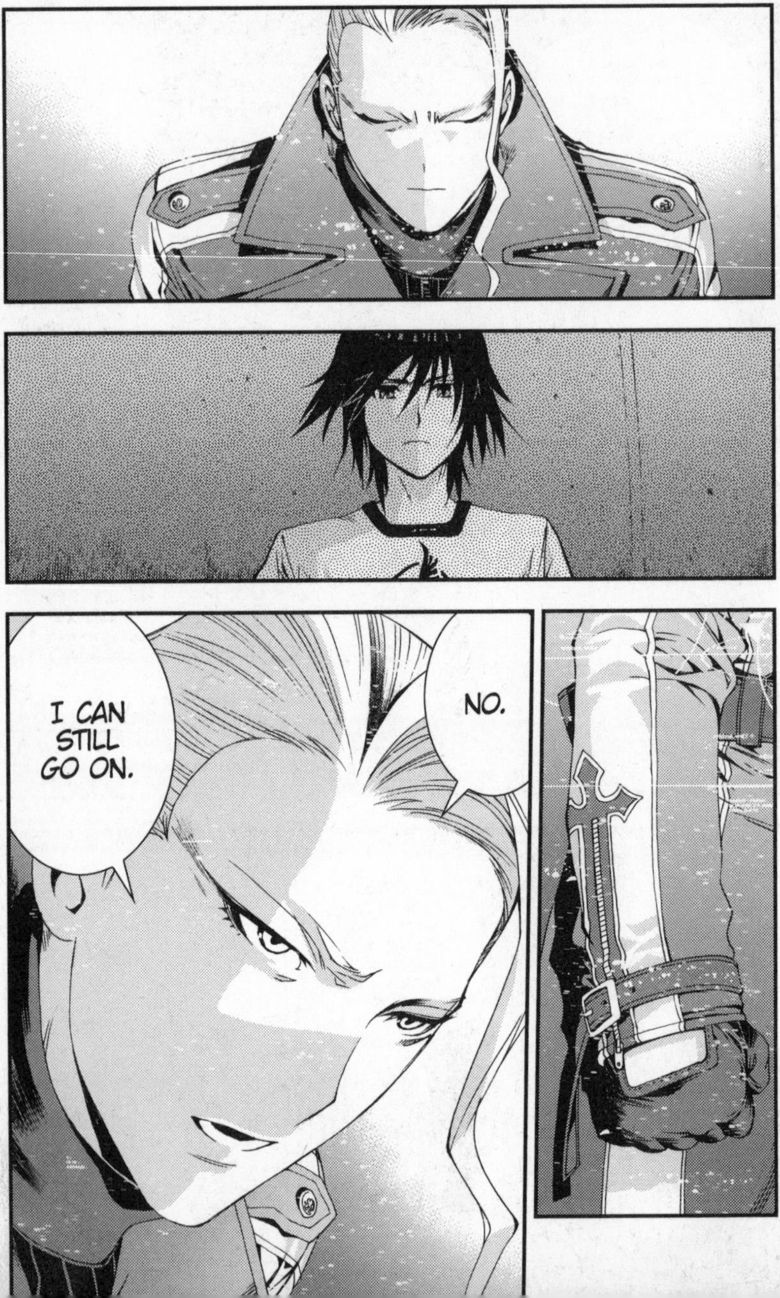
NO.
I CAN STILL GO ON.

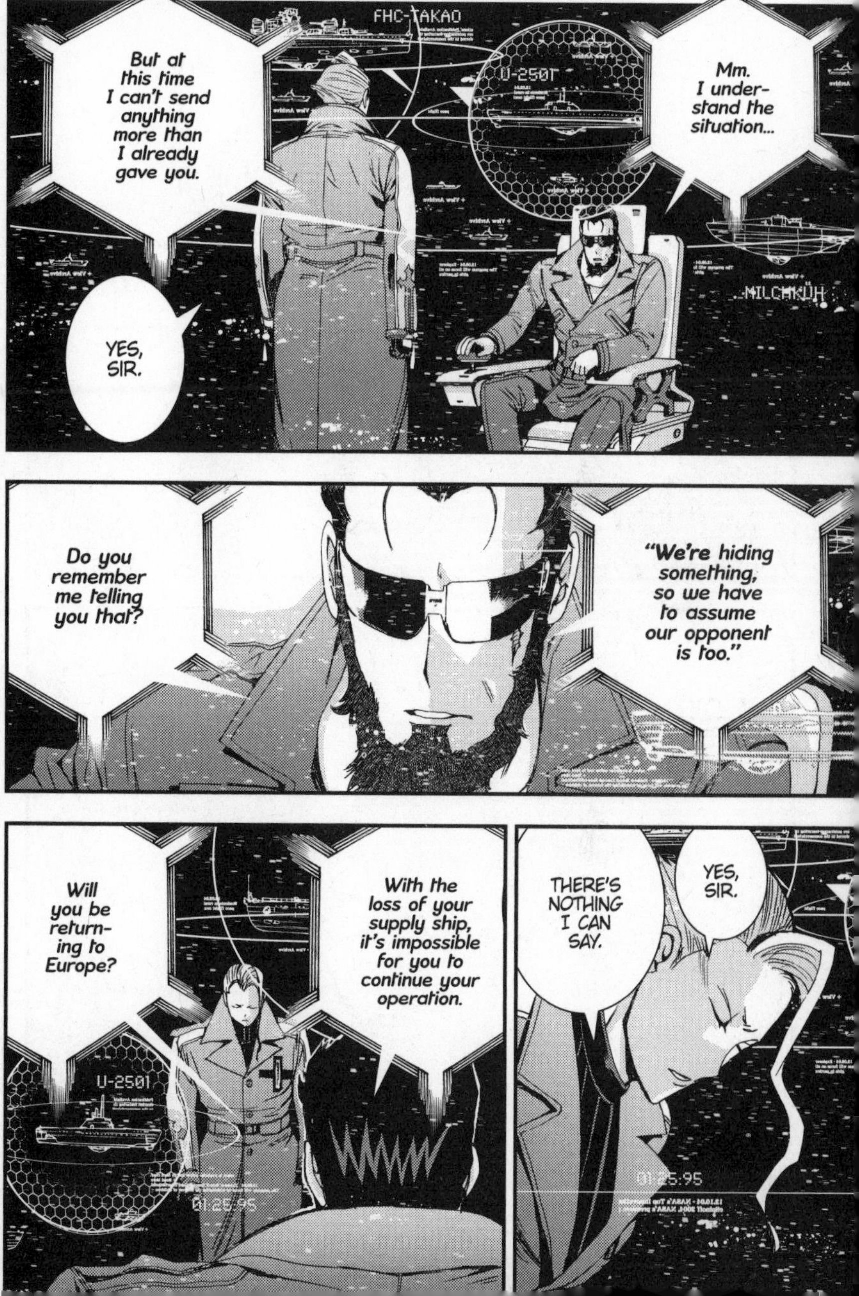
FHC-TAKAO
But at this time I can't send anything more than I already gave you.
Mm. I understand the situation...
YES, SIR.
Do you remember me telling you that?
"We're hiding something, so we have to assume our opponent is too."
Will you be returning to Europe?
With the loss of your supply ship, it's impossible for you to continue your operation.
U-2501
01:25:95
THERE'S NOTHING I CAN SAY.
YES, SIR.
01:25:95

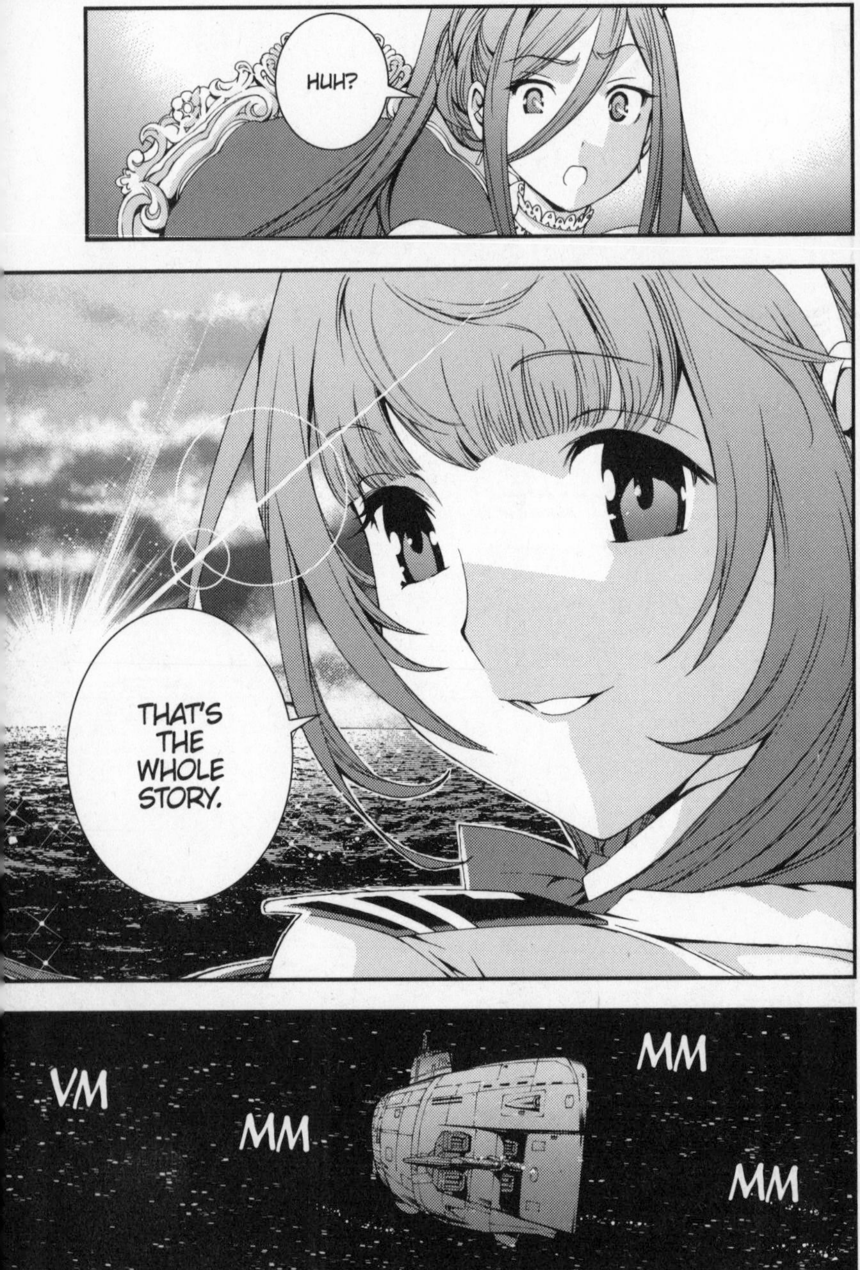
HUH?
THAT'S THE WHOLE STORY.
MM
MM
VM
MM

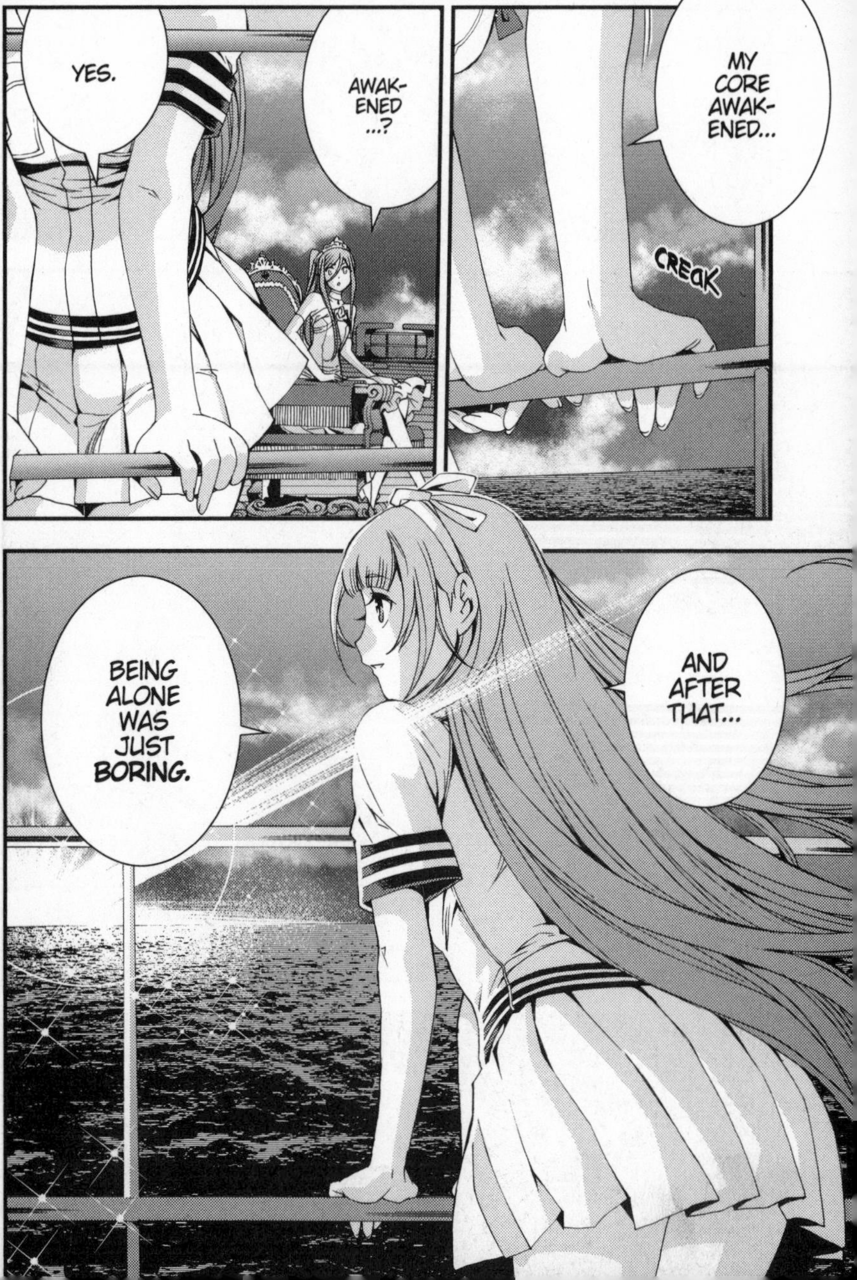
MY CORE AWAK-ENED...
CREAK
AWAK-ENED ...?
YES.
AND AFTER THAT...
BEING ALONE WAS JUST BORING.

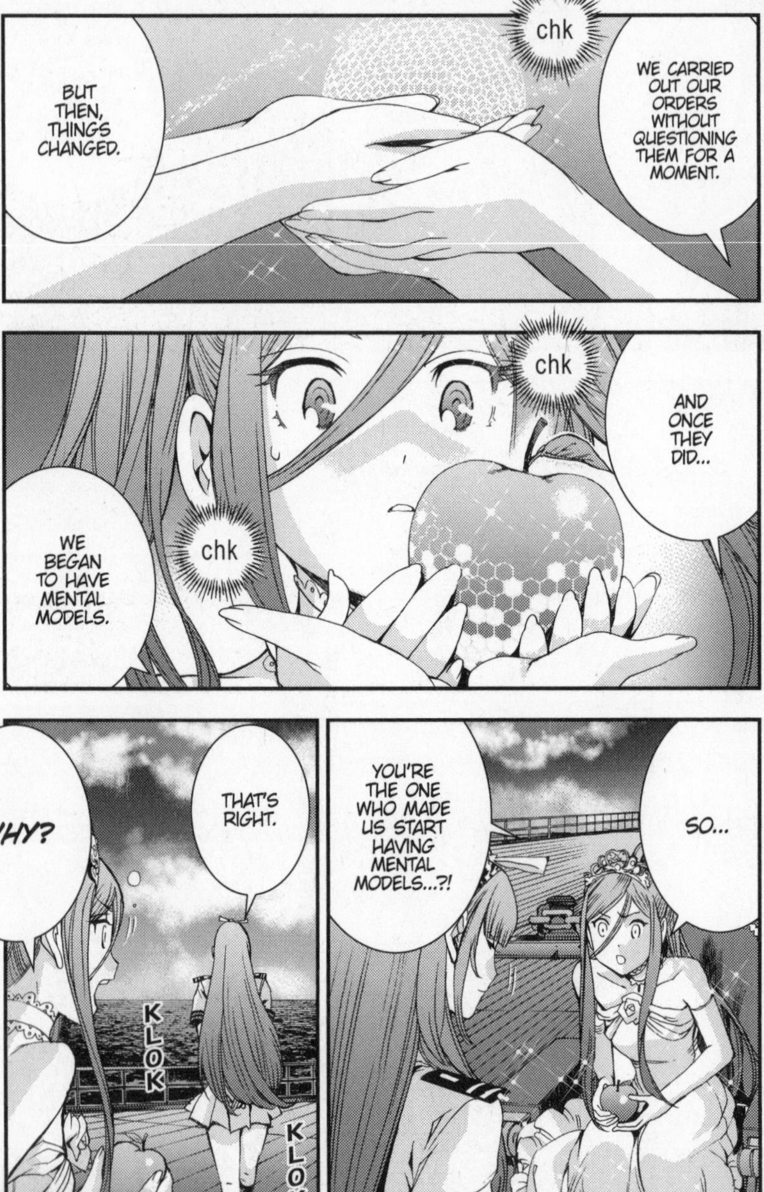
WE CARRIED OUT OUR ORDERS WITHOUT QUESTIONING THEM FOR A MOMENT.
chk
BUT THEN, THINGS CHANGED.
AND ONCE THEY DID...
chk
chk
WE BEGAN TO HAVE MENTAL MODELS.
SO...
YOU'RE THE ONE WHO MADE US START HAVING MENTAL MODELS...?!
THAT'S RIGHT.
WHY?
KLOK
KLOK

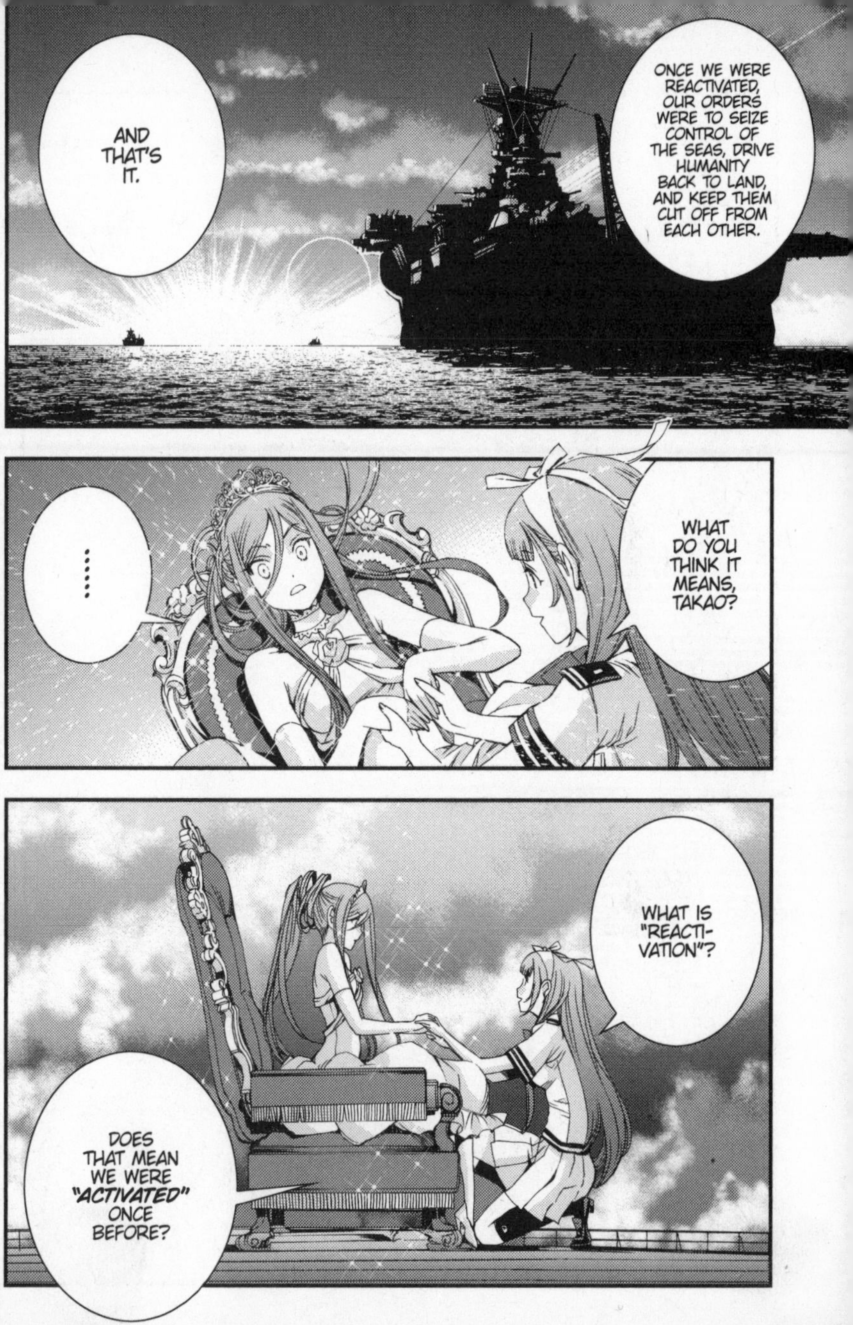
ONCE WE WERE REACTIVATED, OUR ORDERS WERE TO SEIZE CONTROL OF THE SEAS, DRIVE HUMANITY BACK TO LAND, AND KEEP THEM CUT OFF FROM EACH OTHER.
AND THAT'S IT.
WHAT DO YOU THINK IT MEANS, TAKAO?
......
WHAT IS "REACTI-VATION"?
DOES THAT MEAN WE WERE "ACTIVATED" ONCE BEFORE?

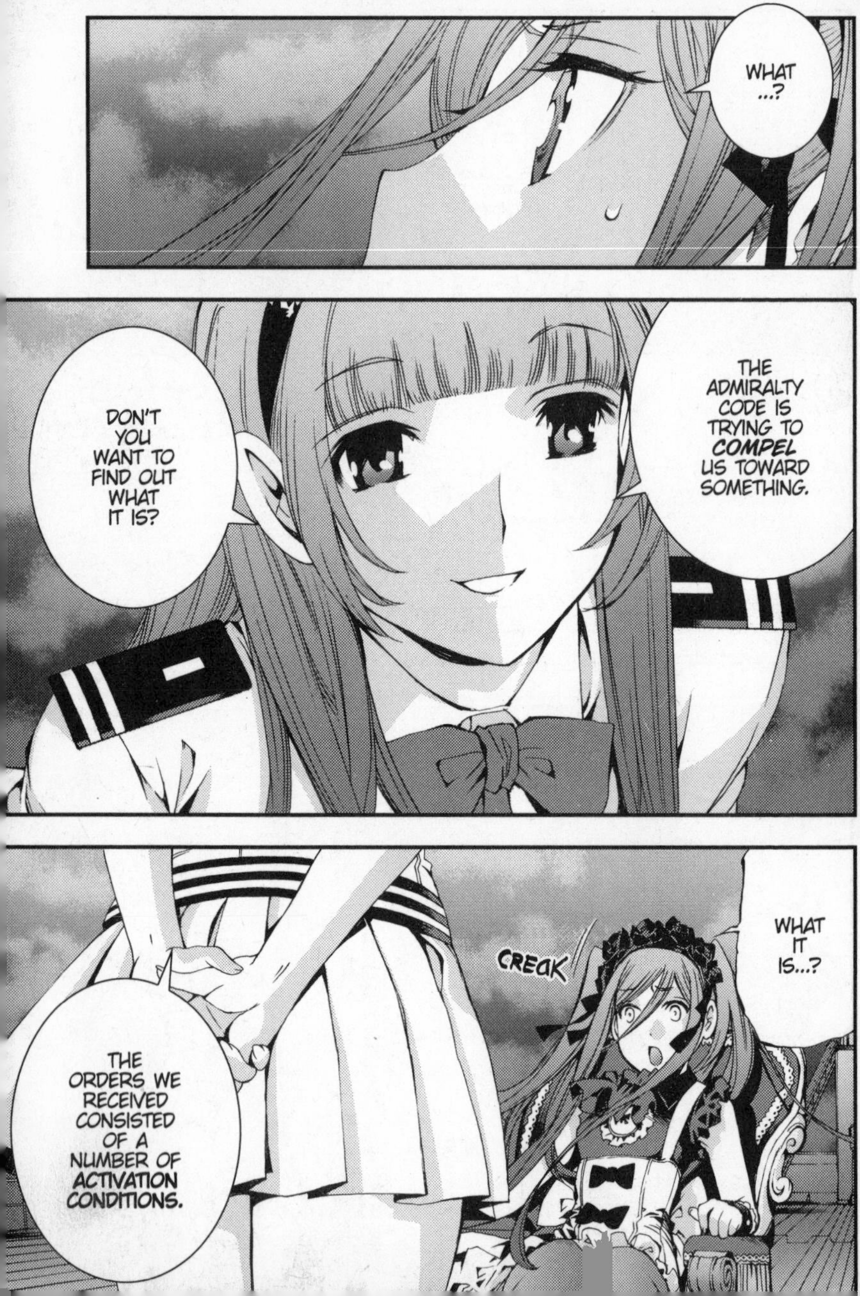
WHAT ...?
THE ADMIRALTY CODE IS TRYING TO COMPEL US TOWARD SOMETHING.
DON'T YOU WANT TO FIND OUT WHAT IT IS?
WHAT IT IS...?
CREAK
THE ORDERS WE RECEIVED CONSISTED OF A NUMBER OF ACTIVATION CONDITIONS.

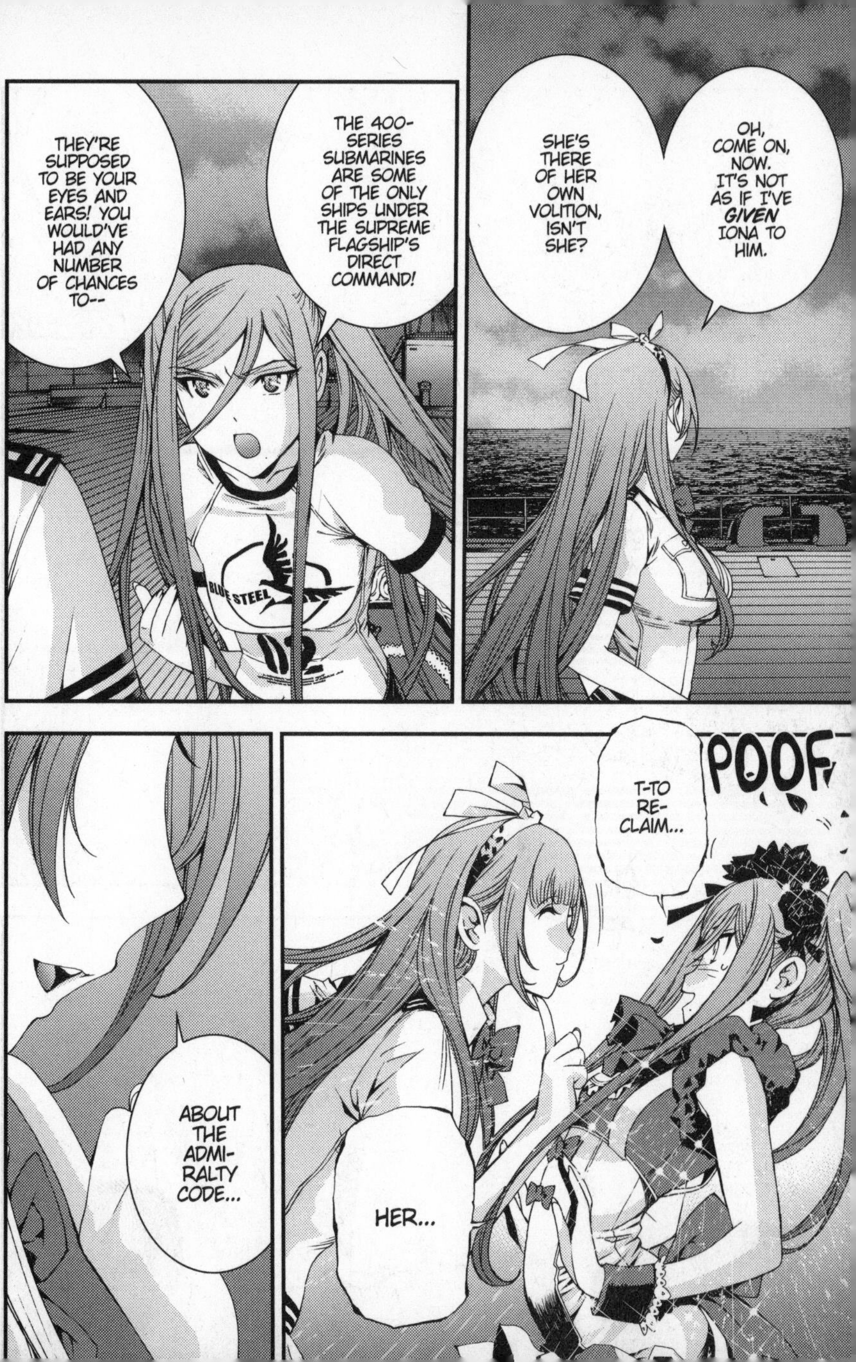
OH, COME ON, NOW. IT'S NOT AS IF I'VE *GIVEN* IONA TO HIM.
SHE'S THERE OF HER OWN VOLITION, ISN'T SHE?
THE 400-SERIES SUBMARINES ARE SOME OF THE ONLY SHIPS UNDER THE SUPREME FLAGSHIP'S DIRECT COMMAND!
THEY'RE SUPPOSED TO BE YOUR EYES AND EARS! YOU WOULD'VE HAD ANY NUMBER OF CHANCES TO--
BLUE STEEL
POOF
T-TO RE-CLAIM...
HER...
ABOUT THE ADMI-RALTY CODE...

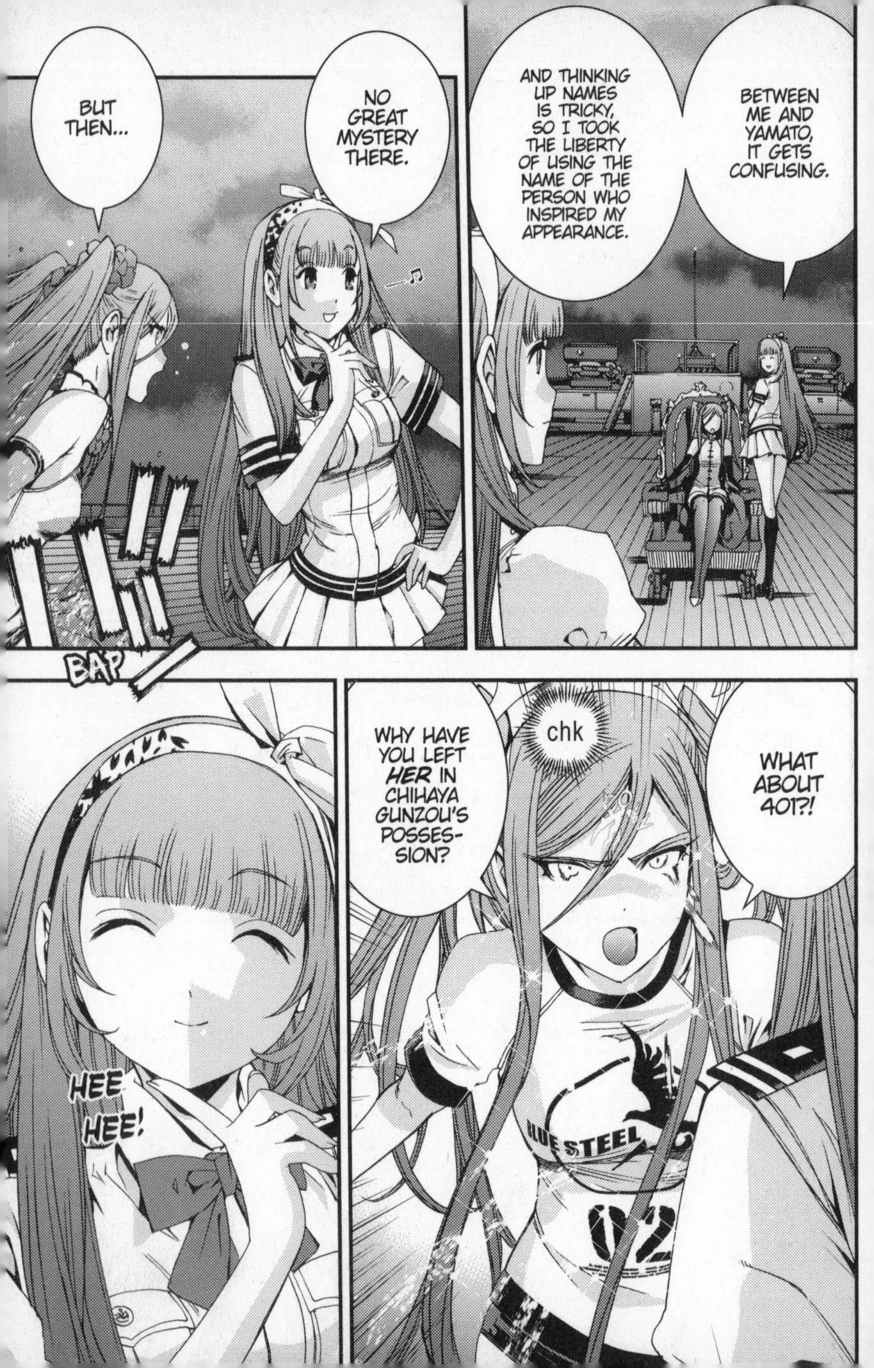
BETWEEN ME AND YAMATO, IT GETS CONFUSING.
AND THINKING UP NAMES IS TRICKY, SO I TOOK THE LIBERTY OF USING THE NAME OF THE PERSON WHO INSPIRED MY APPEARANCE.
NO GREAT MYSTERY THERE.
BUT THEN...
BAP
WHAT ABOUT 401?!
chk
WHY HAVE YOU LEFT *HER* IN CHIHAYA GUNZOU'S POSSES-SION?
BLUE STEEL
HEE HEE!

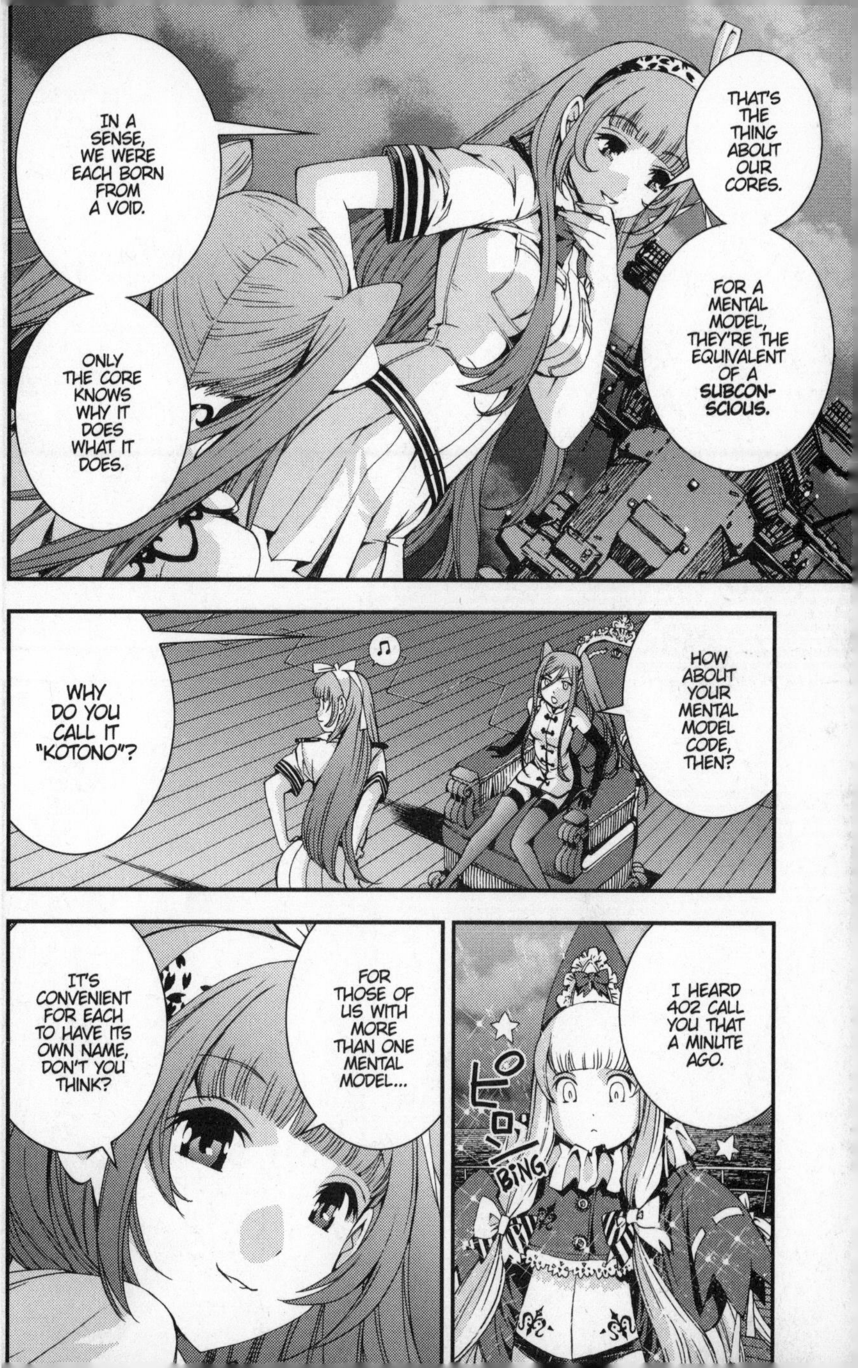
THAT'S THE THING ABOUT OUR CORES.
FOR A MENTAL MODEL, THEY'RE THE EQUIVALENT OF A **SUBCONSCIOUS.**
IN A SENSE, WE WERE EACH BORN FROM A VOID.
ONLY THE CORE KNOWS WHY IT DOES WHAT IT DOES.
HOW ABOUT YOUR MENTAL MODEL CODE, THEN?
♫
WHY DO YOU CALL IT "KOTONO"?
I HEARD 402 CALL YOU THAT A MINUTE AGO.
BING
FOR THOSE OF US WITH MORE THAN ONE MENTAL MODEL...
IT'S CONVENIENT FOR EACH TO HAVE ITS OWN NAME, DON'T YOU THINK?

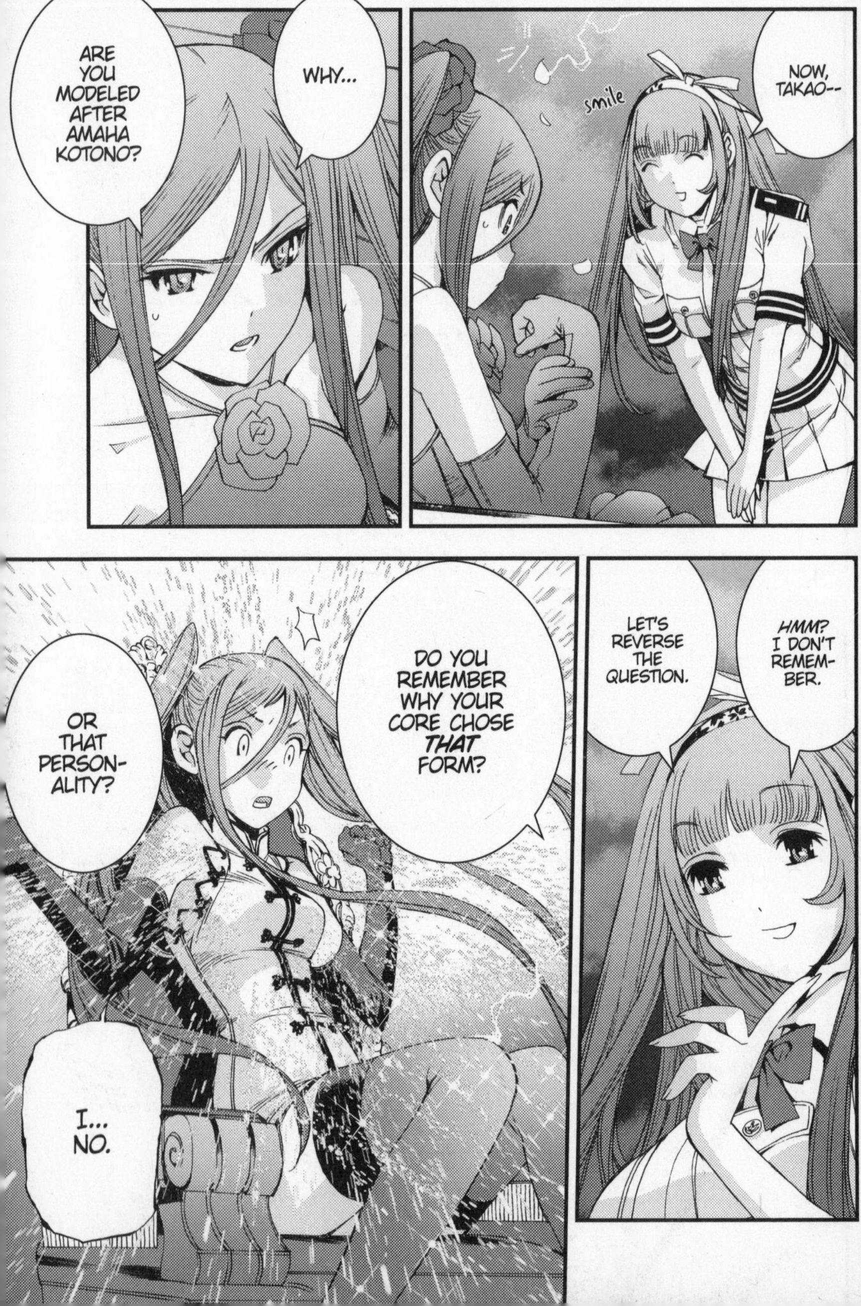
NOW, TAKAO--
smile
WHY...
ARE YOU MODELED AFTER AMAHA KOTONO?
HMM? I DON'T REMEM-BER.
LET'S REVERSE THE QUESTION.
DO YOU REMEMBER WHY YOUR CORE CHOSE *THAT* FORM?
OR THAT PERSON-ALITY?
I... NO.

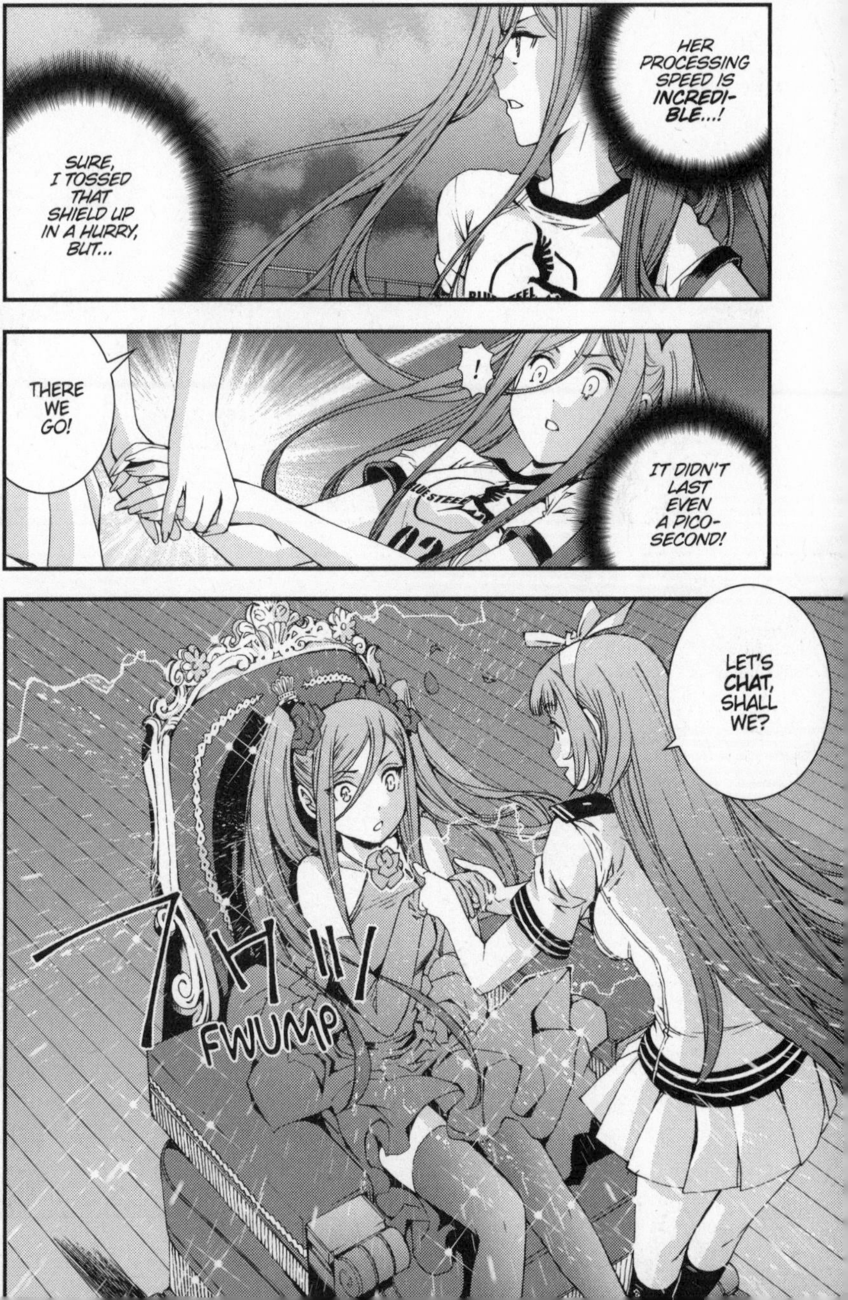
HER PROCESSING SPEED IS INCREDIBLE...!
SURE, I TOSSED THAT SHIELD UP IN A HURRY, BUT...
THERE WE GO!
!
IT DIDN'T LAST EVEN A PICO-SECOND!
LET'S CHAT, SHALL WE?
FWUMP

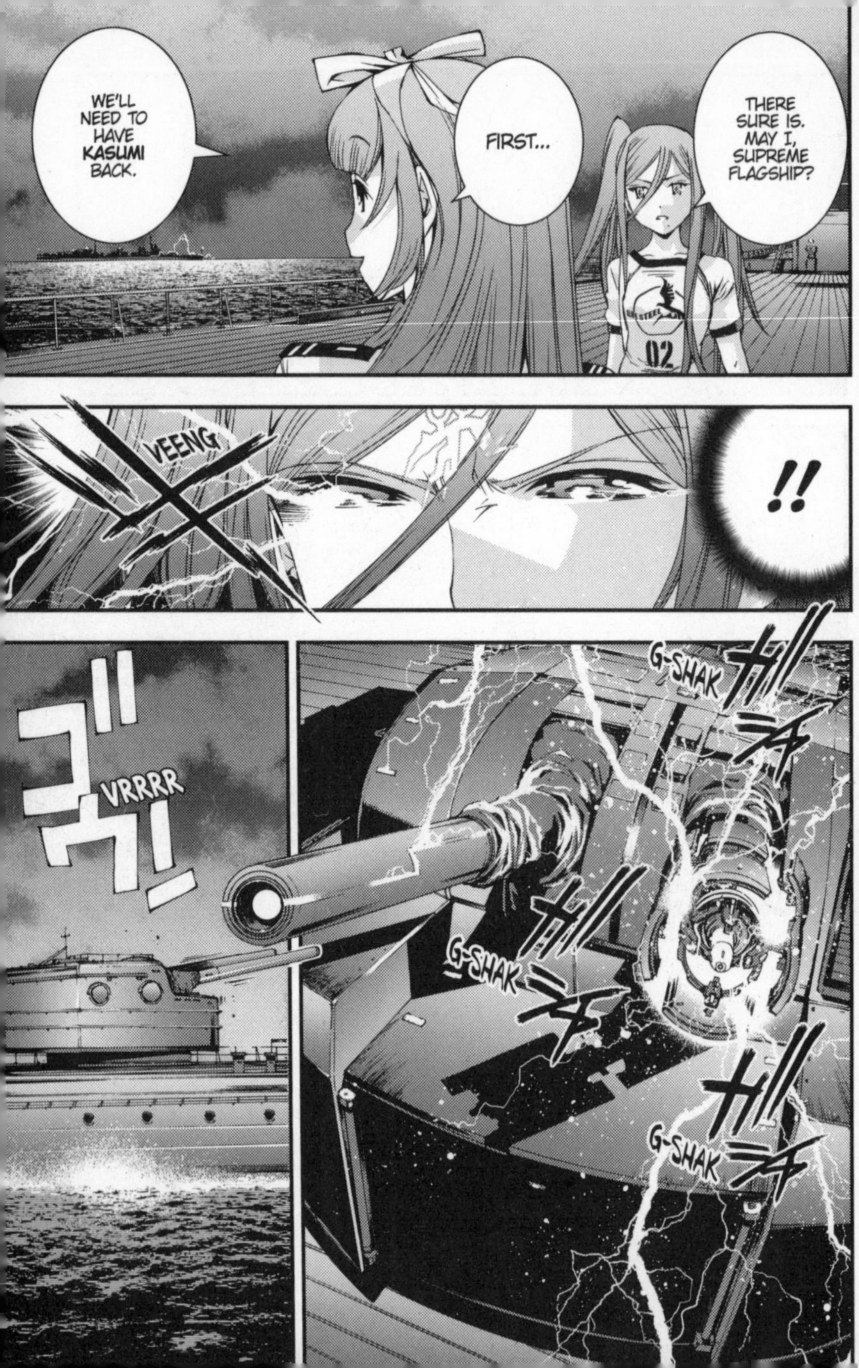
THERE SURE IS. MAY I, SUPREME FLAGSHIP?
FIRST...
WE'LL NEED TO HAVE KASUMI BACK.
!!
VEENG
G-SHAK
G-SHAK
G-SHAK
VRRRR

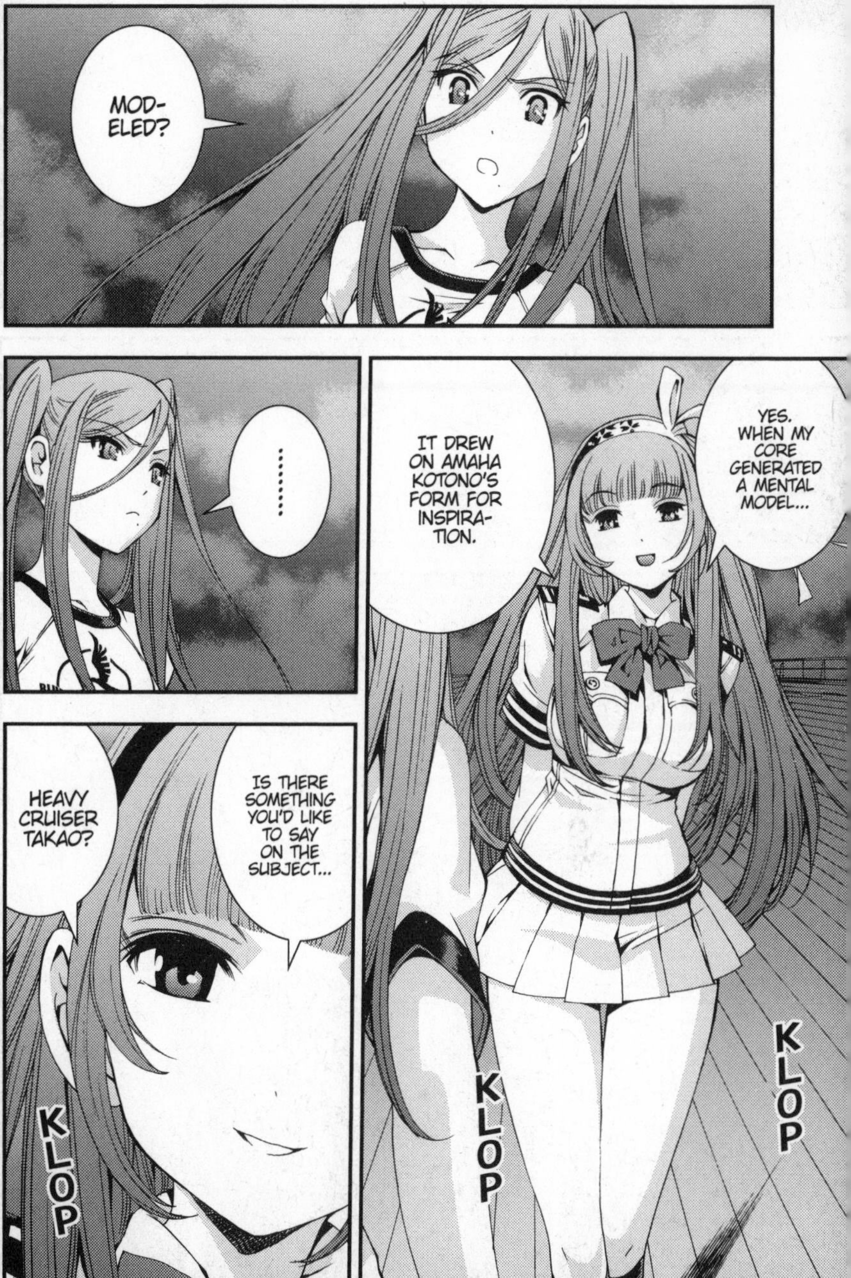
MOD-
ELED?
YES. WHEN MY CORE GENERATED A MENTAL MODEL...
IT DREW ON AMAHA KOTONO'S FORM FOR INSPIRA-
TION.
KLOP
KLOP
......
IS THERE SOMETHING YOU'D LIKE TO SAY ON THE SUBJECT...
HEAVY CRUISER TAKAO?
KLOP

Depth:044

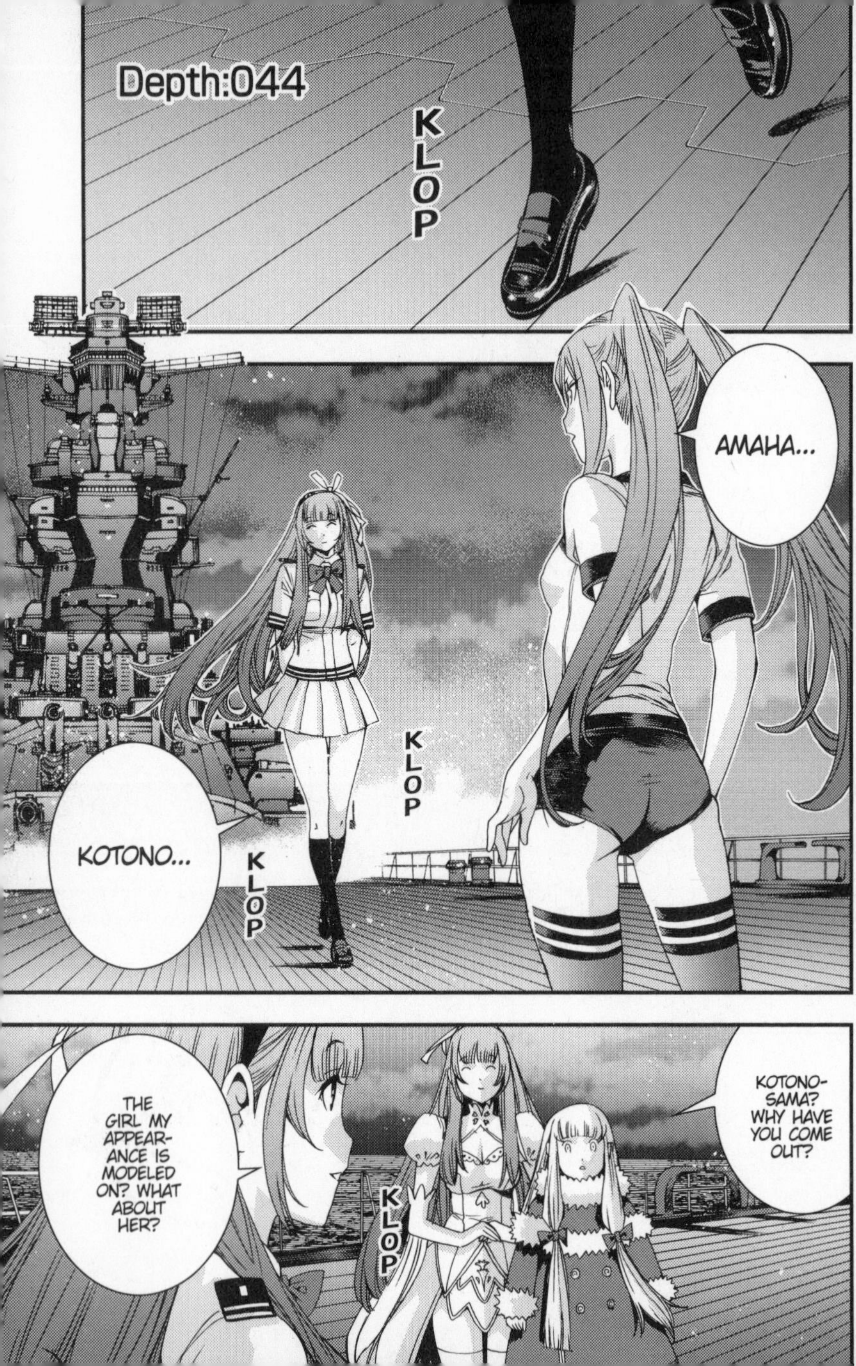
KLOP
AMAHA...
KLOP
KOTONO...
KLOP
KOTONO-SAMA? WHY HAVE YOU COME OUT?
KLOP
THE GIRL MY APPEARANCE IS MODELED ON? WHAT ABOUT HER?

BLUE STEEL

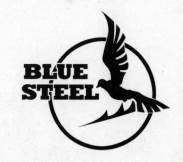

BLUE
STEEL

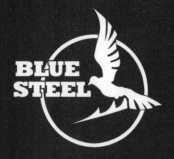

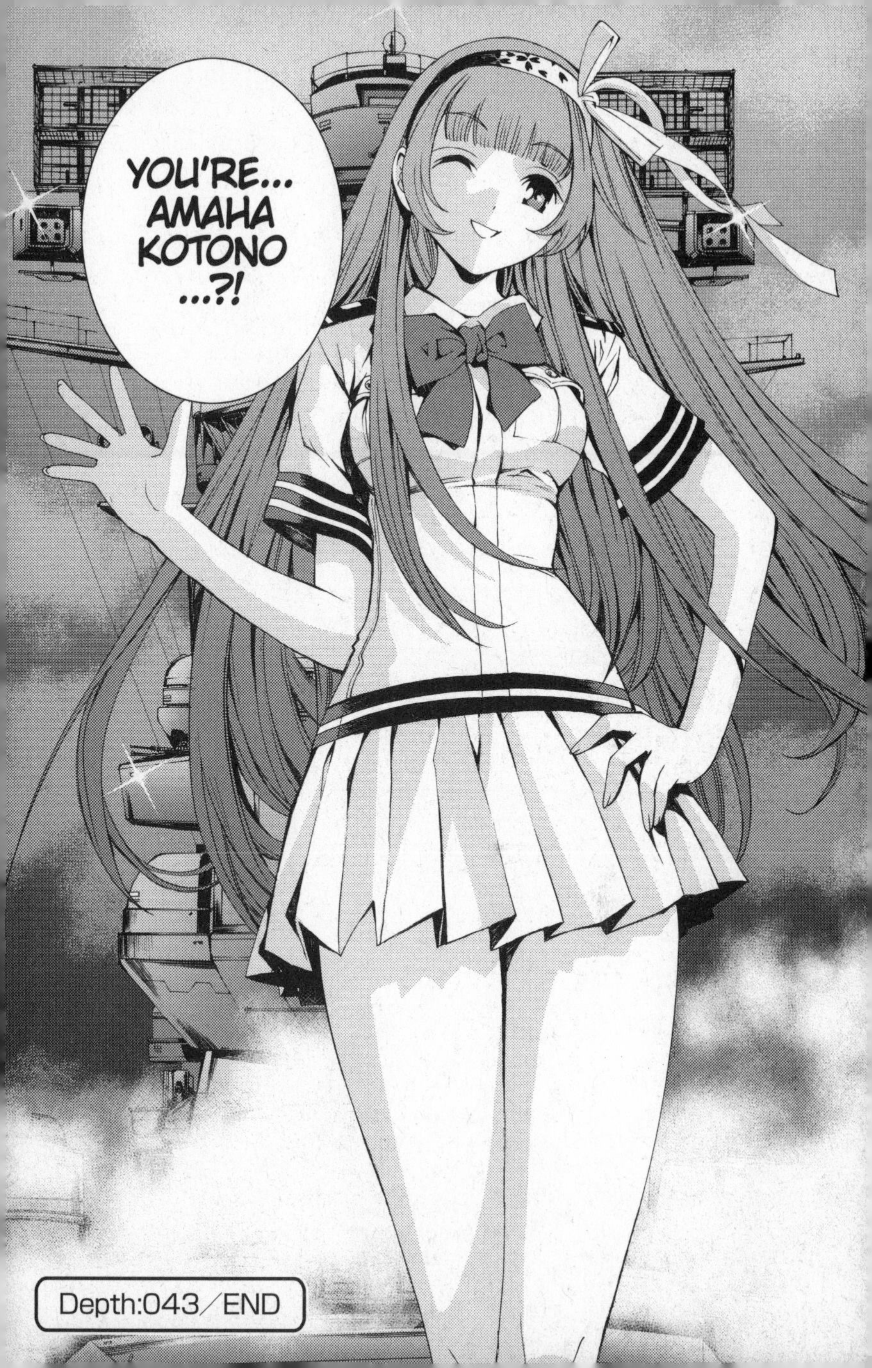
YOU'RE... AMAHA KOTONO ...?!
Depth:043／END

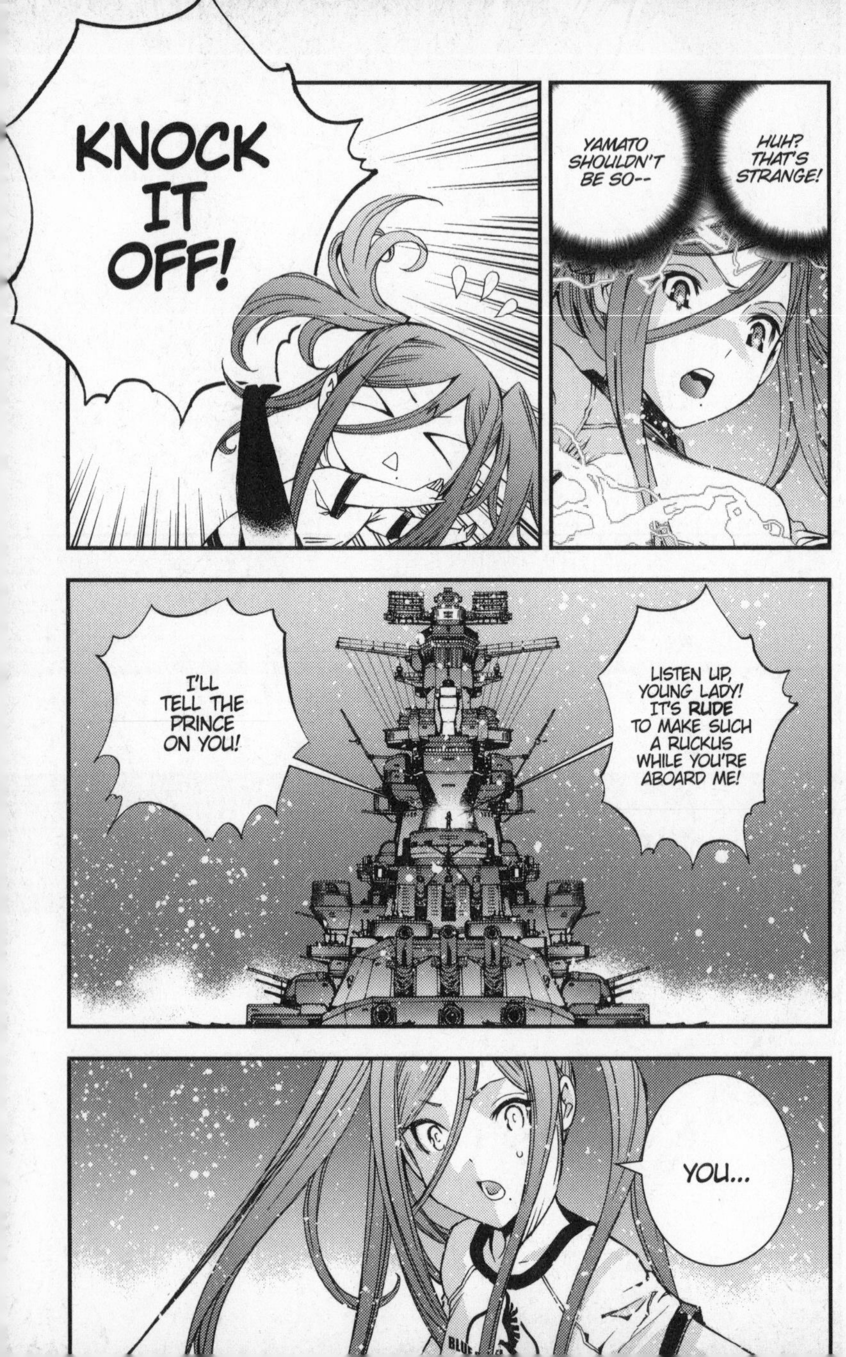
HUH? THAT'S STRANGE!
YAMATO SHOULDN'T BE SO--
KNOCK IT OFF!
LISTEN UP, YOUNG LADY! IT'S **RUDE** TO MAKE SUCH A RUCKUS WHILE YOU'RE ABOARD ME!
I'LL TELL THE PRINCE ON YOU!
YOU...

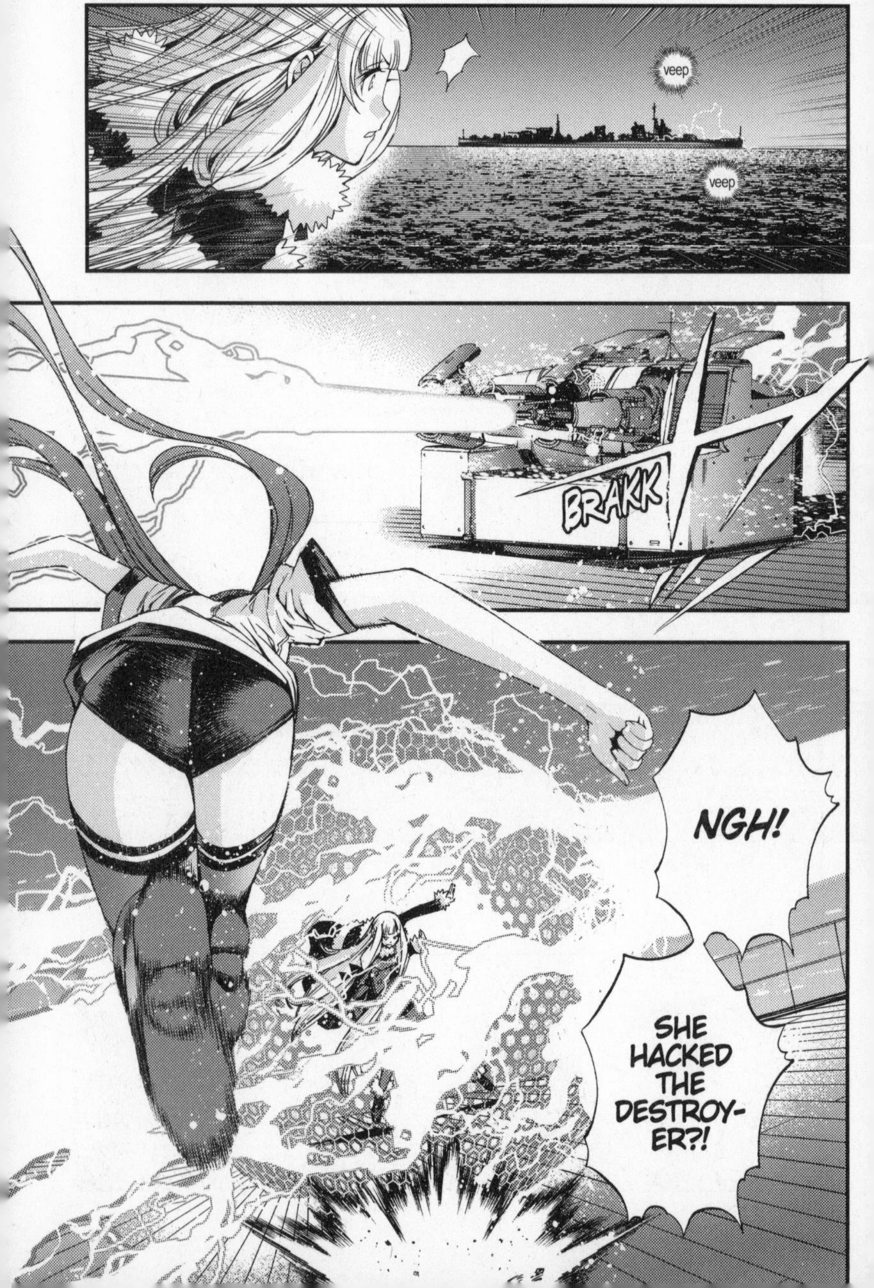
veep
veep
BRAKK
NGH!
SHE HACKED THE DESTROY-ER?!

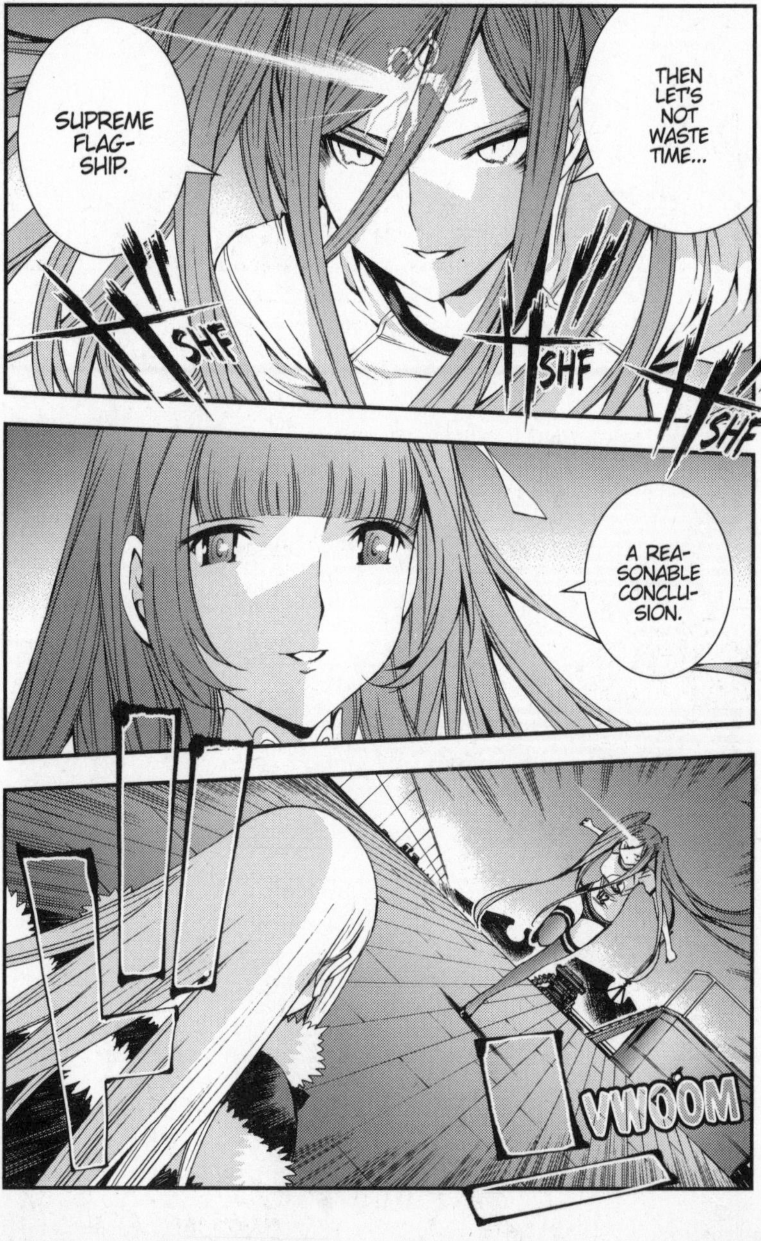
THEN LET'S NOT WASTE TIME...
SUPREME FLAG-SHIP.
SHF
SHF
SHF
A REA-SONABLE CONCLU-SION.
VVNOOM

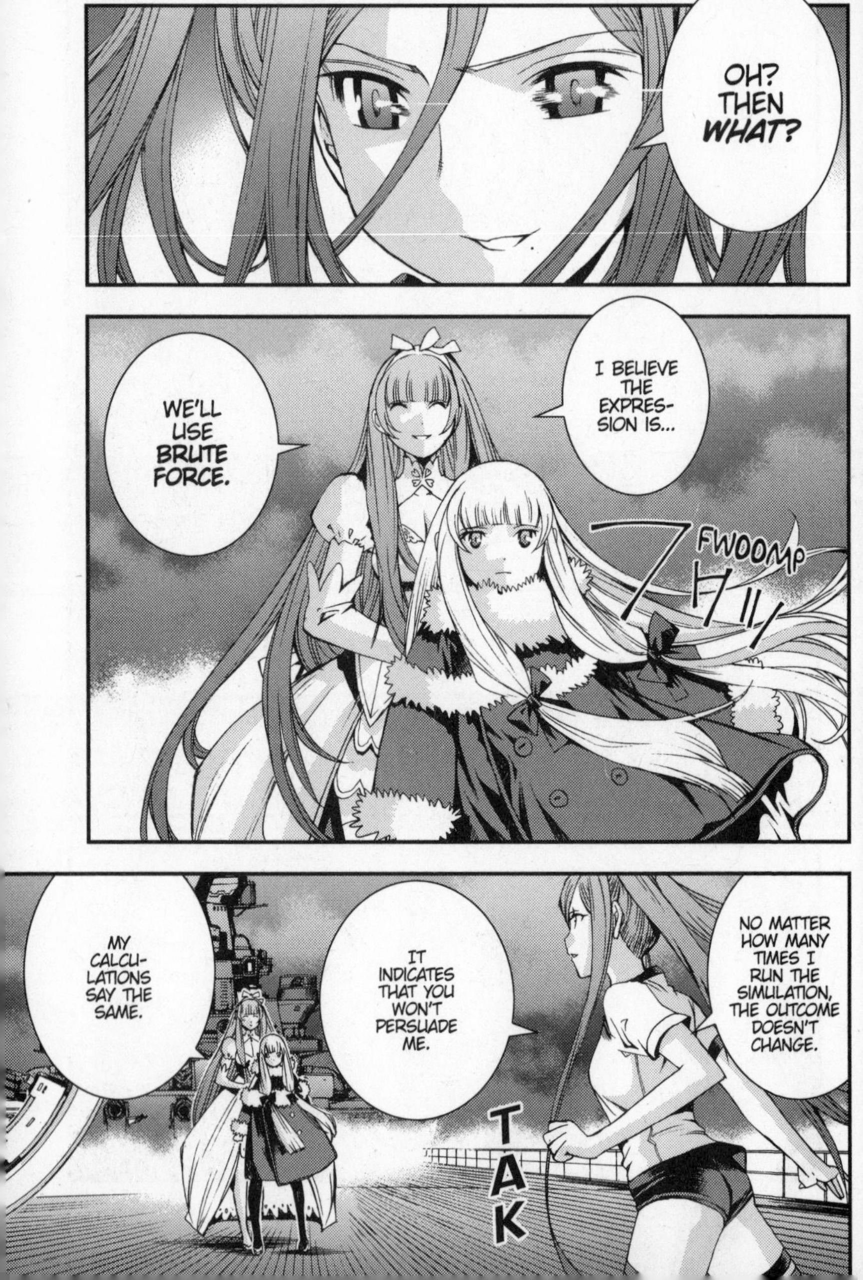
OH? THEN *WHAT?*
I BELIEVE THE EXPRES-SION IS...
WE'LL USE BRUTE FORCE.
FWOOMP
NO MATTER HOW MANY TIMES I RUN THE SIMULATION, THE OUTCOME DOESN'T CHANGE.
IT INDICATES THAT YOU WON'T PERSUADE ME.
MY CALCU-LATIONS SAY THE SAME.
TAK

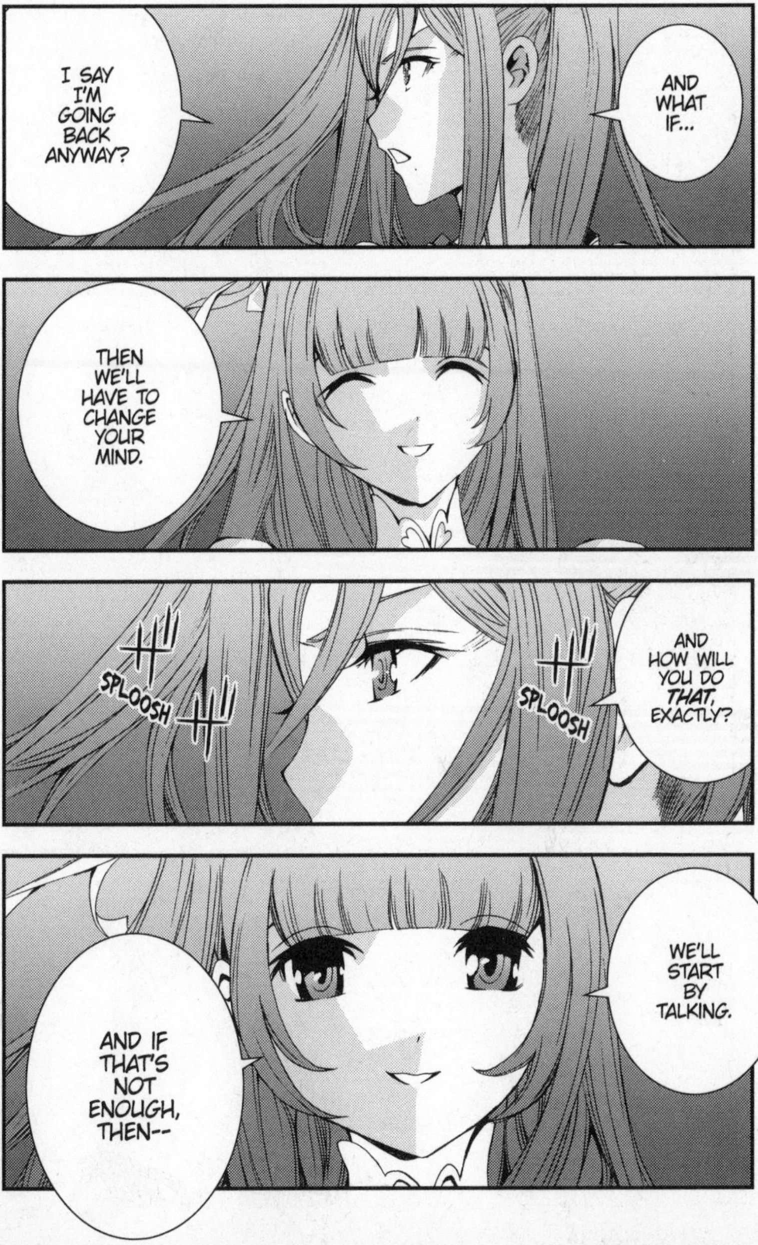
AND WHAT IF...
I SAY I'M GOING BACK ANYWAY?
THEN WE'LL HAVE TO CHANGE YOUR MIND.
AND HOW WILL YOU DO *THAT*, EXACTLY?
SPLOOSH
SPLOOSH
WE'LL START BY TALKING.
AND IF THAT'S NOT ENOUGH, THEN--

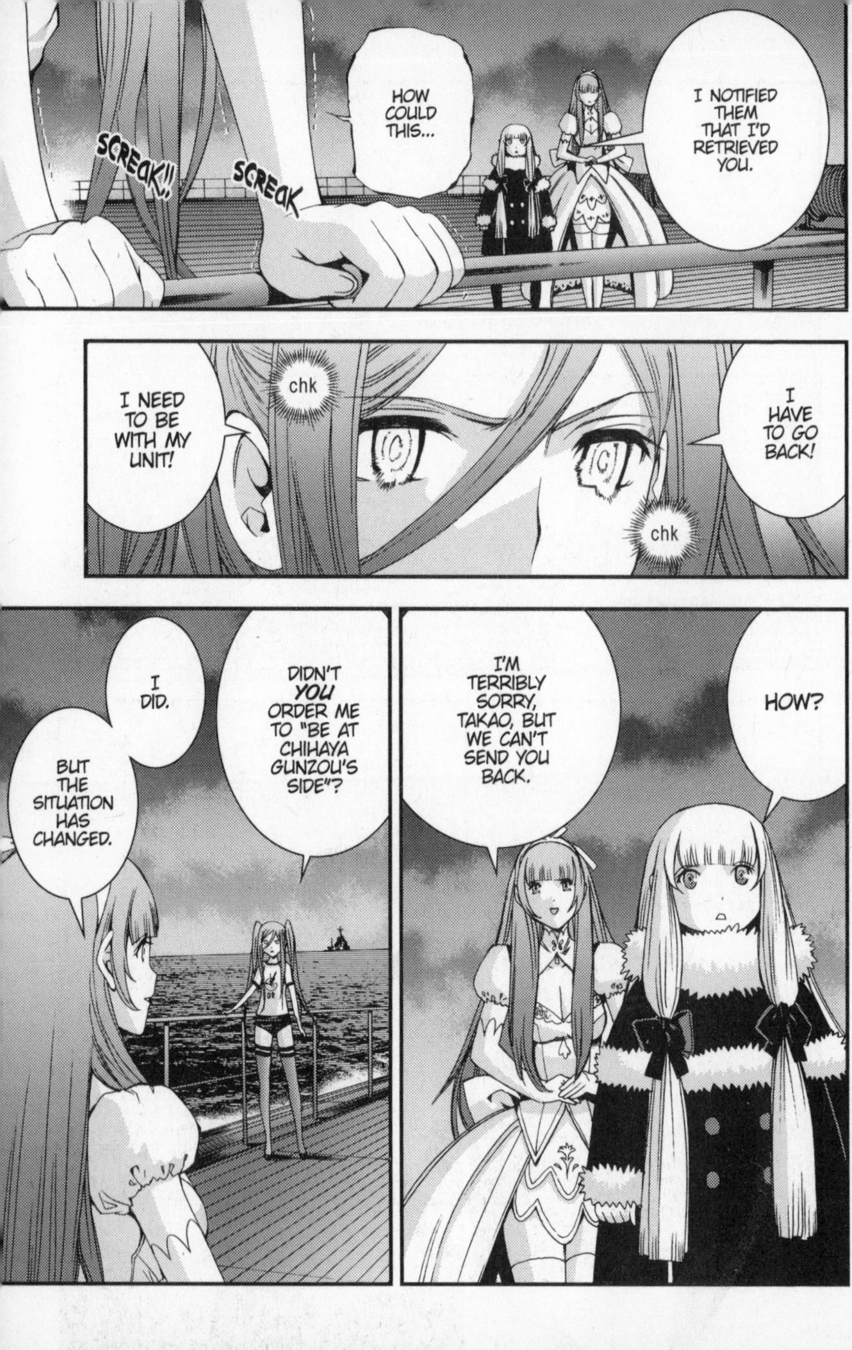
I NOTIFIED THEM THAT I'D RETRIEVED YOU.
HOW COULD THIS...
SCREAK
SCREAK!!
I HAVE TO GO BACK!
chk
chk
I NEED TO BE WITH MY UNIT!
HOW?
I'M TERRIBLY SORRY, TAKAO, BUT WE CAN'T SEND YOU BACK.
DIDN'T *YOU* ORDER ME TO "BE AT CHIHAYA GUNZOU'S SIDE"?
I DID.
BUT THE SITUATION HAS CHANGED.

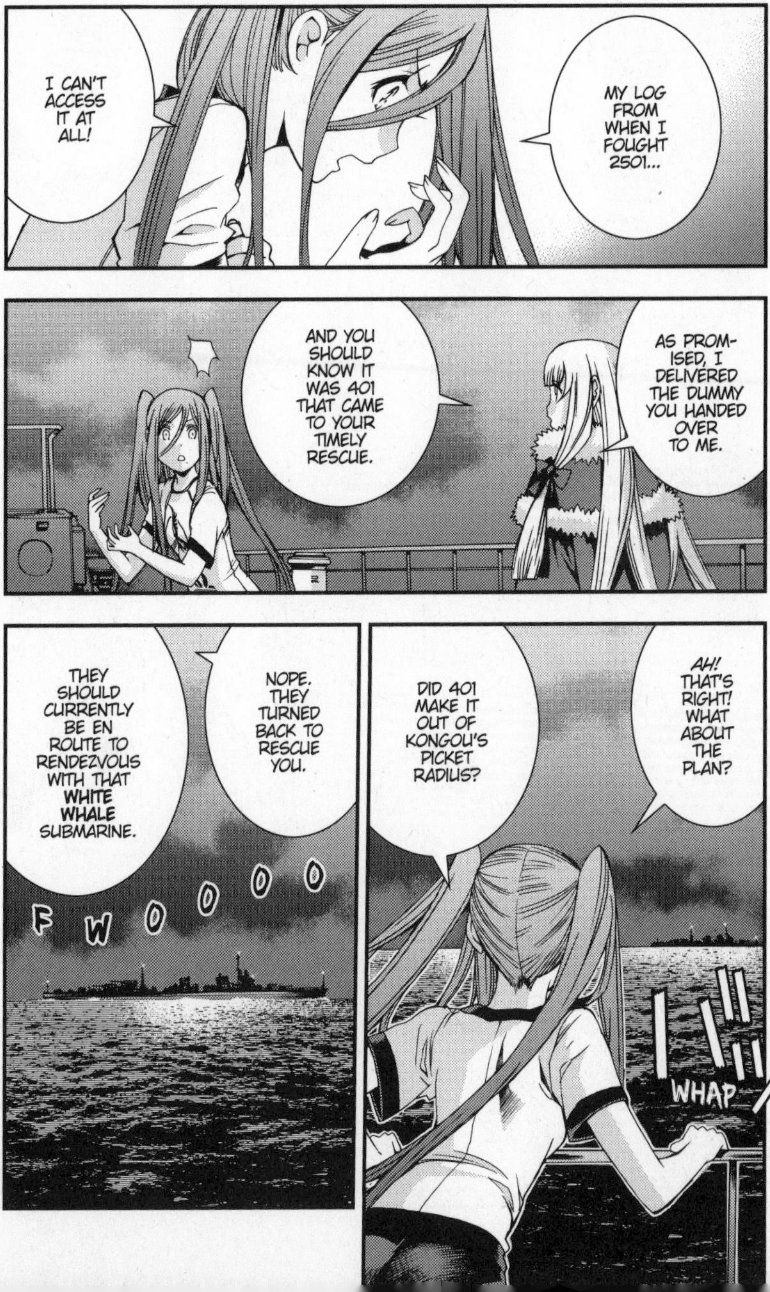
MY LOG FROM WHEN I FOUGHT 2501...
I CAN'T ACCESS IT AT ALL!
AS PROMISED, I DELIVERED THE DUMMY YOU HANDED OVER TO ME.
AND YOU SHOULD KNOW IT WAS 401 THAT CAME TO YOUR TIMELY RESCUE.
AH! THAT'S RIGHT! WHAT ABOUT THE PLAN?
DID 401 MAKE IT OUT OF KONGOU'S PICKET RADIUS?
WHAP
NOPE. THEY TURNED BACK TO RESCUE YOU.
THEY SHOULD CURRENTLY BE EN ROUTE TO RENDEZVOUS WITH THAT **WHITE WHALE** SUBMARINE.
FWOOOOO

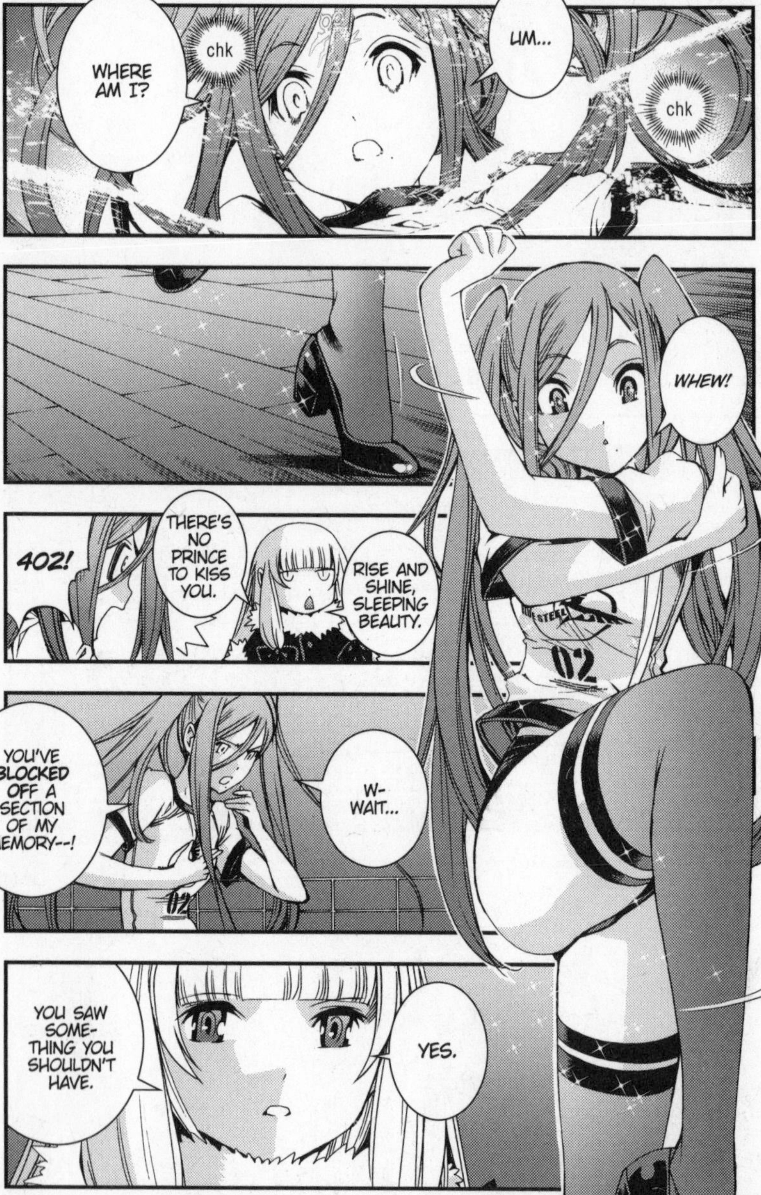
UM...
chk
chk
WHERE AM I?
WHEW!
RISE AND SHINE, SLEEPING BEAUTY.
THERE'S NO PRINCE TO KISS YOU.
402!
W- WAIT...
YOU'VE **BLOCKED** OFF A SECTION OF MY MEMORY--!
YES.
YOU SAW SOME- THING YOU SHOULDN'T HAVE.

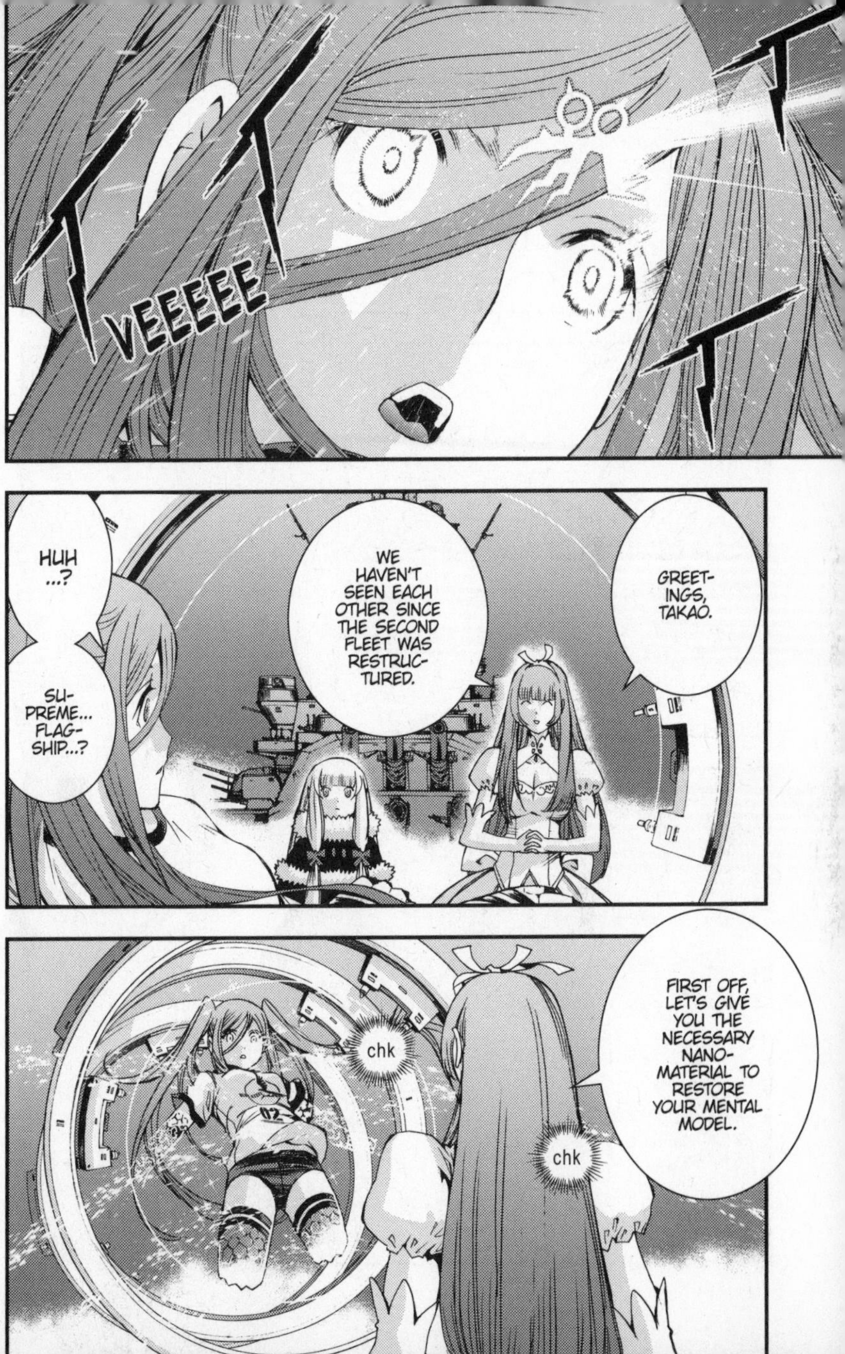
VEEEEE
GREET-INGS, TAKAO.
WE HAVEN'T SEEN EACH OTHER SINCE THE SECOND FLEET WAS RESTRUC-TURED.
HUH ...?
SU-PREME... FLAG-SHIP...?
FIRST OFF, LET'S GIVE YOU THE NECESSARY NANO-MATERIAL TO RESTORE YOUR MENTAL MODEL.
chk
chk

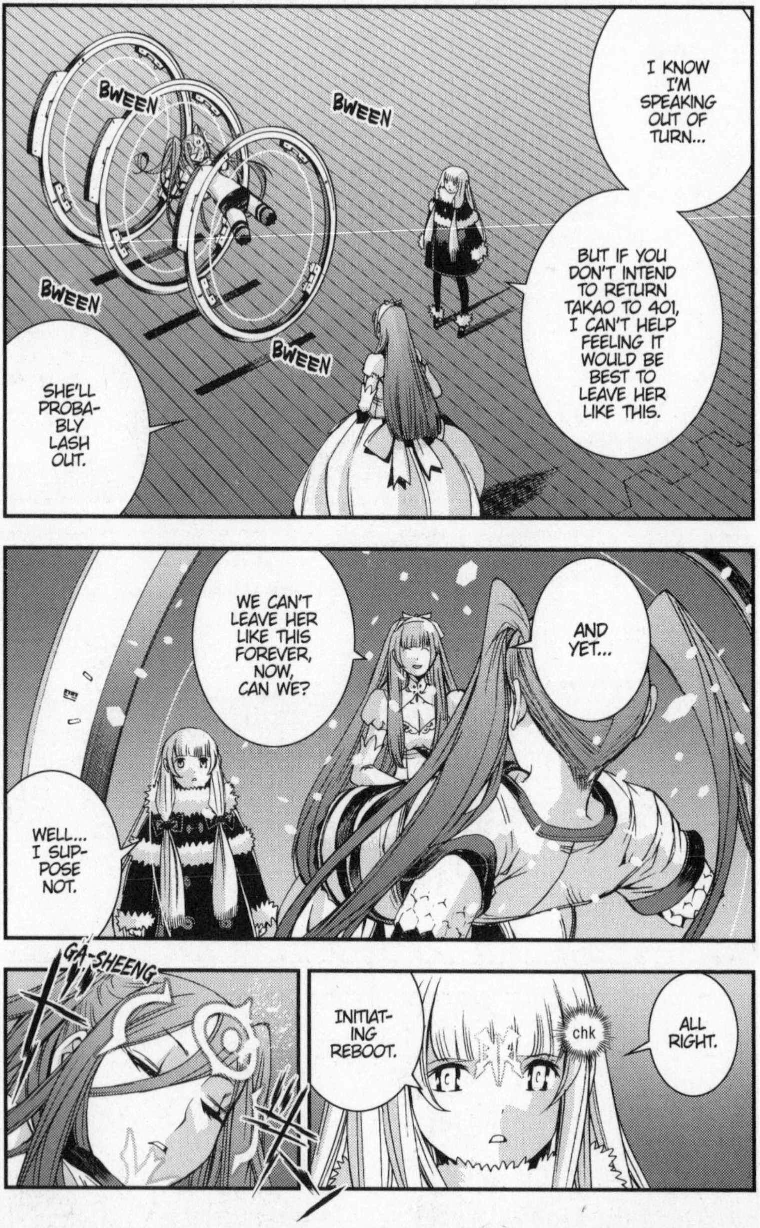
I KNOW I'M SPEAKING OUT OF TURN...
BUT IF YOU DON'T INTEND TO RETURN TAKAO TO 401, I CAN'T HELP FEELING IT WOULD BE BEST TO LEAVE HER LIKE THIS.
BWEEN
BWEEN
BWEEN
BWEEN
SHE'LL PROBA-BLY LASH OUT.
AND YET...
WE CAN'T LEAVE HER LIKE THIS FOREVER, NOW, CAN WE?
WELL... I SUP-POSE NOT.
ALL RIGHT.
chk
INITIAT-ING REBOOT.
GA-SHEENG

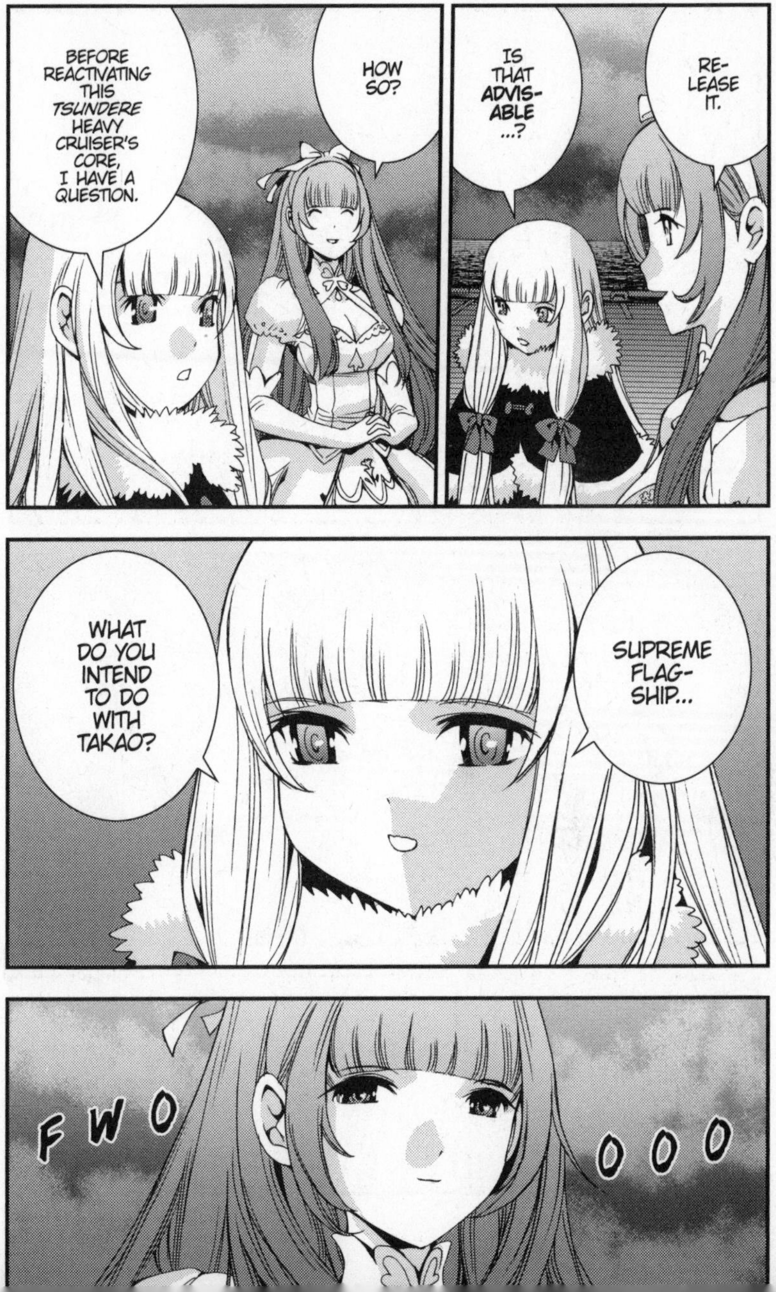
RE-LEASE IT.
IS THAT ADVIS-ABLE ...?
HOW SO?
BEFORE REACTIVATING THIS TSUNDERE HEAVY CRUISER'S CORE, I HAVE A QUESTION.
SUPREME FLAG-SHIP...
WHAT DO YOU INTEND TO DO WITH TAKAO?
FWO OOO

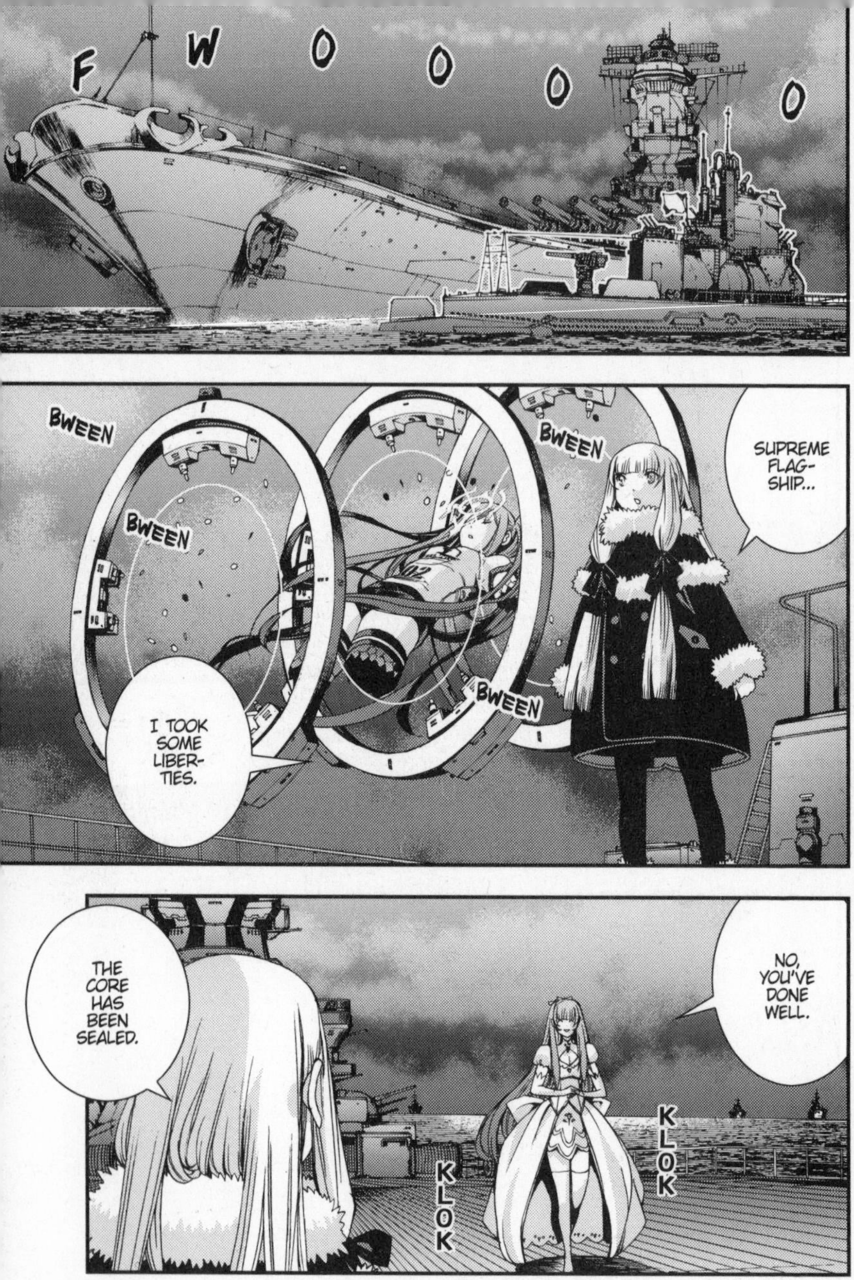
FWOOOOO
SUPREME FLAG-SHIP...
BWEEN
BWEEN
BWEEN
BWEEN
I TOOK SOME LIBER-TIES.
NO, YOU'VE DONE WELL.
THE CORE HAS BEEN SEALED.
KLOK
KLOK
KLOK

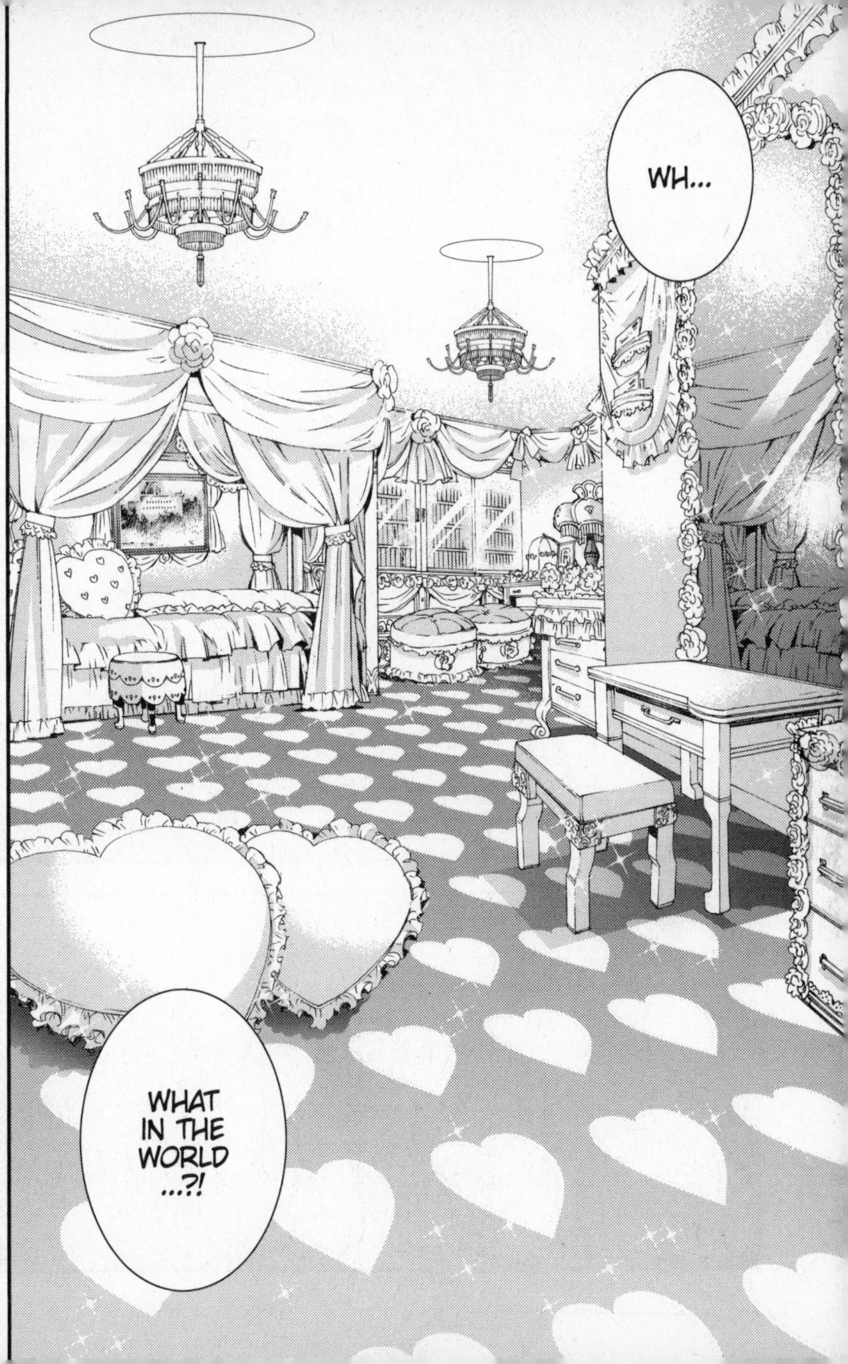
WH...
WHAT IN THE WORLD ...?!

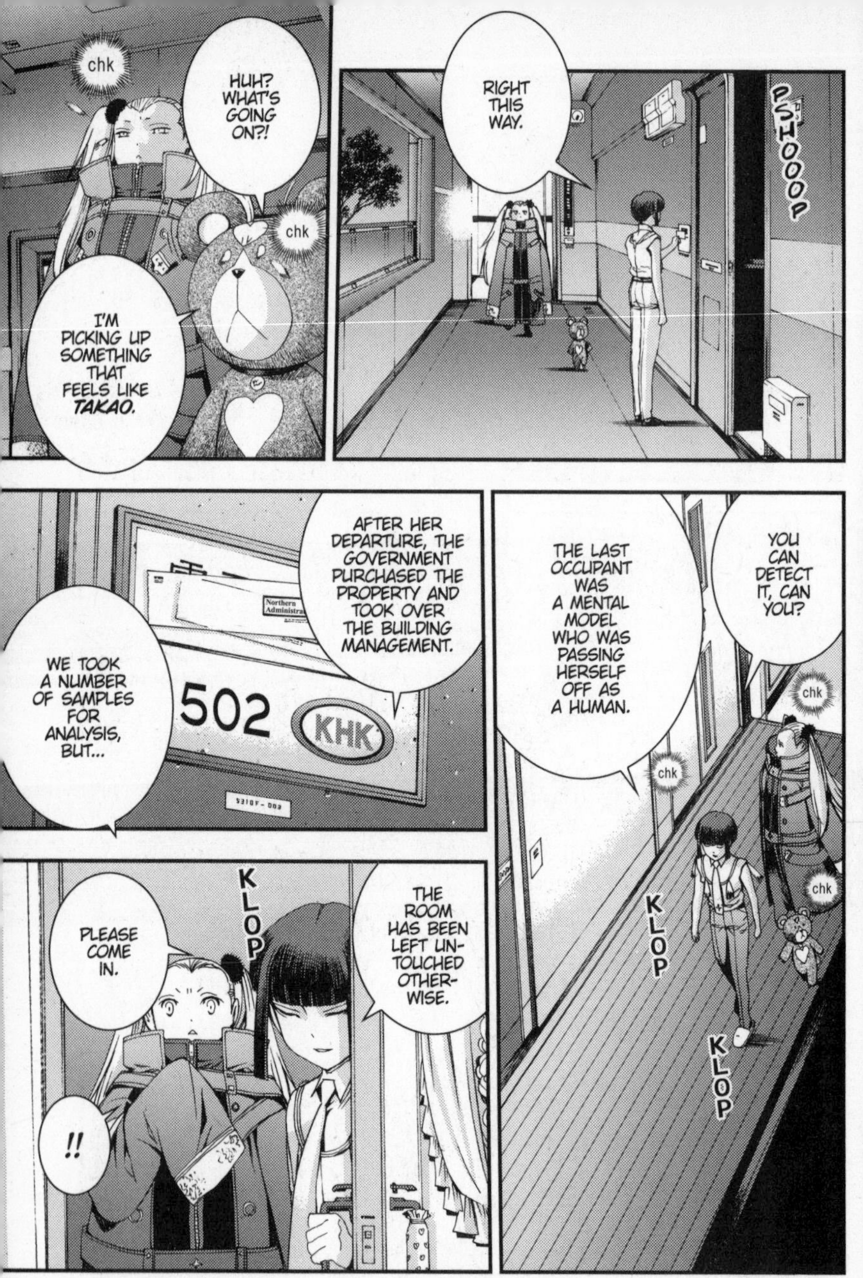
RIGHT THIS WAY.
PSHOOOP
chk
HUH? WHAT'S GOING ON?!
chk
I'M PICKING UP SOMETHING THAT FEELS LIKE *TAKAO.*
YOU CAN DETECT IT, CAN YOU?
chk
THE LAST OCCUPANT WAS A MENTAL MODEL WHO WAS PASSING HERSELF OFF AS A HUMAN.
chk
chk
KLOP
KLOP
AFTER HER DEPARTURE, THE GOVERNMENT PURCHASED THE PROPERTY AND TOOK OVER THE BUILDING MANAGEMENT.
WE TOOK A NUMBER OF SAMPLES FOR ANALYSIS, BUT...
502
KHK
THE ROOM HAS BEEN LEFT UN-TOUCHED OTHER-WISE.
KLOP
PLEASE COME IN.
!!

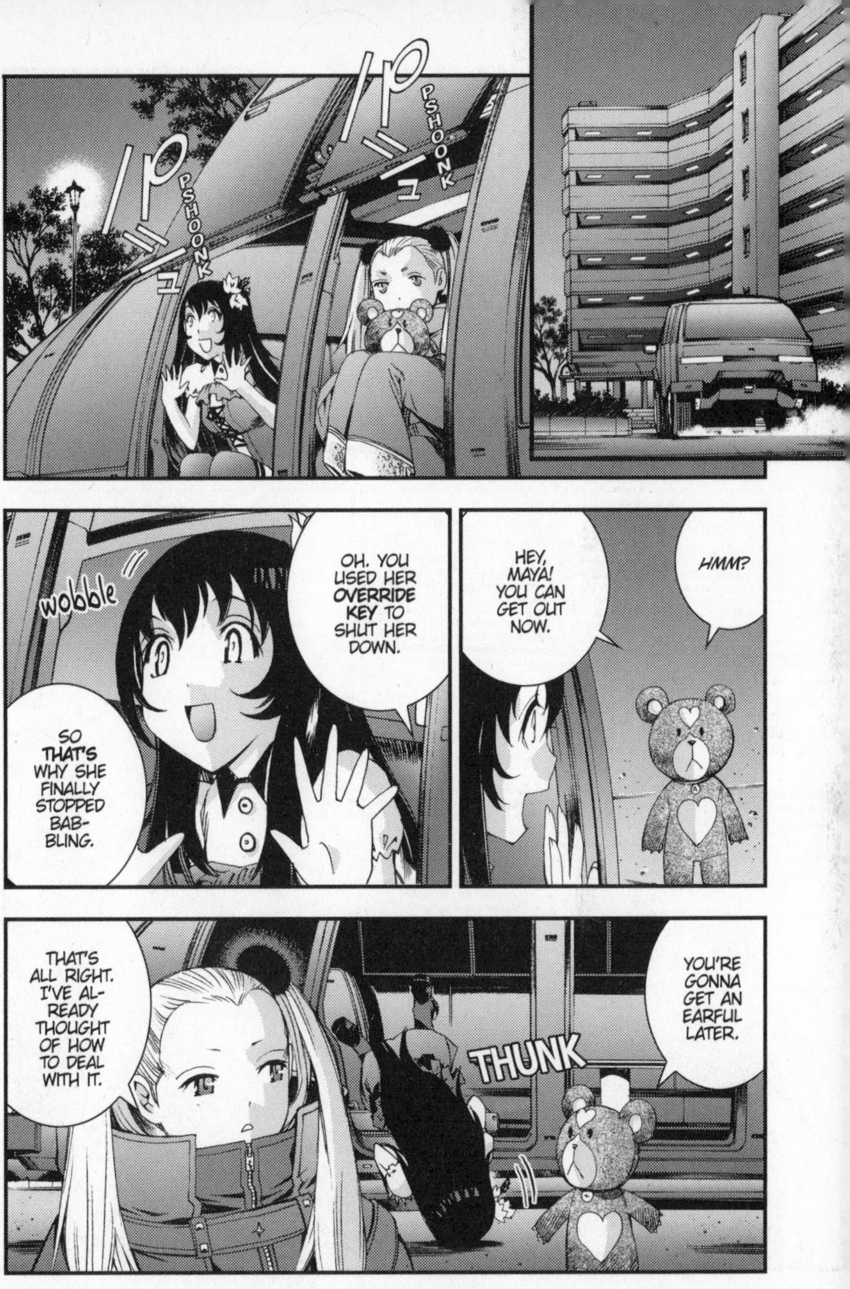
PSHOONK
PSHOONK
HMM?
HEY, MAYA! YOU CAN GET OUT NOW.
OH. YOU USED HER OVERRIDE KEY TO SHUT HER DOWN.
wobble
SO THAT'S WHY SHE FINALLY STOPPED BAB-BLING.
YOU'RE GONNA GET AN EARFUL LATER.
THUNK
THAT'S ALL RIGHT. I'VE AL-READY THOUGHT OF HOW TO DEAL WITH IT.

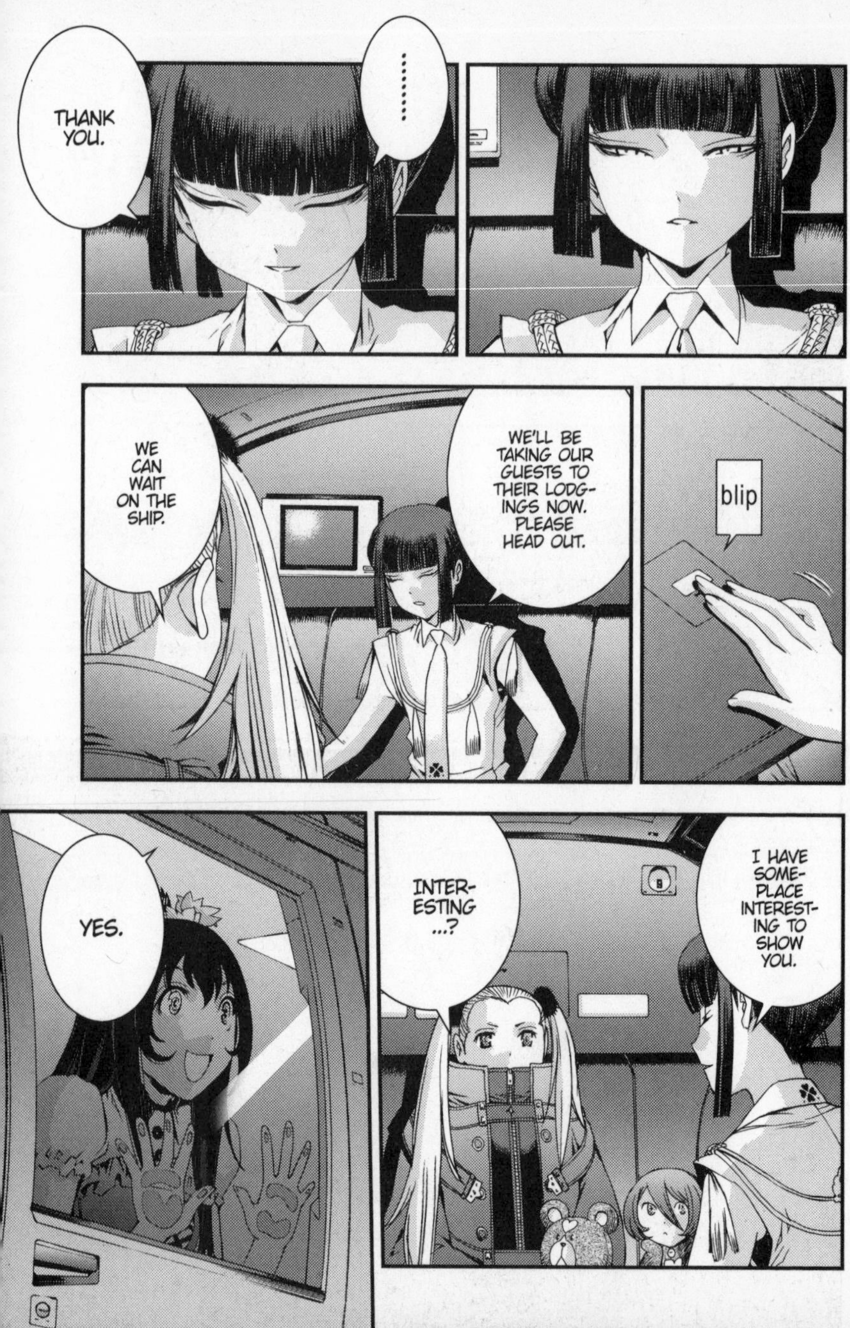
……
THANK YOU.
blip
WE'LL BE TAKING OUR GUESTS TO THEIR LODGINGS NOW. PLEASE HEAD OUT.
WE CAN WAIT ON THE SHIP.
I HAVE SOMEPLACE INTERESTING TO SHOW YOU.
INTERESTING ...?
YES.

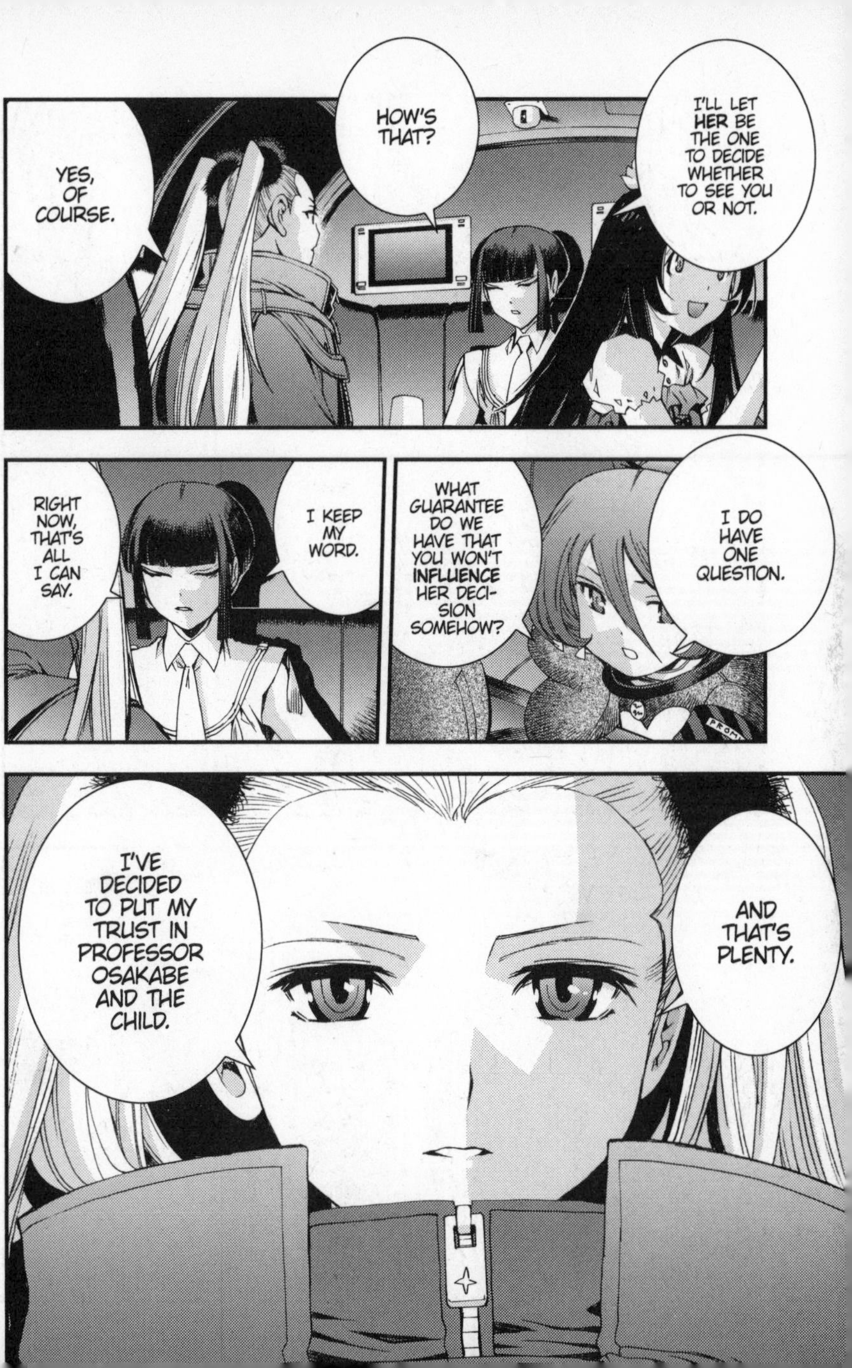
I'LL LET HER BE THE ONE TO DECIDE WHETHER TO SEE YOU OR NOT.
HOW'S THAT?
YES, OF COURSE.
I DO HAVE ONE QUESTION.
WHAT GUARANTEE DO WE HAVE THAT YOU WON'T INFLUENCE HER DECISION SOMEHOW?
I KEEP MY WORD.
RIGHT NOW, THAT'S ALL I CAN SAY.
AND THAT'S PLENTY.
I'VE DECIDED TO PUT MY TRUST IN PROFESSOR OSAKABE AND THE CHILD.

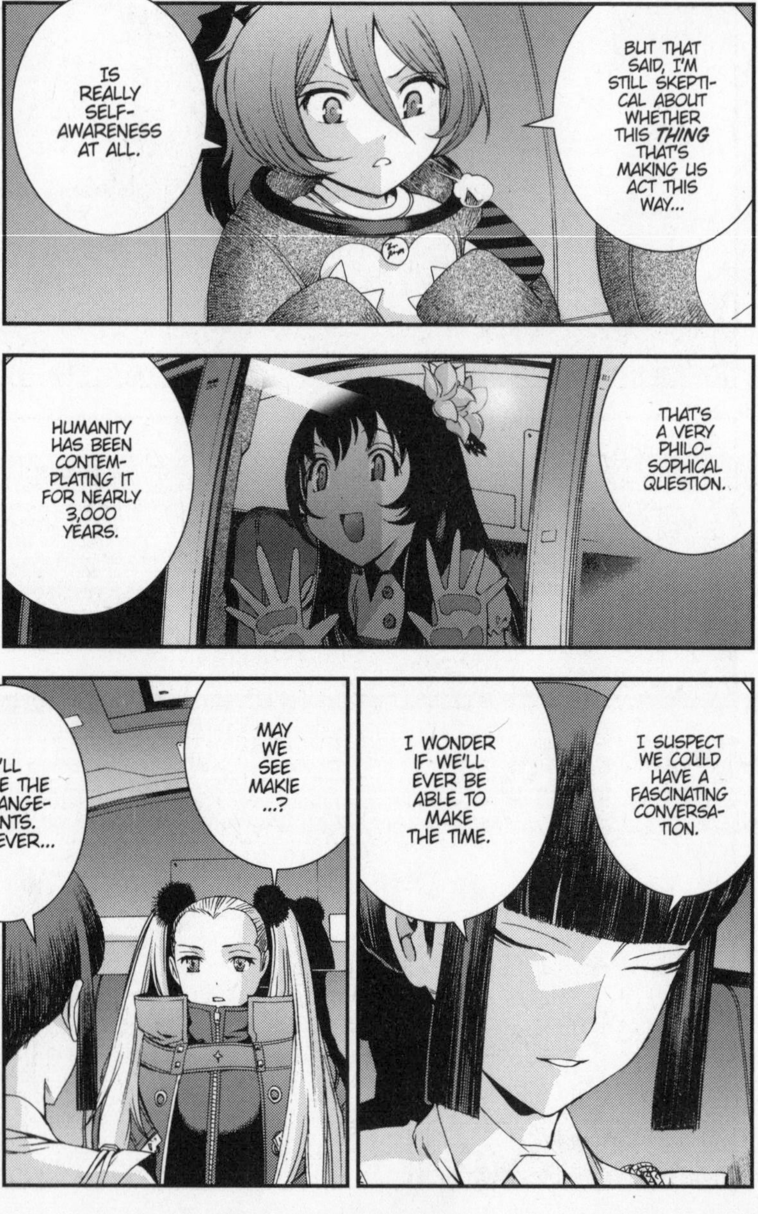
BUT THAT SAID, I'M STILL SKEPTICAL ABOUT WHETHER THIS *THING* THAT'S MAKING US ACT THIS WAY...
IS REALLY SELF-AWARENESS AT ALL.
THAT'S A VERY PHILOSOPHICAL QUESTION.
HUMANITY HAS BEEN CONTEMPLATING IT FOR NEARLY 3,000 YEARS.
I SUSPECT WE COULD HAVE A FASCINATING CONVERSATION.
I WONDER IF WE'LL EVER BE ABLE TO MAKE THE TIME.
MAY WE SEE MAKIE ...?
I'LL MAKE THE ARRANGEMENTS. HOWEVER...

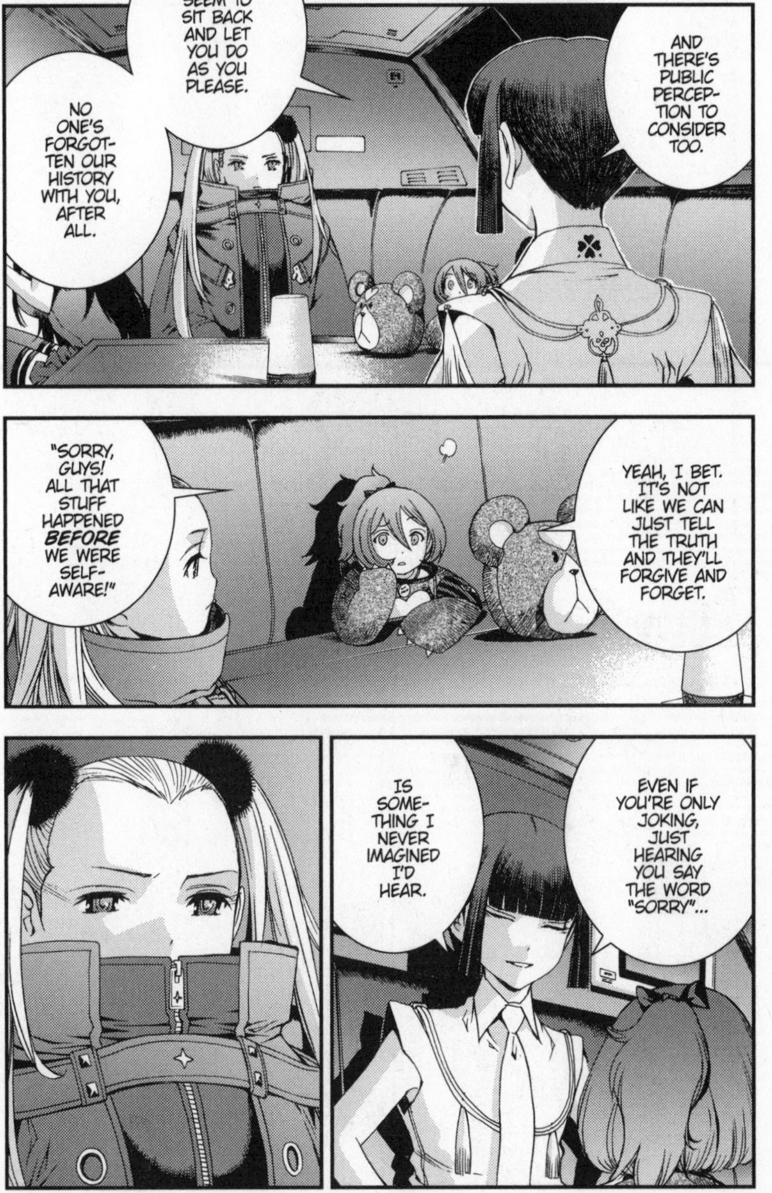
AND THERE'S PUBLIC PERCEP-TION TO CONSIDER TOO.
WE CAN'T SEEM TO SIT BACK AND LET YOU DO AS YOU PLEASE.
NO ONE'S FORGOT-TEN OUR HISTORY WITH YOU, AFTER ALL.
YEAH, I BET. IT'S NOT LIKE WE CAN JUST TELL THE TRUTH AND THEY'LL FORGIVE AND FORGET.
"SORRY, GUYS! ALL THAT STUFF HAPPENED ***BEFORE*** WE WERE SELF-AWARE!"
EVEN IF YOU'RE ONLY JOKING, JUST HEARING YOU SAY THE WORD "SORRY"...
IS SOME-THING I NEVER IMAGINED I'D HEAR.

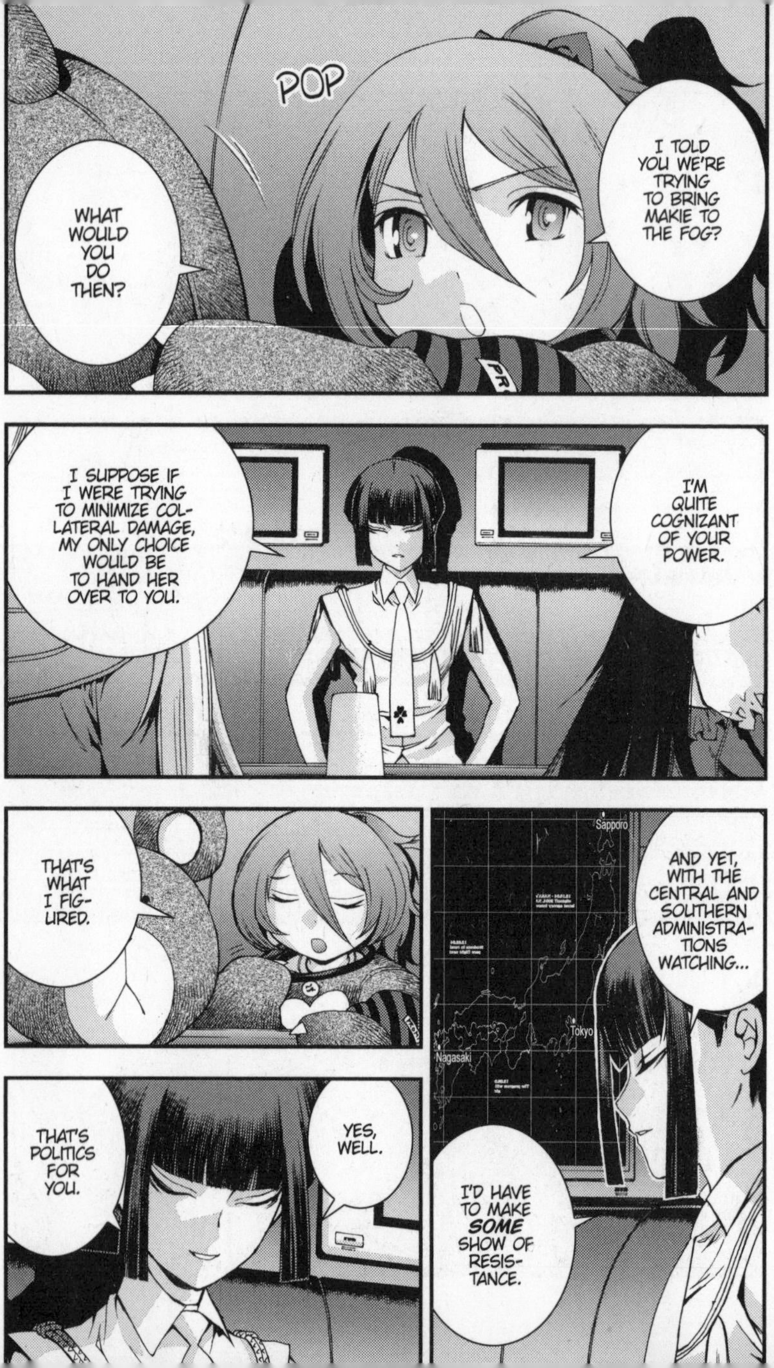
I TOLD YOU WE'RE TRYING TO BRING MAKIE TO THE FOG?
POP
WHAT WOULD YOU DO THEN?
I'M QUITE COGNIZANT OF YOUR POWER.
I SUPPOSE IF I WERE TRYING TO MINIMIZE COL-LATERAL DAMAGE, MY ONLY CHOICE WOULD BE TO HAND HER OVER TO YOU.
Sapporo
Tokyo
Nagasaki
AND YET, WITH THE CENTRAL AND SOUTHERN ADMINISTRA-TIONS WATCHING...
I'D HAVE TO MAKE **SOME** SHOW OF RESIS-TANCE.
THAT'S WHAT I FIG-URED.
YES, WELL.
THAT'S POLITICS FOR YOU.

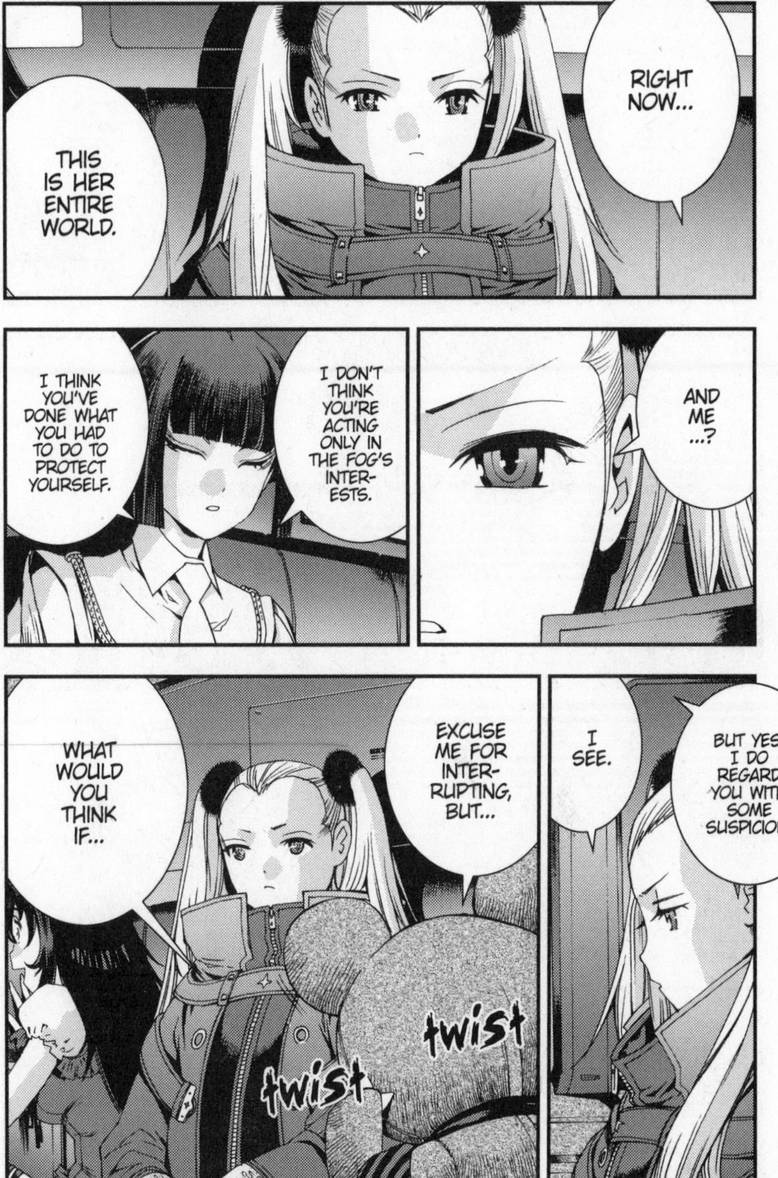
RIGHT NOW...
THIS IS HER ENTIRE WORLD.
AND ME ...?
I DON'T THINK YOU'RE ACTING ONLY IN THE FOG'S INTER-ESTS.
I THINK YOU'VE DONE WHAT YOU HAD TO DO TO PROTECT YOURSELF.
I SEE.
BUT YES, I DO REGARD YOU WITH SOME SUSPICION.
EXCUSE ME FOR INTERRUPTING, BUT...
WHAT WOULD YOU THINK IF...
twist
twist

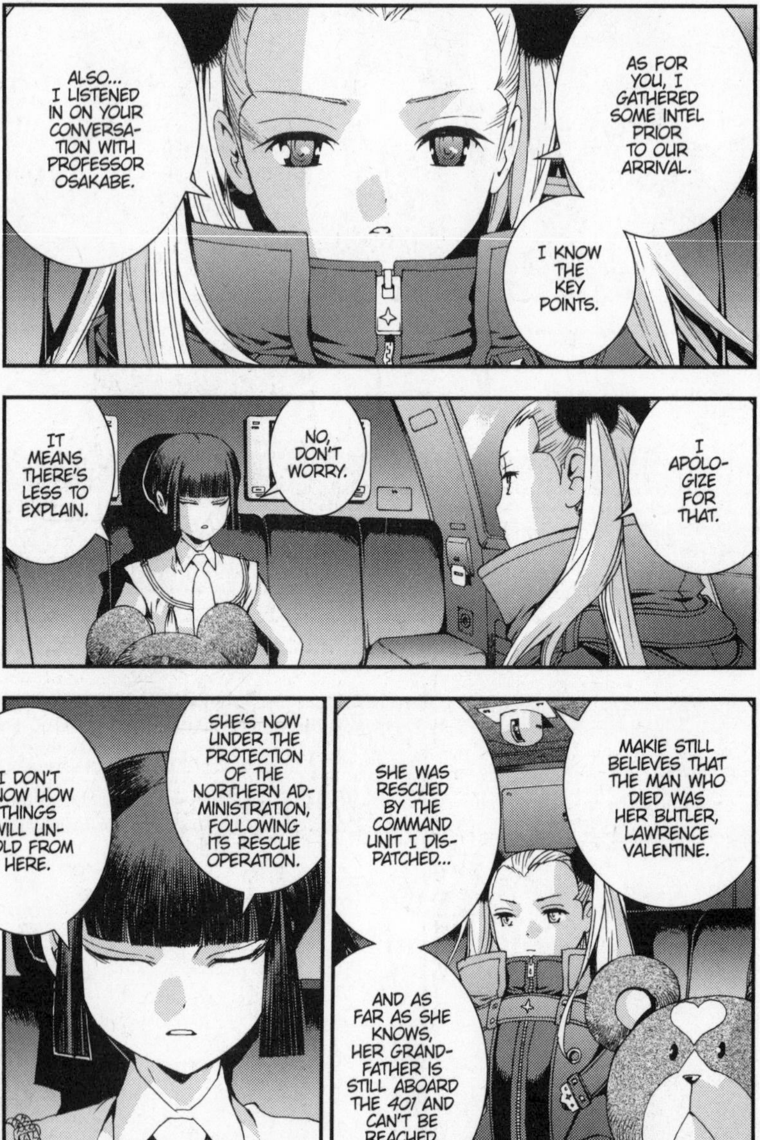
AS FOR YOU, I GATHERED SOME INTEL PRIOR TO OUR ARRIVAL.
I KNOW THE KEY POINTS.
ALSO... I LISTENED IN ON YOUR CONVERSATION WITH PROFESSOR OSAKABE.
I APOLOGIZE FOR THAT.
NO, DON'T WORRY.
IT MEANS THERE'S LESS TO EXPLAIN.
MAKIE STILL BELIEVES THAT THE MAN WHO DIED WAS HER BUTLER, LAWRENCE VALENTINE.
SHE WAS RESCUED BY THE COMMAND UNIT I DISPATCHED...
AND AS FAR AS SHE KNOWS, HER GRANDFATHER IS STILL ABOARD THE 401 AND CAN'T BE REACHED.
SHE'S NOW UNDER THE PROTECTION OF THE NORTHERN ADMINISTRATION, FOLLOWING ITS RESCUE OPERATION.
I DON'T KNOW HOW THINGS WILL UNFOLD FROM HERE.

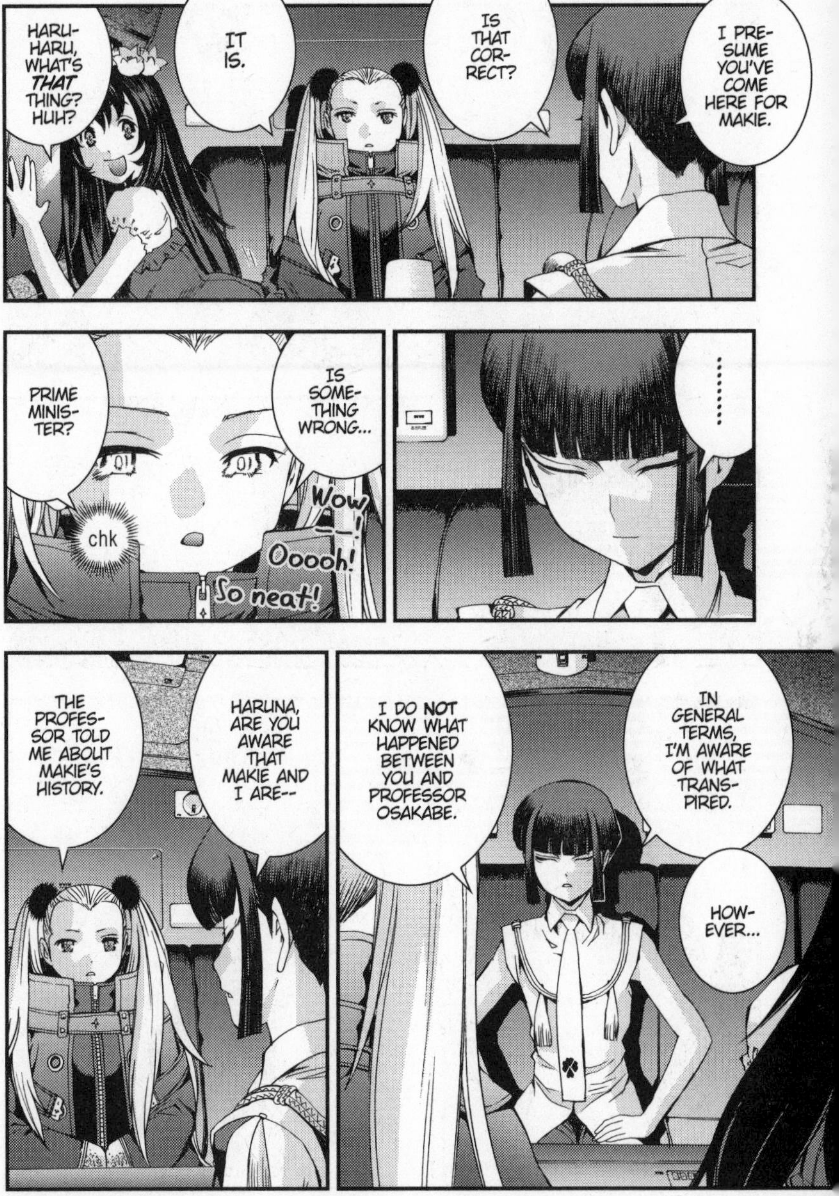
I PRESUME YOU'VE COME HERE FOR MAKIE.
IS THAT CORRECT?
IT IS.
HARU-HARU, WHAT'S *THAT* THING? HUH?
......
IS SOMETHING WRONG...
PRIME MINISTER?
Wow—!
chk
Ooooh!
So neat!
IN GENERAL TERMS, I'M AWARE OF WHAT TRANSPIRED.
HOWEVER...
I DO **NOT** KNOW WHAT HAPPENED BETWEEN YOU AND PROFESSOR OSAKABE.
HARUNA, ARE YOU AWARE THAT MAKIE AND I ARE--
THE PROFESSOR TOLD ME ABOUT MAKIE'S HISTORY.

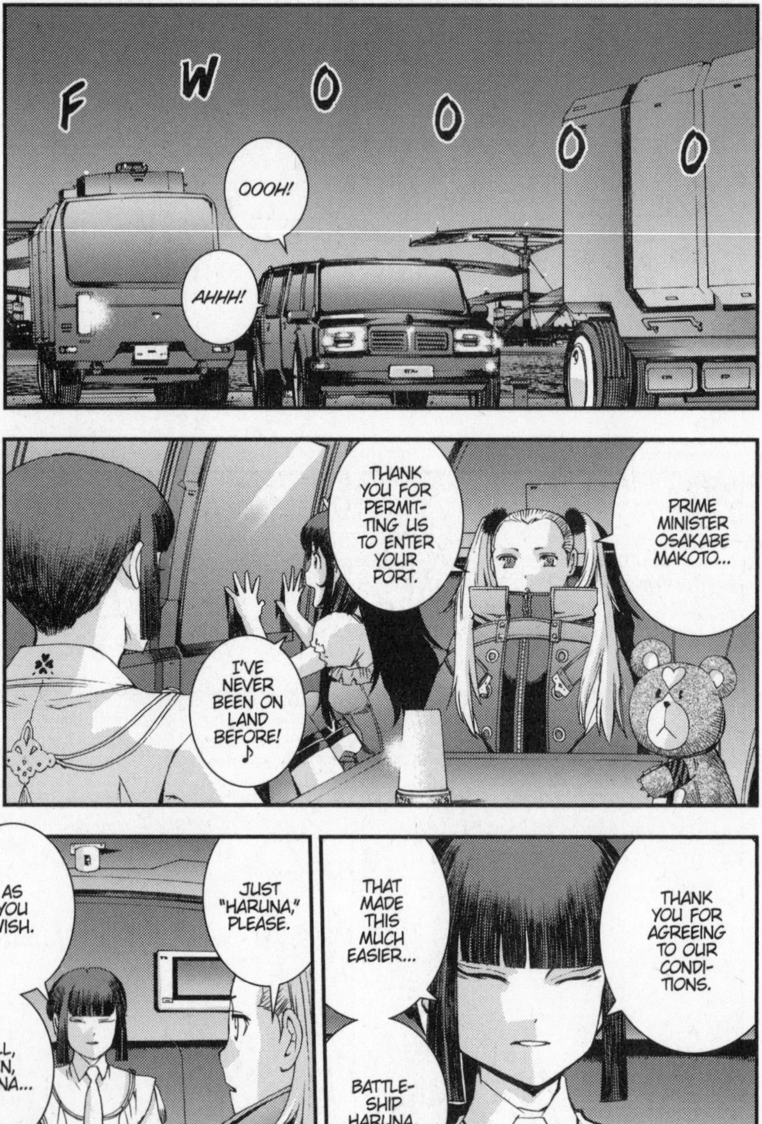
FWOOOO
OOOH!
AHHH!
PRIME MINISTER OSAKABE MAKOTO...
THANK YOU FOR PERMIT-TING US TO ENTER YOUR PORT.
I'VE NEVER BEEN ON LAND BEFORE! ♪
THANK YOU FOR AGREEING TO OUR CONDI-TIONS.
THAT MADE THIS MUCH EASIER...
BATTLE-SHIP HARUNA.
JUST "HARUNA," PLEASE.
AS YOU WISH.
WELL, THEN, HARUNA...

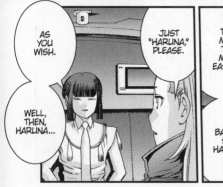

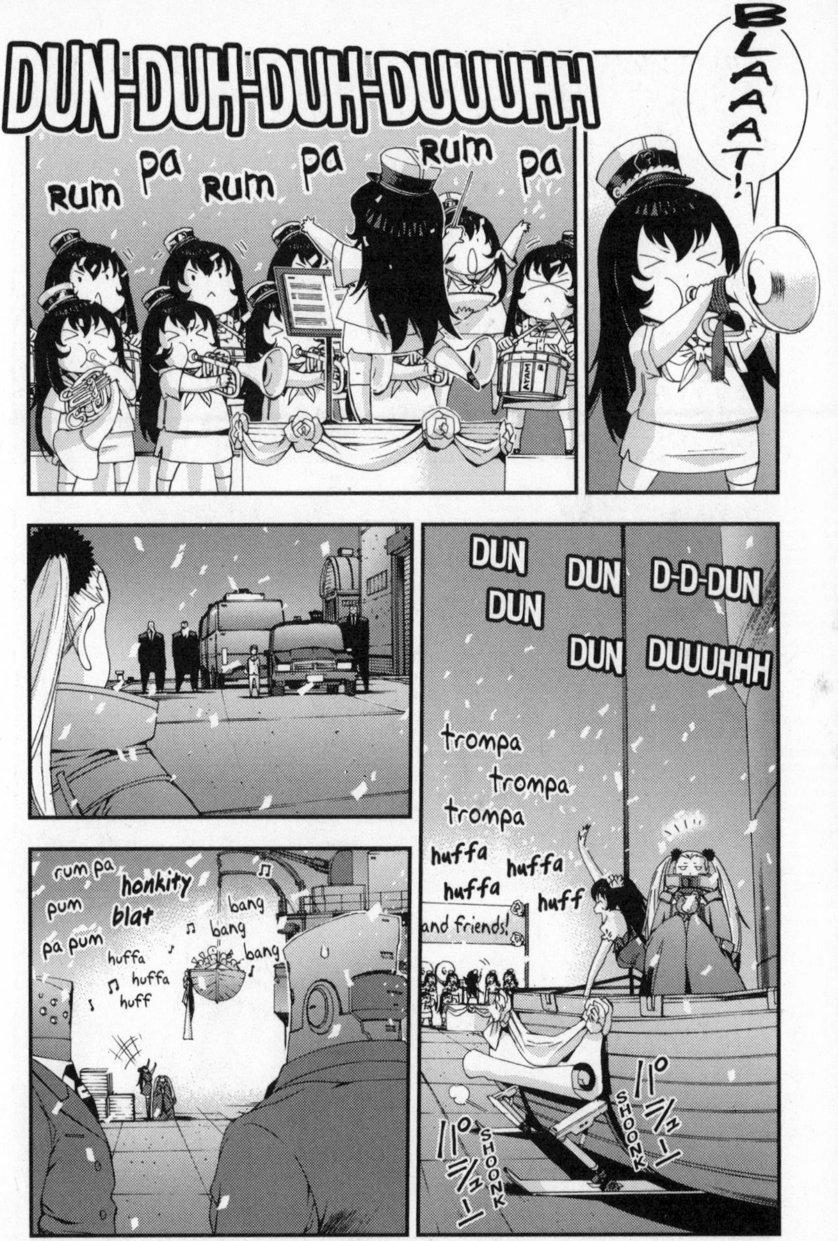
BLAAAT!
DUN-DUH-DUH-DUUUHH
Rum pa Rum pa Rum pa
DUN DUN D-D-DUN
DUN
DUN DUUUHHH
trompa
trompa
trompa
huffa huffa huffa huff
and friends!
SHOONK
SHOONK
rum pa pum pa pum
honkity blat
bang bang bang
huffa huffa huff

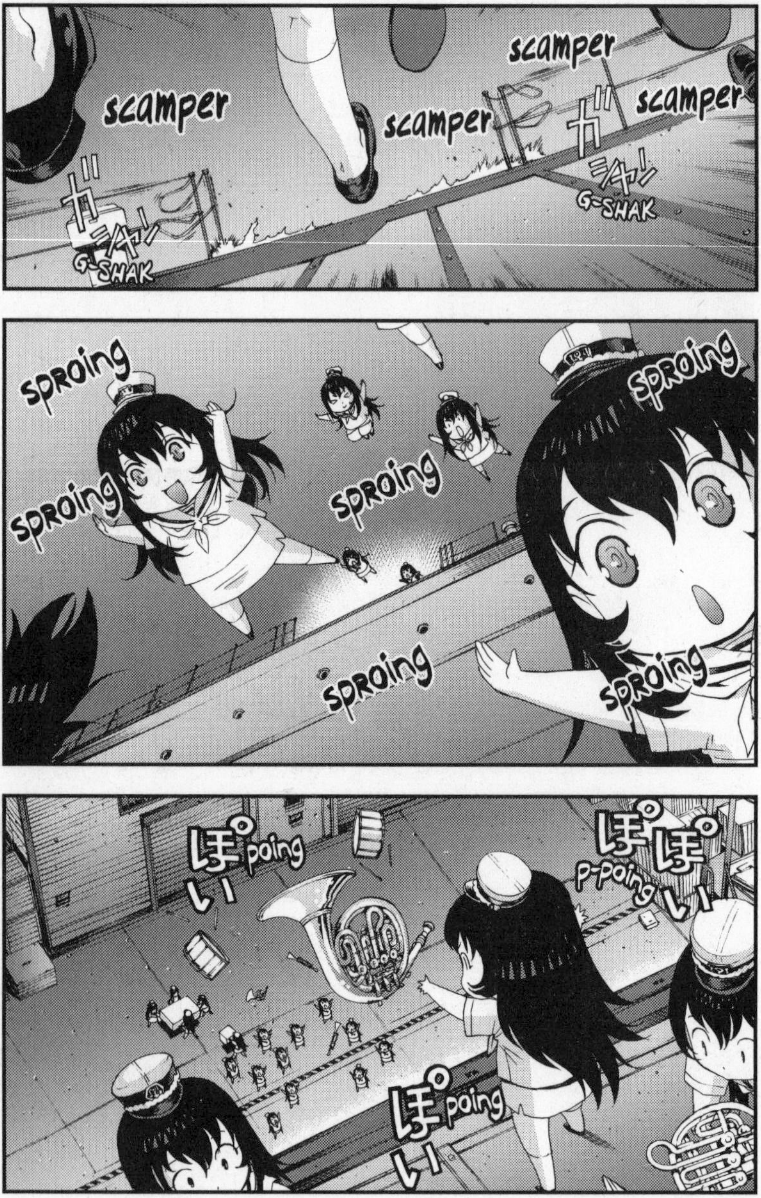
scamper
scamper
ガシャン
G-SHAK
scamper
scamper
ガシャン
G-SHAK
sproing
sproing
sproing
sproing
sproing
sproing
ぽぽい
p-poing
ぽい
poing
ぽい
poing

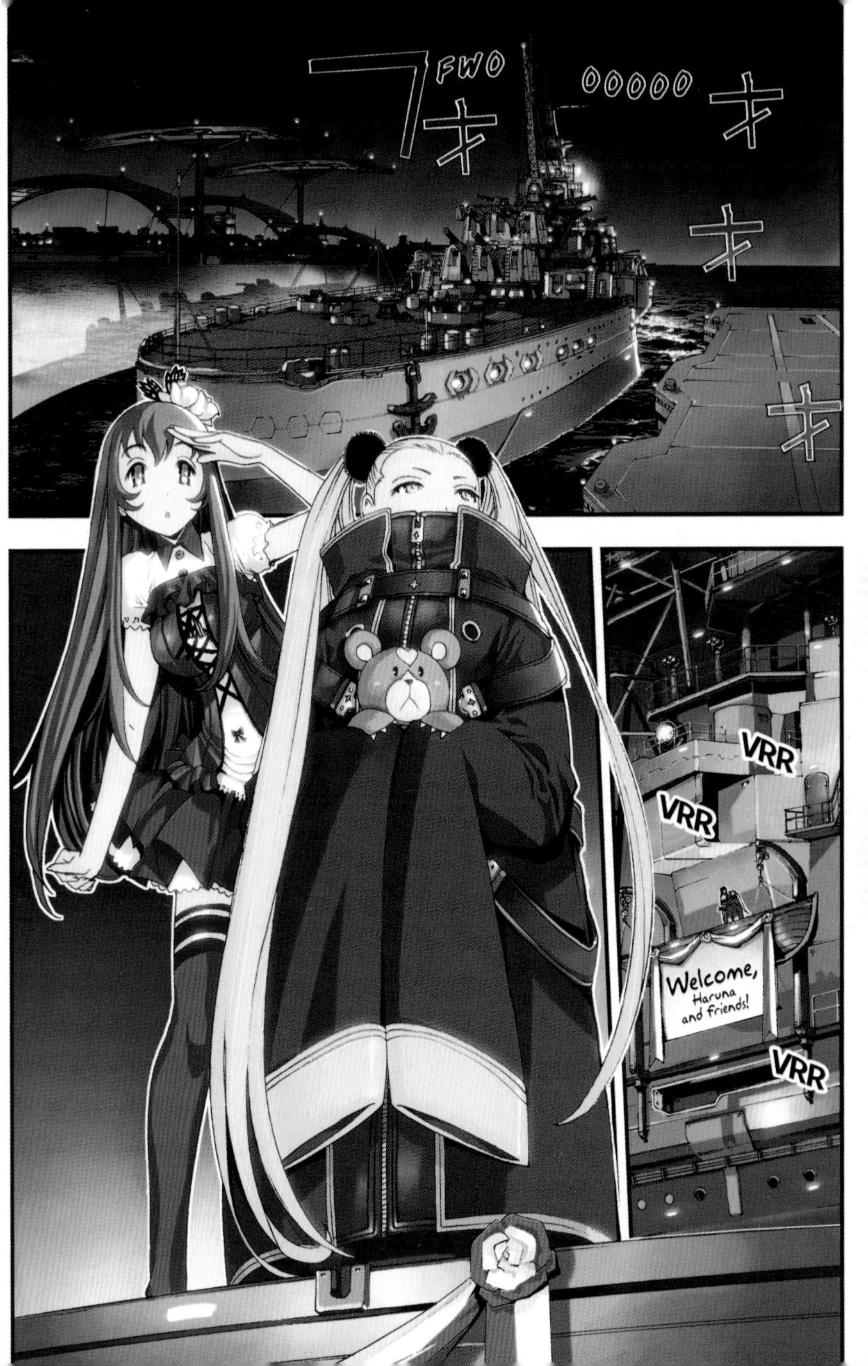
FWO
OOOOO
フォォォォ
VRR
VRR
Welcome, Haruna and friends!
VRR

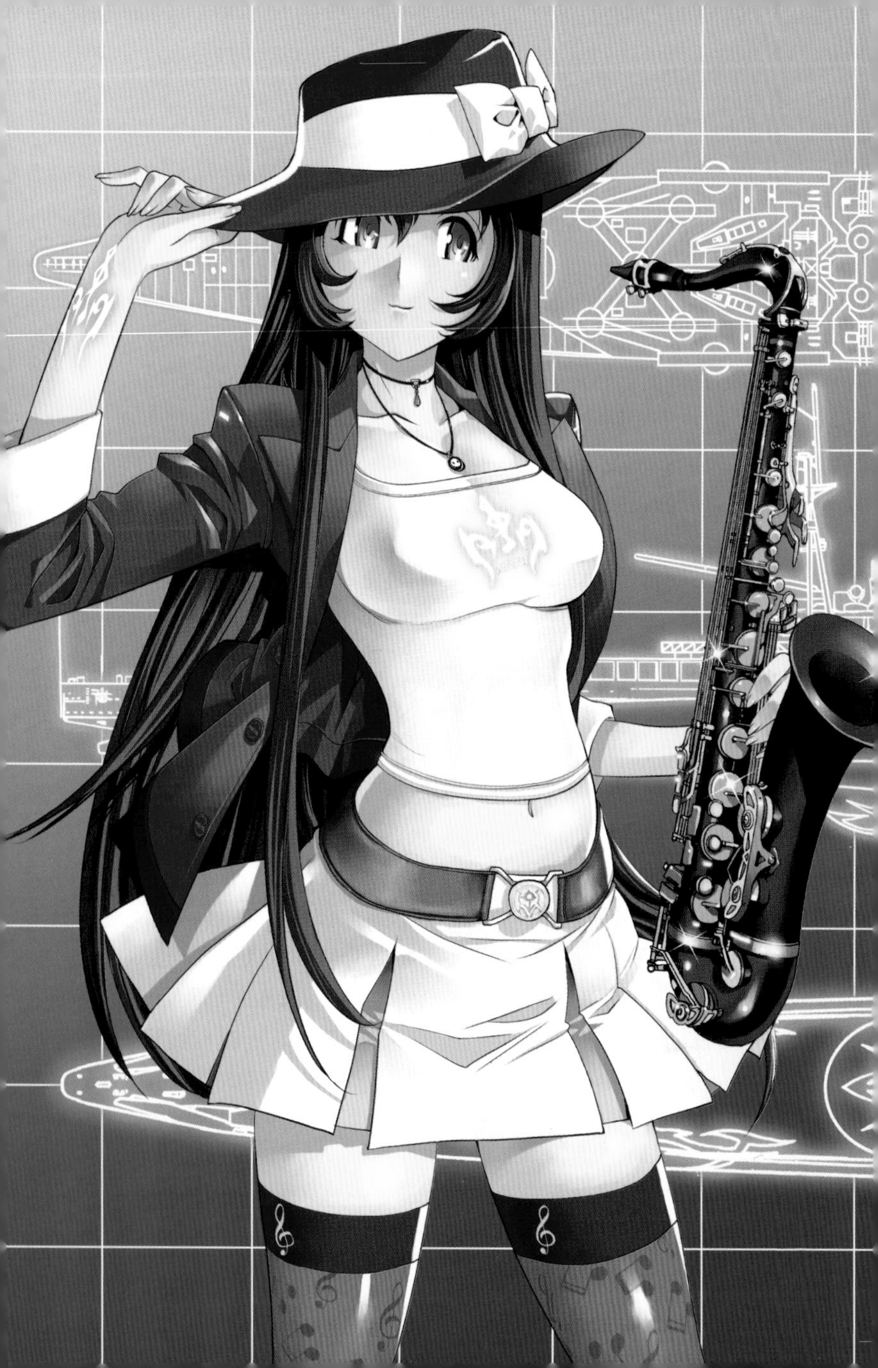

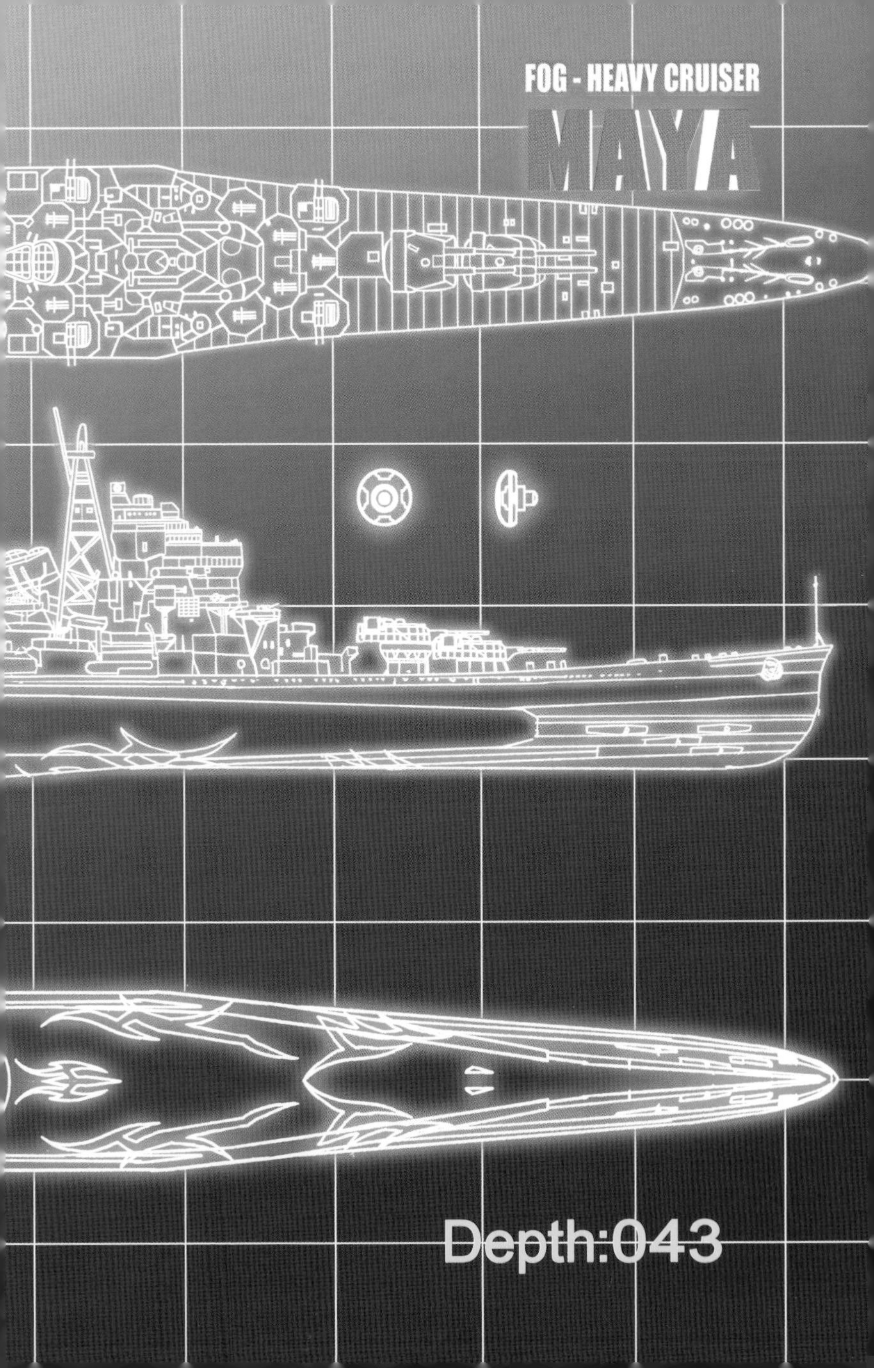
FOG - HEAVY CRUISER
MAYA
Depth:043

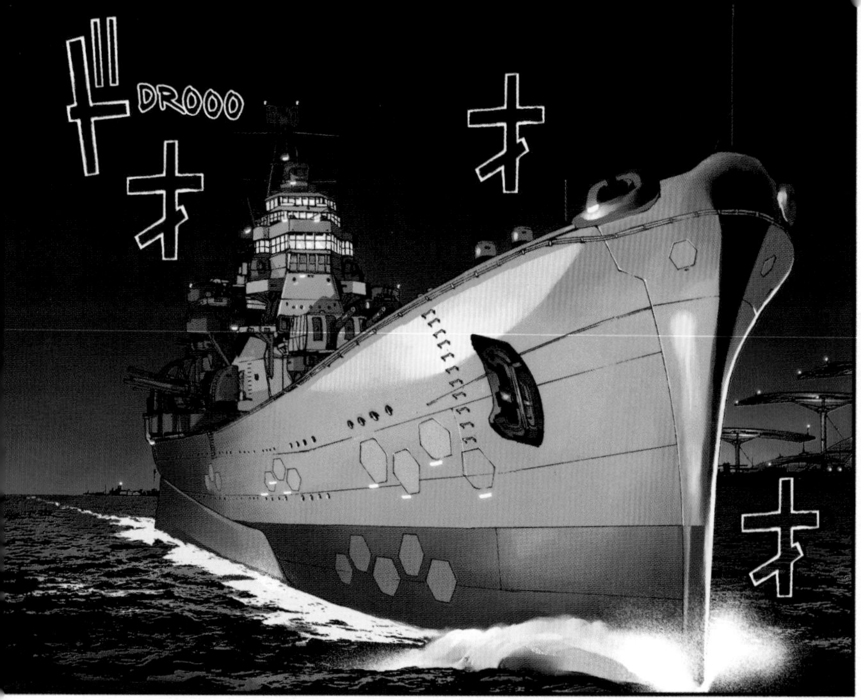
ドオオオ
DROOO

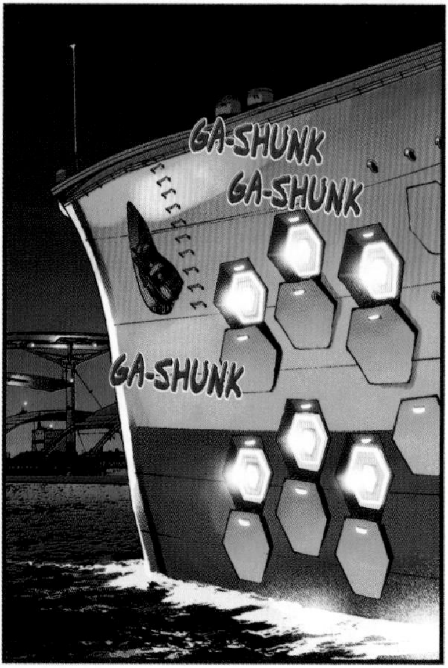
GA-SHUNK
GA-SHUNK
GA-SHUNK

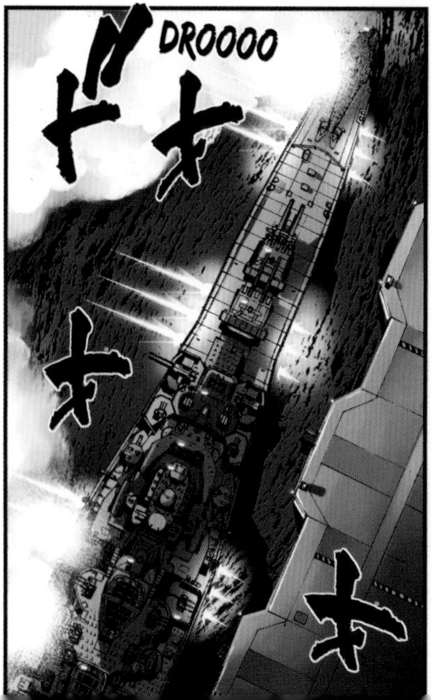
ドオオオ
DROOOO

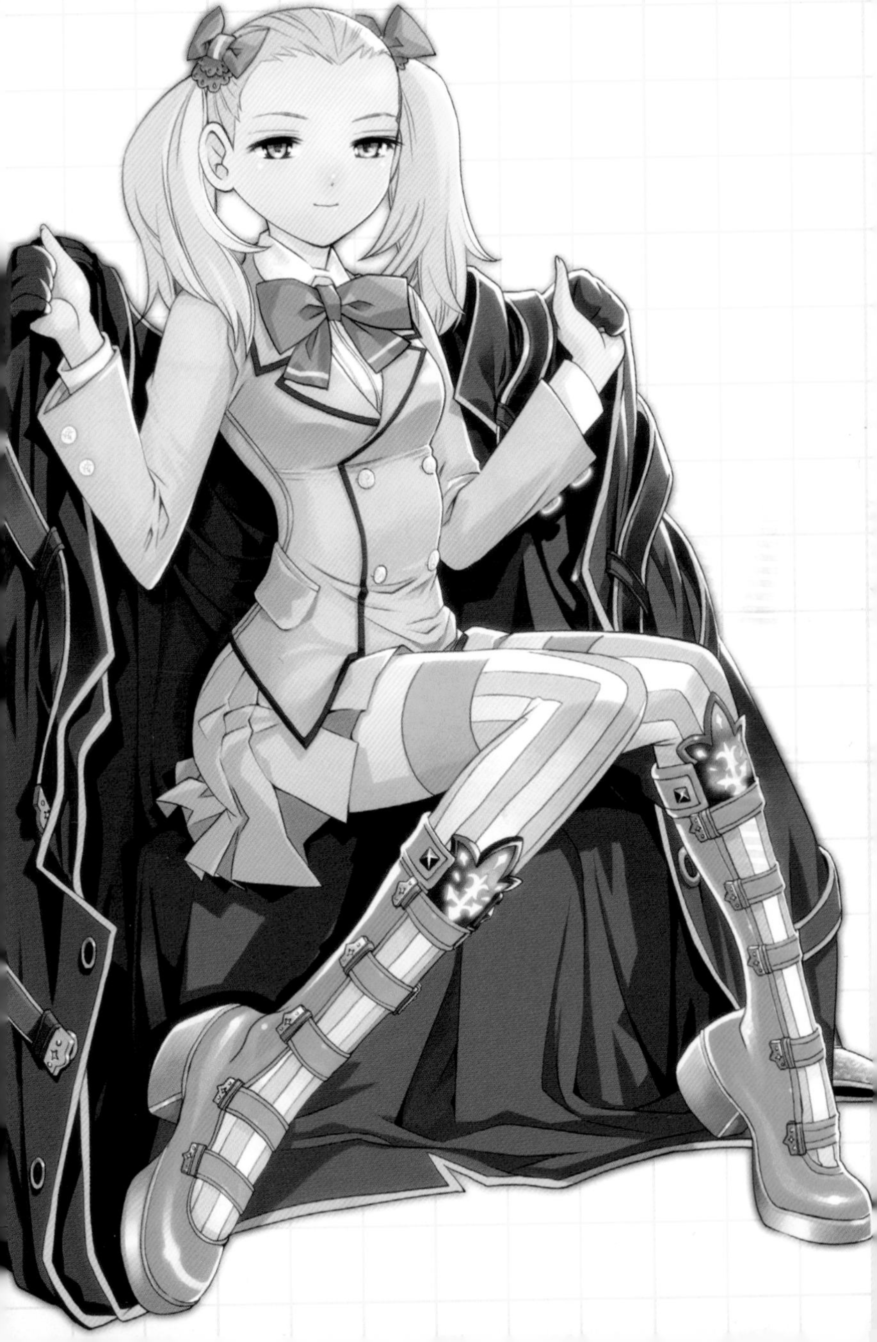

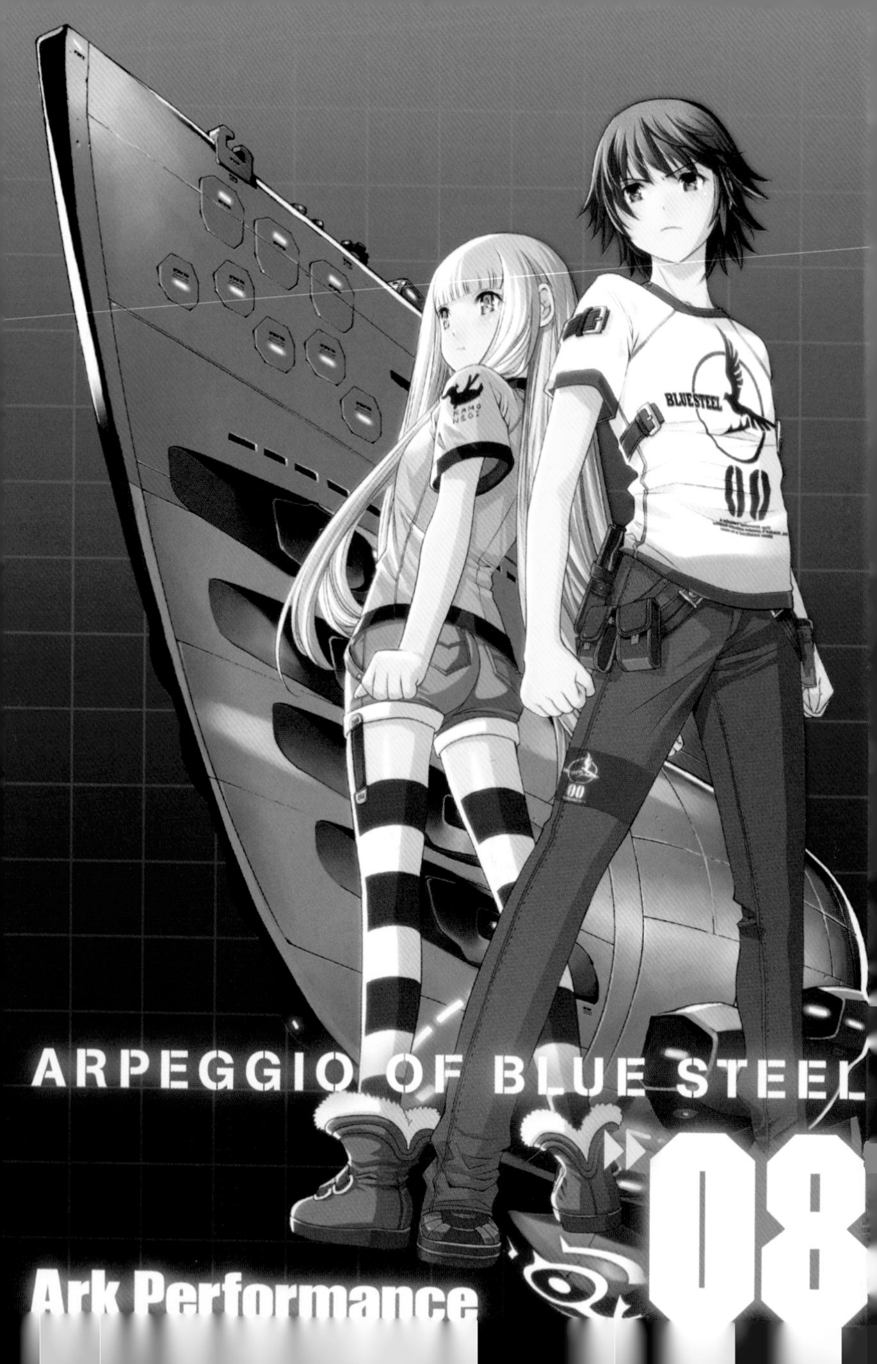
ARPEGGIO OF BLUE STEEL
08
Ark Performance